Towards a Global Consensus against Corruption

Corruption has long been identified as a governance challenge, yet it took states until the 1990s to adopt binding agreements to combat it. While the rapid spread of anti-corruption treaties appears to mark a global consensus, a closer look reveals that not all regional and international organizations are moving on similar trajectories. This book seeks to explain similarities and differences between international anti-corruption agreements.

In this volume Lohaus develops a comprehensive analytical framework to compare international agreements in the areas of prevention, criminalization, jurisdiction, domestic enforcement, and international cooperation. Outcomes range from narrow enforcement cooperation to broad commitments that often lack follow-up mechanisms. Lohaus argues that agreements vary because they are designed to signal anti-corruption commitment to different audiences. To demonstrate such different approaches to anti-corruption, he draws on two starkly different cases—the Organization of American States and the African Union.

Contributing to debates on decision-making in international organizations, this work showcases how global governance is shaped by processes of diffusion that involve state and non-state actors. The book highlights challenges as well as opportunities linked to the patchwork of international rules. It will be of great interest to students and scholars of IR theory, global governance, international organizations, and regionalism.

Mathis Lohaus is a postdoctoral researcher at the Otto Suhr Institute of Political Science at Freie Universität Berlin, Germany. His research interests include international and regional organizations, global efforts to promote anti-corruption and good governance, and the diffusion of ideas. He holds a doctoral degree in political science from Berlin Graduate School for Transnational Studies and Freie Universität Berlin.

Global Institutions

Edited by Thomas G. Weiss
The CUNY Graduate Center, New York, USA
and Rorden Wilkinson
University of Sussex, Brighton, UK

The "Global Institutions Series" provides cutting-edge books about many aspects of what we know as "global governance." It emerges from our shared frustrations with the state of available knowledge—electronic and print-wise—for research and teaching. The series is designed as a resource for those interested in exploring issues of international organization and global governance. And since the first volumes appeared in 2005, we have taken significant strides toward filling many conceptual gaps.

The series consists of two related "streams" distinguished by their blue and red covers. The blue volumes, comprising the majority of the books in the series, provide user-friendly and short (usually no more than 50,000 words) but authoritative guides to major global and regional organizations, as well as key issues in the global governance of security, the environment, human rights, poverty, and humanitarian action among others. The books with red covers are designed to present original research and serve as extended and more specialized treatments of issues pertinent for advancing understanding about global governance.

The books in each of the streams are written by experts in the field, ranging from the most senior and respected authors to first-rate scholars at the beginning of their careers. In combination, the components of the series serve as key resources for faculty, students, and practitioners alike. The works in the blue stream have value as core and complementary readings in courses on, among other things, international organization, global governance, international law, international relations, and international political economy; the red volumes allow further reflection and investigation in these and related areas.

The books in the series also provide a segue-way to the foundation volume that offers the most comprehensive textbook treatment available dealing with all the major issues, approaches, institutions, and actors in contemporary global governance. The second edition of our edited work International Organization and Global Governance (2018) contains essays by many of the authors in the series.

Understanding global governance—past, present, and future—is far from a finished journey. The books in this series nonetheless represent significant steps toward a better way of conceiving contemporary problems and issues as well as, hopefully, doing something to improve world order. We value the feedback from our readers and their role in helping shape the on-going development of the series.

A complete list of titles can be viewed online here: https://www.routledge.com/Global-Institutions/book-series/GI.

Global Governance and China
edited by Scott Kennedy

Global Business Associations
by Karsten Ronit

A League of Democracies
Cosmopolitanism, Consolidation Arguments, and Global Public Goods
by John Davenport

Moral Obligations and Sovereignty in International Relations
A Genealogy of Humanitarianism
by Andrea Paras

Protecting the Internally Displaced
Rhetoric and Reality
by Phil Orchard

Accessing and Implementing Human Rights and Justice
by Kurt Mills and Melissa Labonte

The IMF, the WTO & the Politics of Economic Surveillance
by Martin Edwards

Multinational Rapid Response Mechanisms
by John Karlsrud and Yf Rykers

Towards a Global Consensus Against Corruption
International Agreements as Products of Diffusion and Signals
of Commitment
by Mathis Lohaus

Towards a Global Consensus against Corruption

International Agreements as Products of Diffusion and Signals of Commitment

Mathis Lohaus

LONDON AND NEW YORK

First published 2019 by Routledge

2 Park Square, Milton Park, Abingdon, Oxon OX14 4RN

605 Third Avenue, New York, NY 10017

Routledge is an imprint of the Taylor & Francis Group, an informa business

First issued in paperback 2021

Copyright © 2019 Mathis Lohaus

The right of Mathis Lohaus to be identified as author of this work has been asserted by him in accordance with sections 77 and 78 of the Copyright, Designs and Patents Act 1988.

All rights reserved. No part of this book may be reprinted or reproduced or utilized in any form or by any electronic, mechanical, or other means, now known or hereafter invented, including photocopying and recording, or in any information storage or retrieval system, without permission in writing from the publishers.

Notice:
Product or corporate names may be trademarks or registered trademarks, and are used only for identification and explanation without intent to infringe.

Publisher's Note

The publisher has gone to great lengths to ensure the quality of thisreprint but points out that some imperfections in the original copies may beapparent.

British Library Cataloguing in Publication Data
A catalogue record for this book is available from the British Library.

Library of Congress Cataloging-in-Publication Data
A catalog record has been requested for this book.

ISBN: 978-1-138-58850-9 (hbk)
ISBN: 978-1-03-217834-9 (pbk)
DOI: 10.4324/9780429492235

Typeset in Times New Roman
by Taylor & Francis Books

Contents

	List of illustrations	viii
	Acknowledgments	ix
	Abbreviations	xi
	Introduction	1
1	The argument: Diffusion and signaling motives	25
2	International anti-corruption agreements in comparison	43
3	Organization of American States: Activist governments and domestic reference models	84
4	African Union: Development cooperation, non-state actors, and external reference models	118
5	Conclusion: Lessons to draw from the global patchwork	153
	List of anti-corruption documents	170
	Additional data on scope conditions	172
	List of interviews	175
	Bibliography	177
	Index	179

Illustrations

Figures

I.1	States that have ratified at least one anti-corruption agreement	3
1.1	Theoretical model	38
2.1	Democracy and foreign aid inflows	53
2.2	Agreements in comparison (only core treaties)	68
2.3	Agreements in comparison (including additional documents)	69
3.1	Signing and ratification of the OAS convention	86
4.1	Signing and ratification of the AU convention	120
4.2	Ratification of African anti-corruption agreements	127
A2.1	Control of corruption and foreign aid inflows	172
A2.2	Control of corruption and GDP per capita	173
A2.3	Control of corruption and democracy	174

Tables

I.1	Analytical framework	8
1.1	Mechanisms of diffusion	27
2.1	Binding anti-corruption agreements	50
2.2	Conditions under which agreements have been adopted	55
2.3	The scope of international anti-corruption agreements	58
2.4	Degrees of legalization	62
2.5	Elements of delegation (monitoring and follow-up)	63
2.6	Scope, obligation, and delegation in comparison	66
2.7	Observed frequency of copying and pasting in nine anti-corruption agreements	74
5.1	Four groups of cases	155
5.2	Signaling motives and outcomes	157
A1.1	Overview of relevant anti-corruption documents	170
A3.1	List of interviews	175

Acknowledgments

First and foremost, I thank Tanja A. Börzel for her advice and mentorship. I am grateful for the close friendships that developed through the Berlin Graduate School for Transnational Studies. Many thanks to Sören Stapel, Zoe Phillips Williams, Wiebke Wemheuer-Vogelaar, Kai Striebinger, Tobias Bunde, Christian Kreuder-Sonnen, Luise Müller, Patrick Gilroy, Sophie Eisentraut, Gil Murciano, Maurits Meijers, and the rest of the BTS crowd for their invaluable support. Being a part of the Research College (KFG) "The Transformative Power of Europe" has been another great privilege, and showcased the diffusion of ideas. I look forward to reunions with Dan Berliner, Inken von Borzyskowski, Amanda Clayton, Brooke Coe, Elin Hellquist, Merran Hulse, Mor Mitrani, Stefano Palestini, Clara Portela, Ed Stoddard, Kilian Spandler, and the other alumni. Many thanks to Ines Stavrinakis, Astrid Roos, Anne Morgenstern, and the other members of the coordination team. None of this would have been possible without the generous funding provided by the German Research Foundation (DFG).

Outside of Berlin, three trips had a major impact on this project. In 2014, I was a DAAD visiting fellow at Georgetown University, which was extremely helpful for my research. The following year, I profited from a productive writing retreat at UNC-Chapel Hill. Many thanks to Abe Newman for his generous support and brilliant comments over the years, and to Liesbet Hooghe and Gary Marks for hosting me in North Carolina. I also thank Tina Ruby, Katie Lindner, and my colleagues in Georgetown and Chapel Hill for making me feel at home. During my research stay in Addis Ababa, many practitioners patiently answered my questions and pointed me to sources, despite their busy schedules. I am grateful for their help and their dedicated work to reduce the negative effects of corruption.

x *Acknowledgments*

When it was time to turn my research into a book, my colleagues in Greifswald (particularly Margit Bussmann, Levke Aduda, and Anja Menzel) put up with me when I was distracted and encouraged me when necessary. Comments from the editors of the *Global Institutions Series* as well as the anonymous reviewer were extremely useful and helped to improve the manuscript. Beyond specific feedback, I cannot thank Tom Weiss and Rorden Wilkinson enough for their support and patience. I am also grateful to everyone at Routledge, particularly the managing editor Nina Connelly and the excellent copy-editor Philip Parr.

To Sonja and my parents: thank you a thousand times for your love and support!

Abbreviations

ADB	Asian Development Bank
AfDB	African Development Bank
APEC	Asia–Pacific Economic Cooperation
ASEAN	Association of South-East Asian Nations
AU	African Union
AU ABC	African Union Advisory Board on Corruption
BPI	Bribe Payers Index (Transparency International)
CAN	Andean Community
CARICOM	Caribbean Community
COE	Council of Europe
CPI	Corruption Perceptions Index (Transparency International)
EAC	East African Community
ECOWAS	Economic Community of West African States
EU	European Union
FTAA	Free Trade Agreement of the Americas
GCA	Global Coalition for Africa
GRECO	Group of States against Corruption (Council of Europe)
IACAC	Inter-American Convention Against Corruption
IMF	International Monetary Fund
IO	International organization
IRG	Implementation Review Group (United Nations)
LAS	League of Arab States (also known as Arab League)
MERCOSUR	Southern Common Market
MESICIC	Mechanism for Follow-up on the Implementation of the IACAC
NGO	Non-governmental organization
OAS	Organization of American States

xii *Abbreviations*

OECD	Organisation for Economic Co-operation and Development
OLAF	European Anti-fraud Office (European Union)
OLC	Office of the Legal Counsel (African Union)
SADC	Southern African Development Community
SAHRIT	Southern African Human Rights Trust (NGO)
SICA	Central American Integration System
SIDA	Swedish International Development Cooperation Agency
StAR	Stolen Assets Recovery Initiative
TI	Transparency International
UK	United Kingdom
UN	United Nations
UNCAC	United Nations Convention Against Corruption
UNDP	United Nations Development Programme
UNECA	United Nations Economic Commission for Africa
US	United States
WB	World Bank
WSA	World Society Approach

Introduction

- **The arrival of anti-corruption on the global agenda**
- **Comparing the scope and legal design of agreements**
- **The argument in brief: diffusion and signaling motives**
- **Why study anti-corruption agreements?**
- **Chapter outline**

In December 2017, the Organisation for Economic Co-operation and Development (OECD) marked the twentieth anniversary of its anti-bribery convention; and the United Nations Convention Against Corruption (UNCAC) turned fifteen years old the following year. Recent headlines about corruption, however, provide few reasons to celebrate. Latin America has recently seen bribery and embezzlement on an unprecedented scale. The US federal government is shaken by scandals. Around the world, prosecutors are searching for billions of dollars hidden by former ruling elites. Obscure issues, such as banking secrecy and shell companies, have been popularized via the "Panama Papers." Even sports fans with no interest in international business and politics could hardly escape the topic given the turmoil at the international football association FIFA.[1]

There are many opportunities for international cooperation to reduce corruption or at least mitigate its effects. Yet, before the mid-1990s, no international organization had adopted a binding agreement to combat corruption. The issue was addressed in hortatory language, at best, leading to occasional declarations of intent at the intergovernmental level. Since then, however, initiatives have proliferated around the globe. International and regional organizations, such as the OECD, the Council of Europe (COE), and the United Nations (UN), have adopted documents committing member states to implement domestic reforms and strengthen international cooperation. This wave of agreements appears to reflect a new global consensus against corruption.

2 Introduction

Yet, a closer look reveals significant differences between the various organizations. Their agreements vary in the scope of issues covered and the degree of legal obligation and follow-up provisions included in the documents. While some contain binding commitments on many aspects of anti-corruption, others are quite narrow in scope or use less obligatory language. Some organizations have not adopted binding agreements at all, apparently resisting the global trend. Motivated by this diffusion and differentiation, I address the following research question: which factors explain the similarities and differences between international anti-corruption agreements?

Rather than making independent choices, international organizations influence each other when they negotiate and draft agreements. This observation draws on a rich literature on the international diffusion of norms and policies, which has identified several mechanisms, such as persuasion and lesson-drawing. I further argue that diffusion processes are subject to scope conditions: international organizations adopt binding agreements if their members want to signal their anti-corruption credentials to domestic constituents, within the group of member states, or to external audiences such as international donors. In the absence of such signaling motives, organizations will resist the global anti-corruption trend. Beyond explaining the decision to adopt an agreement or not, I argue that the signaling scope condition also affects the contents of documents.

To compare international anti-corruption agreements systematically, I disaggregate the main research question into two parts. First, why do some regional and international organizations adopt agreements that include mandatory clauses whereas others do not? Second, how can we explain differences and similarities in the scope of issues covered and the legal design among the binding agreements? I address these questions through a comparison of fourteen international and regional organizations and their respective anti-corruption efforts. Two case-study chapters then analyze how member-state delegates, international bureaucrats, and non-state actors reached consensus in the Organization of American States (OAS) and the African Union (AU).

The remainder of this chapter provides some detail on the background, analytical framework, argument, and empirical relevance of this approach.

The arrival of anti-corruption on the global agenda

Since the mid-1990s, international organizations (IOs) around the world have adopted multilateral anti-corruption agreements. This has

Introduction 3

been variously characterized as an "eruption," a growing "industry," and a "campaign" or "movement."[2] Several authors have applied Nadelmann's notion of "prohibition regimes" to anti-corruption.[3] The 2003 UNCAC is at the center of these developments and enjoys almost universal ratification today. However, as I discuss in Chapter 2, the UN was neither the first nor the only forum to address corruption. Due to the patchwork of regional and global initiatives, virtually every independent state today has ratified between one and five international anti-corruption agreements (see Figure I.1).

In hindsight, it seems logical for international organizations to tackle the transnational challenges of corruption. Yet, it took decades for them to overcome obstacles to cooperation and reach the first binding agreement in this field. I will briefly address two questions. First, why did anti-corruption finally take center stage in the mid-1990s after being sidelined for so long? One possible answer is that the end of the Cold War provided the necessary permissive conditions for anti-corruption to receive more attention from the global community. Second, which actors were central in setting the agenda? Whereas the structural changes during the 1990s allowed anti-corruption to evolve as a global issue, agency was also necessary to facilitate its development.

During the 1990s, two broad trends resulted in conditions under which governments sought to reach agreements about fighting corruption. Democratization and economic globalization led to a change in public

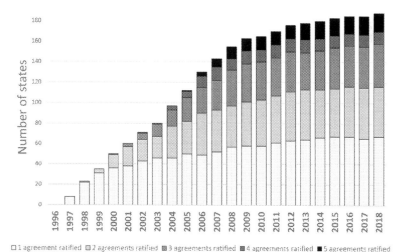

Figure I.1 States that have ratified at least one anti-corruption agreement
Source: Author, based on official records.

4 *Introduction*

perceptions of corruption, and consequently to increased pressure on governments to address it: "The hardships of global competition have exhausted voters' patience with government excesses and misconduct."[4] This applies directly to transition countries, whose leaders faced high expectations from their newly empowered electorates. A number of politicians in Latin America and South-East Asia were forced to step down due to high-profile corruption cases. With more room for civil society and public debate, corruption gained more attention at the national level.[5]

At the same time, large-scale corruption had been discovered in countries with long traditions of democratic rule. Two major examples are Japan, where Prime Minister Takeshita stepped down in 1989, and Italy's "*mani pulite*" campaign, which began in 1992.[6] For Europe, an additional outcome of democratization was that the post-Soviet states were to be integrated into the Council of Europe and ultimately the European Union (EU). This led policymakers to put anti-corruption at the top of the political agenda. The EU and COE launched a joint program called Octopus, which ran from 1996 to 2000 to assist prospective new members with bringing their domestic legislation up to EU standards.[7] As Western European states asked their Eastern counterparts to enact reforms, they themselves had to commit to anti-corruption in order not to appear hypocritical.[8]

Meanwhile, ever more countries were involved in global trade, and foreign investments reached unprecedented levels. With national markets no longer the most important reference points, corruption scandals in globalized industries started to attract a lot of attention.[9] Whereas domestic political crises could be seen as issues for national lawmakers, their effects on transnational business required international cooperation. To safeguard the benefits of open markets and transnational investments, activists began to argue against the payment of bribes.[10] Even among countries with different ideological orientations, it made sense to create a level playing field "to increase the confidence of their prospective trading partners."[11] In a similar vein, the Asian financial crisis was partly blamed on "crony capitalism," further emphasizing the need to tackle unethical behavior in international business.[12] Several authors have criticized this linkage of anti-corruption to market liberalization without denying its importance as a permissive condition for the new set of policies to emerge.[13]

Also in the early 1990s, US foreign policy and security objectives changed as a consequence of the end of the Cold War: "compliant or friendly policies towards superpowers ceased to be the driving criterion for foreign relations, and other principles such as democratic

Introduction 5

governance, trade relations, human rights, and transparent governments could take center stage."[14] Put more bluntly, the end of the Cold War eliminated the need to protect every ally, regardless of their shortcomings. Priorities for development assistance and diplomatic relations changed, and exposing corrupt leaders was no longer unthinkable.[15]

Closely related to the change in ideological conflicts due to the end of the Cold War is the evolution of the US debate on global security. The emphasis on traditional military threats and the stand-off between the superpowers gave way to worries about alternative forms of conflict. Promoting good governance and the rule of law was framed as a strategy to fight transnational crime and avoid the negative externalities from civil wars associated with failed or weak states. Security concerns in the wake of 9/11 played an important role in the drafting of the 2003 UN Convention Against Corruption, as reflected in official US statements about corruption and its relation to international terrorism.[16]

In addition, the US government was the principal agenda-setter and proponent of banning transnational bribery. This activism was rooted in the 1977 Foreign Corrupt Practices Act (FCPA). In the wake of the Watergate and Lockheed scandals, American legislators had banned US corporations from paying bribes to foreign officials. Export-oriented businesses felt the FCPA put them at a competitive disadvantage because no other country enacted similar laws.[17] Yet, at least initially, the US government was unable to pressurize others to follow suit after it "unilaterally disarmed."[18] After the FCPA was amended in 1988, the United States again tried to create a level playing field. Combining economic arguments with normative claims, in 1997 US negotiators succeeded in convincing their counterparts at the OECD to ban transnational bribery.[19] They thus propelled one aspect of anti-corruption onto the global agenda. Critics argue that the United States' motives were far from altruistic, and that the net result might be an internationalization of US law rather than the creation of a global norm.[20] Yet, as subsequent chapters will show, international anti-corruption efforts cover a broader range of issues than this argument suggests.[21]

Another factor in the promotion of anti-corruption was a change in expert opinion, particularly regarding the detrimental effects of corruption on developing countries. Scathing assessments from economists and social scientists prompted a shift in priorities among the policymakers in multilateral institutions, particularly the World Bank (WB) and the International Monetary Fund (IMF). During the 1990s, a quite benevolent attitude toward corruption finally started to give way

6 Introduction

to increasingly negative appraisals. Huntington is often cited as an example of the former perspective, but others, such as Nye and Leff, similarly did not consider the fight against corruption a priority. However, as ever more research incorporated surveys and quantitative indicators, a wealth of new evidence in support of anti-corruption efforts came to the fore.[22] For instance, IMF economist Paolo Mauro published a series of highly influential working papers and journal articles in which he likened corruption to sand in the wheels of growth.[23] Principal-agent models and institutionalist perspectives were embraced as this new generation of research revealed corruption's negative impact on a vast range of economic and social variables.[24]

The academic discourse was closely linked to the WB and the IMF, which hosted researchers and publicized their findings. James Wolfensohn became the WB's president in 1995 and began prioritizing bribery the following year.[25] Indeed, in his 1996 presidential address, he stated that the WB must "deal with the cancer of corruption."[26] Compared to the previous non-interventionist stance, this was a significant change of direction. Wolfensohn's World Bank became an important teacher of norms in the field of anti-corruption, both through anti-corruption provisions in its own programs and by publicly advocating for reform.[27] While the level of action did not necessarily match the rhetoric, let alone achieve positive effects on the ground,[28] the change in policy did inspire others. Among the first to follow the WB's lead was the IMF, which "adopted stringent guidelines for public sector transparency and accounting as part of its standard conditionality" in 1996.[29] Whereas researchers and policy experts had previously been undecided, by the middle of the 1990s there was almost universal acceptance of a strong anti-corruption stance.

Finally, Transparency International (TI) is often considered the key non-governmental organization (NGO) in terms of advancing the anti-corruption agenda. Founded in 1993 by Peter Eigen, a German economist with long experience working for the WB in Africa, and several colleagues, it quickly became "the most visible non-governmental player in the anti-corruption movement."[30] Since 1995, TI has published the annual Corruption Perceptions Index (CPI), in which countries are ranked according to their perceived levels of corruption. Yet, overall, the organization is regarded as diplomatic and cooperative rather than confrontational.[31] It relies on cooperation with governments, a combination of advocacy for legal reform with general awareness-raising, and a decentralized structure with national chapters around the world.[32] At first, it focused on bribery and tried to address the prisoner's dilemma among export-oriented countries by engaging with key

Introduction 7

business leaders and national politicians. Of course, this approach corresponded with the US government's efforts to ban transnational bribery.[33] In addition, TI aims to shape public opinion by naming and shaming miscreants in the widely publicized CPI and the Bribe Payers Index (BPI).[34] As early as 1998, the organization claimed that the CPI "influences the policies of major aid agencies and is a factor in the foreign investment decisions of multinational corporations."[35] Nevertheless, some commentators are critical of TI due to its close links to Western governments and the WB.[36] Indeed, because its initial funding came almost exclusively from government sources, it has even been labeled "*quasi*-nongovernmental."[37] Still, there is no doubt that the organization has been a crucial agent of change in the anti-corruption movement. Later, it was joined by the International Chamber of Commerce, the International Bar Association, and the American Bar Association, among other NGOs.[38] However, no other non-state actor has received as much attention and credit in the literature as TI.

This brief account of how anti-corruption made its way up the global policy agenda provides a useful starting point for my analysis. Yet, research that focuses exclusively on norm emergence neglects subsequent developments and important variations between cases. Other studies might discuss case-specific arguments about the emergence and design of agreements but lack a comparative approach.[39] Meanwhile, comparative studies by legal scholars might address the implications of variations between cases but fail to present causal arguments.[40] This study, in contrast, not only compares international anti-corruption agreements but also explains the similarities and differences between them.

Comparing the scope and legal design of agreements

When international organizations draft and adopt agreements to combat corruption, the results are far from uniform in form and scale. At one end of the spectrum, there are short statements about corruption in non-binding language. Such provisions are often adopted at the end of high-level meetings and characterized by hortatory language. To conclude the first Summit of the Americas in Miami in 1994, for instance, the heads of state and government adopted a five-page declaration of principles, including one sentence on corruption as an issue to be tackled.[41] At the other end of the spectrum, there are international treaties with legally binding provisions. A case in point is the UNCAC, which contains 71 articles that cover a vast range of

8 *Introduction*

issues.[42] Action plans, protocols, and additional documents occupy the middle ground between these two extremes.

To allow for valid comparisons, the analysis in this book is limited to treaties and comparable documents with a minimum degree of legal obligation. Furthermore, the relevant dimensions and criteria for the comparisons need to be specified: first, the *scope* of anti-corruption efforts; and second, their *legal design* (see Table I.1). To measure the scope of agreements, I disaggregate anti-corruption into five categories:

- What do states commit to do to prevent corruption?
- Which acts of corruption are to be criminalized domestically?
- What do agreements say about how states should define jurisdiction over corruption cases?
- Which provisions exist on standards for domestic enforcement?
- Which provisions does an agreement encompass about international cooperation?

Guided by these categories, I track which items occur in each document. The result is a mapping that covers 57 elements, which jointly represent the scope of each anti-corruption agreement.

The second analytical dimension—legal design—captures how the agreements are set up. Here, I follow the suggestions contained within the legalization framework.[43] First, I consider obligation: for each element of scope, the language in the agreement indicates the extent to which states are legally bound to comply. Phrases such as "shall" or "will" indicate a high level of obligation, whereas states that "consider" an issue are merely making an aspirational statement. This aspect of legal design can be coded separately for each element covered in the scope dimension. Second, I analyze delegation, which takes a single value for the whole case. The crucial question here is: does an agreement establish a body or forum to fulfill tasks related to enforcement or monitoring? Empirically, the range of outcomes is quite

Table I.1 Analytical framework

Scope: What is covered?	Legal design: How is the agreement set up?
Prevention	Obligation: high–low
Criminalization	Delegation: Follow-up, monitoring
Jurisdiction	
Domestic enforcement	
International cooperation	

Introduction 9

limited. For instance, no international organization has ever created a specialist court to adjudicate only on corruption cases. In practice, anti-corruption follow-up is either non-existent or reaches the monitoring level of delegation (see Chapter 2).

Analyzing scope and legal design allows for nuanced comparisons between agreements. Of course, two international organizations may be completely dissimilar if one adopts an agreement with binding anti-corruption commitments and the other refuses to do so. Or they can be very similar if their respective documents share virtually every characteristic regarding scope and legal design, which would suggest that one was modeled on the other in its entirety. Yet, most importantly, my focus is on the middle range of varying similarities and differences. Regarding scope, this means comparing which issues are covered in each agreement. Moreover, the wording of individual provisions might be similar across multiple cases. In terms of legal design, two agreements might be almost identical or very different in their degree of obligation and how this varies between issue areas. Finally, I compare how their follow-up mechanisms are designed.

Based on this analytical framework, I analyze and compare the anti-corruption agreements created by nine international organizations mostly between 1996 and 2003. Four IOs may be described as early adopters: the OAS, COE, OECD, and EU all started negotiations around the same time and adopted binding documents between 1996 and 1999. The COE and the OECD included follow-up mechanisms immediately, while the OAS added one in 2001. Between 2001 and 2003, three African organizations—the Economic Community of West African States (ECOWAS), the Southern African Development Community (SADC), and the African Union (AU)—followed suit and adopted their own anti-corruption documents. This global trend culminated in December 2003, when the UN Convention Against Corruption was adopted after three years of preparation and negotiations. A review mechanism was added six years later. Finally, the League of Arab States (LAS) adopted a convention in 2010.

While the LAS was rather lethargic, some regional organizations have shown even less appetite for drafting a binding agreement. For instance, in Latin America, neither the Southern Common Market (MERCOSUR) nor the Andean Community (CAN) has created its own anti-corruption protocol; instead, they both defer to the OAS. Similarly, neither the Caribbean Community (CARICOM) nor the East African Community (EAC) had signed up to a binding agreement at the time of writing, although negotiations were at least under way in the latter (see Chapter 4). The Association of South-East Asian

10 *Introduction*

Nations (ASEAN) is another outlier, making Asia the only continent with no binding anti-corruption agreement.

Another difference between organizations is that some have become active only once, whereas others have addressed corruption in several documents. The OECD, COE, and EU have all added multiple recommendations and supplementary documents to their main agreements. These have either expanded on issues established in the original agreements or introduced new ones. To a lesser extent, the OAS and AU have also added some extra documents that address corruption. In contrast, the ECOWAS and SADC agreements appear to be singular declarations as neither has been amended or developed since adoption.

How do the organizations with at least one binding agreement compare with one another? Simply put, researchers and practitioners must carefully consider the contents of each agreement because both scope and legal design differ markedly from case to case. For instance, the OECD's convention is relatively narrow in scope in terms of criminalization and enforcement related to transnational bribery, but it contains a high degree of obligation plus delegation to a strong follow-up mechanism. Some other issues are addressed too, but mostly as non-binding recommendations. Meanwhile, the OAS and UN agreements are much broader in scope and display either more or less obligation, depending on the issue. In both cases, follow-up mechanisms were created a few years after ratification. All of the agreements adopted by African organizations share a broad scope and a high degree of obligation for most provisions. Yet, in terms of delegation, they have either no or only weak follow-up mechanisms.

In sum, anti-corruption agreements present a mixed picture in terms of overall legalization. On the one hand, there are some narrow but strongly enforced commitments; on the other, a number of broad and binding documents are stymied by a lack of delegation. As a further consequence of the choices made by different organizations, there is variation from region to region. In the Americas, the OAS is the only organization with a binding agreement; all of the others have either not addressed corruption at all or they defer to the OAS, at best adding technical, non-binding documents. In Europe, multiple anti-corruption agreements have developed in parallel to achieve specific objectives, with the COE and the EU prioritizing different issues. The OECD, with its focus on transnational bribery, also fits into this pattern. Among the African organizations, by contrast, there is already an overlapping set of agreements, with another currently under negotiation.

Introduction 11

The argument in brief: diffusion and signaling motives

I argue that these similarities and differences among international organizations' approaches to anti-corruption are best explained by a diffusion perspective that incorporates scope conditions. Diffusion generally refers to processes of interdependent decision-making.[44] When applied to the subject of this study, it implies that the choices relating to anti-corruption that are made in one international organization are systematically influenced by the choices that are made in others. Rather than expecting all organizations to engage in independent attempts to solve the problem, or to be driven by other idiosyncratic factors, I assume that decisions on how to draft an effective agreement are influenced by other actors' prior—or anticipated—decisions.

These influences may be based on direct mechanisms of diffusion. Outside actors might offer positive or negative incentives as well as capacity-building to induce a change of behavior. They might also engage in normative pressure and persuasion in the hope of triggering desired outcomes, for instance by arguing that corruption is morally wrong and ought to be addressed by every international organization. Yet, diffusion does not depend on any such direct attempts to exert influence; indeed, it could be driven by indirect mechanisms alone. For instance, an IO might reach a decision solely to keep pace with others that are competing for similar resources. Alternatively, decision-makers might draw lessons from an external model when seeking solutions for a particular policy problem. Finally, the literature on diffusion highlights the importance of normative emulation, when an organization is influenced by the actions of peers with high prestige or legitimacy.[45]

However, I do not assume that diffusion affects all cases uniformly. Because the member states are the primary decision-makers in international organizations, their motives serve as scope conditions for diffusion. I argue that the choice to adopt an anti-corruption agreement is driven by member states' motives to use treaties for signaling purposes. These signals may be intended for domestic, intra-group, or external audiences. In organizations whose member states are more democratic (on average), one may expect the domestic signaling motive to play a decisive role. Because corruption is a highly relevant issue for many constituents, adopting an international agreement to tackle this issue is a useful way to display commitment to the electorate. The second motive—intra-group signaling—applies to situations in which member states draft an agreement to codify their commitments to one another, for instance to solve cooperation problems. This is likely when at least one member of the group pushes for the agreement and seeks

12 *Introduction*

commitments from its peers, as illustrated by the US government lobbying the other member states of the OECD to adopt similar laws against bribery in transnational business. Finally, the external signaling motive applies in organizations whose member states are highly dependent on inflows of development aid. In such cases, anti-corruption efforts are primarily driven by the wish to react to actual or perceived external pressure and therefore avert demands for further action.

Organizations are unlikely to adopt binding anti-corruption agreements in the absence of a signaling motive. This explains ASEAN's and the LAS's reluctance to follow the global anti-corruption trend. Beyond their impact on the core decision to become active or not, the scope conditions also influence both the scope and the legal design of agreements. If either domestic or intra-group signaling is the principal motive, agreements tend to display a trade-off between scope and obligation as well as strong follow-up provisions to foster compliance. This outcome is most obvious in the OAS, COE, and OECD agreements. By contrast, when external signaling is the main motive, agreements tend to be broad in scope and highly obligatory, but with weak follow-up mechanisms. Therefore, it is safe to assume that the African regional organizations were signaling primarily to donors and the international community when drafting their agreements.

Beyond the study of corruption and the political responses to it, this study contributes to broader debates in international relations. Depending on their theoretical point of departure, researchers may focus on the emergence of specific issues on the global agenda, the resulting patterns of institutional convergence and differentiation, or the processes and mechanisms through which ideas spread. One such research approach is comparative regionalism: that is, the comparative study of regional orders and regional governance. A subset of this literature investigates how regional organizations shape domestic governance structures, including the rule of law and good governance.[46] International anti-corruption agreements may be viewed through this lens.

Moreover, these agreements are relevant for research into norm and policy diffusion. The starting point here is that decision-making in international organizations is seen as interdependent, meaning that each decision is systematically influenced by those in other units. The structural variant of this perspective—the World Society Approach (WSA)—sees the broad trend towards anti-corruption as an instance of convergence or isomorphism.[47] Fighting corruption, in this interpretation, has become part of a shared script of rationality and modernity. Other diffusion researchers are more interested in the agency of various actors and the possibility that different mechanisms might be at play.[48]

Introduction 13

The more nuanced differentiation of agreements analyzed in this study speaks to debates about direct and indirect mechanisms of diffusion. For structural as well as agency-centered approaches, the emergence and further development of the international agenda to combat corruption presents an opportunity to test and develop causal arguments. In addition, this study contributes to the literature on international regimes and institutional design by analyzing decision-making in IOs and the design choices of international institutions. Addressing the question of what motivates member states to adopt anti-corruption agreements within a diffusion approach allows studies of institutional design to be linked to research into commitment to treaties and the signaling logic behind international law.[49]

Why study anti-corruption agreements?

While the campaign against transnational bribery and the US government's efforts to promote it have received the bulk of the academic attention, anti-corruption is much broader both conceptually and empirically. A commitment to combat corruption can have different meanings depending on the terminology used in the document. For instance, if an IO's member states agree to ban one specific practice but nothing else, that is very different from a commitment to address a wide range of corruption-related issues.

In 1964, US Supreme Court Justice Potter Stewart suggested that it was almost impossible to define pornography, so he would refrain from trying. Instead, he simply stated, "I know it when I see it."[50] Arguably, the same could be said for corruption. TI has suggested the widely cited definition "abuse of entrusted power for private gain," and further differentiates between "grand," "petty," and "political" corruption, based on the actors involved and their motives.[51] However, this still leaves a great deal of room for interpretation.

This approach to defining corruption follows the commonly used public-office or breach-of-duty perspective. "Entrusted power" here includes what earlier authors have labeled "public office," although TI's phrase allows for private-sector corruption to be included in a more holistic definition. Such definitions are based on the notion that some individuals occupy positions of power that are linked to norms of behavior, which corrupt actors violate by seeking gains for themselves or others. I will refrain from a more thorough discussion of the various perspectives on how to define corruption.[52] Suffice to say that a wide range of behavior has been categorized as corruption, and violations of impartiality norms are a common denominator.

14 *Introduction*

As part of this study, I track how international agreements define corruption. If there is no explicit definition, we can at least explore how corrupt behavior is circumscribed in these documents. It makes sense to treat definitions as part of the empirical variation to explain, as both they and implicit assumptions can shape the contents of agreements. Importantly, the concept of corruption is not free of normative or moral connotations. Even relatively technical definitions must refer to some normative basis to be meaningful. Therefore, it is crucial to study which norms have spread in the international system and thus potentially contradict and/or influence those at the domestic level.

Moreover, international agreements to combat corruption affect international and domestic politics. Most obviously, they have direct effects on national law-making and thus potentially contribute to combating corruption. National laws are supposed to curb undesirable behavior, as national authorities define and enforce mandatory rules. Ostensibly, this is what international anti-corruption agreements, with their focus on obliging member states to change their domestic laws, aim to achieve. Yet, critics have argued that betting on laws to reduce corruption betrays "naive confidence" with "little concrete evidence to support this belief."[53] Even with the best of intentions, some governments might simply be unable to address the deep-rooted causes of corruption in their societies. Indeed, quantitative empirical research has found little or no evidence of a causal link between commitments to international agreements and reductions in corruption at the national level.[54]

Nevertheless, there is no doubt that the international anti-corruption agenda has had some impact on national political systems. National laws to combat corruption have evolved around the world in tandem with the international agreements. Indeed, "virtually every country has domestic [anti-corruption] laws covering its public officials."[55] For African countries in particular, "the coming into force of [the African Union and the United Nations conventions] had a dramatic effect on the development of anti-corruption and good governance laws and institutions."[56] The OECD's influence on its member states' anti-bribery laws is another case in point.[57]

In addition to standard-setting at the domestic level, international agreements enable cooperation between member states. If bribes are paid in the context of transnational business, successful prosecution often depends on international cooperation to collect and share evidence. Mutual legal assistance, extradition, and the freezing of assets are further aspects of the international cooperation relating to

Introduction 15

corruption. International agreements are meant to facilitate and promote such interactions, which ultimately depend on case-by-case political will.[58]

Anti-corruption agreements are also significant focal points and benchmarks. Several of them have established follow-up mechanisms, with peer review being the most typical design choice. When an organization's member states regularly review one another's performance regarding treaty commitments, this constitutes an inherent means of information collection, sharing, and benchmarking. Such mechanisms are meant to induce higher levels of compliance by applying peer pressure and reputational costs. Anti-corruption agreements can thus become focal points for naming and shaming.[59]

Less directly, they also become focal points by setting the agenda on corruption and raising awareness of the problem. International efforts are most likely to reach their goals when they facilitate local stakeholders and policy entrepreneurs.[60] TI, the leading NGO in the field, publishes regular "progress reports" on the UN and OECD conventions. In this sense, the international agreements focus the attention of activists, who are able to highlight non-compliance among parties to the various treaties or pressurize states to commit to anti-corruption compacts in the first place. For instance, TI called on Germany and Japan to ratify the UNCAC when it felt they were dragging their feet. Moreover, while the official monitoring mechanisms associated with international agreements stop short of ranking member-state performance, TI uses the OECD's data on the application of foreign-bribery clauses to do just that.[61]

In developing countries and emerging markets, curbing corruption has become a benchmark for both donor agencies and investors. As discussed above, the WB reversed its stance on corruption in the 1990s. Now, it aims to help countries implement domestic good-governance reforms, but also considers corruption indicators when it assesses country performance and makes procurement decisions.[62] Specific expectations as to what governments should implement draw on international agreements, and the UN convention in particular has become a model for domestic legislation.[63] This provides outsiders with leverage on domestic policy. As one expert explained, the fact that countries see the need to implement conventions has "helped donors and people who provide technical assistance in building cooperation with recipient countries."[64] This goes hand in hand with naming and shaming on the basis of corruption indices, and both trends indicate the "huge ambition of international donors to have an impact on national governance."[65]

16 *Introduction*

Whatever normative position one might adopt in these debates, it is an indisputable fact that international agreements have become important benchmarks and focal points. In addition to the theoretical appeal of studying the political processes leading to international anti-corruption agreements, this study is motivated by their political relevance, both internationally and domestically.

Chapter outline

Chapter 1 deals with the theoretical building blocks that are used to explain similarities and differences among international agreements. I first address diffusion as a theoretical framework, emphasizing the processes and mechanisms of interdependent decision-making. This is complemented by a discussion of agency in international organizations. I argue that activists and international bureaucrats as well as member-state delegates can play important roles. The third building block relates to international law as signaling, showing how agreements serve to send messages to various audiences. My theoretical model applies the signaling logic as a scope condition for diffusion mechanisms.

Chapter 2 starts with a short overview of the agreements that various organizations have adopted. To account for the existence or absence of agreements, I then discuss member states' signaling motives as scope conditions for diffusion. Next, I focus on the organizations that have created binding agreements and present detailed comparisons of their scope and legal design. I discuss how differences in the underlying signaling motives correspond to different outcomes in terms of scope and legal design. Finally, I compare the agreements' contents in greater detail and emphasize that many provisions are copied verbatim. The comparison thus demonstrates the plausibility of the diffusion approach, setting the scene for the two case-studies that follow.

In Chapter 3, I analyze the process that led up to the Organization of American States adopting its anti-corruption convention in 1996. This is a typical case of domestic and intra-group signaling motives shaping the decision-making process. Under the leadership of a US-led coalition of member states, the organization swiftly drafted and adopted an agreement, then added a monitoring mechanism at a later date. This case illustrates how documents can be influenced by different national as well as international reference models. The resulting agreement focuses on a relatively narrow set of issues, reflecting the varied interests of member states.

Chapter 4 focuses on the African Union, which adopted an anti-corruption agreement in 2003. In this case, the impetus to address

Introduction 17

corruption came primarily from donors and multilateral institutions, rather than advocates within the organization itself. Thereafter, regional bureaucrats, legal experts, and civil society activists dominated the drafting and negotiation process. The resulting agreement is a typical case of diffusion conditioned by external signaling motives. The evidence points to multiple mechanisms of diffusion, showing how the drafters drew on a variety of international reference models. The final convention covers many issues in mandatory language but lacks delegation.

In Chapter 5, I summarize and discuss the scope and legal design of these agreements. International anti-corruption agreements range from narrow enforcement cooperation to broad but poorly enforced agreements that I label "illusionary giants." OAS and AU were driven by contrasting signaling motives, and they also differ with respect to the diffusion mechanisms that drove the process. The book concludes with a discussion of the theoretical and practical implications of these findings.

Notes

1 Sérgio Fernando Moro, "Preventing Systemic Corruption in Brazil," *Daedalus* 147, no. 3 (2018): 157–168; Matthew Stephenson, *Tracking Corruption and Conflicts in the Trump Administration*, GAB: The Global Anticorruption Blog, 2018, https://perma.cc/6RYF-5L2Q; Hannes Munzinger and Frederik Obermaier, *Lost Treasure: Where is Gaddafi's Money?*, Süddeutsche Zeitung, *Panama Papers*, 2016, http://panamapapers.sueddeutsche.de/articles/573aea c75632a39742ed39a0/; J. C. Sharman, *The Despot's Guide to Wealth Management: On the International Campaign against Grand Corruption* (Ithaca, NY: Cornell University Press, 2017); Alexander Cooley, John Heathershaw, and J. C. Sharman, "Laundering Cash, White Washing Reputations," *Journal of Democracy* 29, no. 1 (2018): 39–53; Nicholas Casey and Andrea Zarate, "Corruption Scandals with Brazilian Roots Cascade across Latin America," *New York Times*, 13 February 2017; Dan Hough and William R. Heaston, "The Art of Missing the Point: FIFA and the Control of Corruption," in *Corruption and Norms: Why Informal Rules Matter*, ed. Ina Kubbe and Annika Engelbert (London: Palgrave Macmillan, 2018), 329–346.
2 Patrick Glynn, Stephen J. Kobrin, and Moisés Naím, "The Globalization of Corruption," in *Corruption and the Global Economy*, ed. Kimberly Ann Elliott (Washington, DC: Institute for International Economics, 1997), 7–27; Steven Sampson, "The Anti-corruption Industry: From Movement to Institution," *Global Crime* 11, no. 2 (2010): 261–278; Staffan Andersson and Paul M. Heywood, "Anti-corruption as a Risk to Democracy: On the Unintended Consequences of International Anti-corruption Campaigns," in *Governments, NGOs and Anti-Corruption: The New Integrity Warriors*, ed. Luís de Sousa, Peter Larmour, and Barry Hindess (London and New

18   *Introduction*

York: Routledge, 2009), 33–50; Wayne Sandholtz and Mark M. Gray, "International Integration and National Corruption," *International Organization* 57, no. 4 (2003): 761–800; Mlada Bukovansky, *Corruption is Bad: Normative Dimensions of the Anti-corruption Movement* (Canberra: Australian National University, 2002), https://openresearch-repository.anu.edu.au/bit stream/1885/40136/3/02-5.pdf.

3 Ethan A. Nadelmann, "Global Prohibition Regimes: The Evolution of Norms in International Society," *International Organization* 44, no. 4 (1990): 479–526; Sebastian Wolf and Diana Schmidt-Pfister, eds., *International Anti-corruption Regimes in Europe: Between Corruption, Integration, and Culture* (Baden-Baden: Nomos, 2010); Kathleen A. Getz, "The Effectiveness of Global Prohibition Regimes: Corruption and the Antibribery Convention," *Business and Society* 45, no. 3 (2006): 254–281; Anja P. Jakobi, *"E Pluribus Unum?* The Global Anti-corruption Agenda and its Different International Regimes," in *International Anti-corruption Regimes in Europe*, ed. Wolf and Schmidt-Pfister, 87–104.

4 Robert S. Leiken, "Controlling the Global Corruption Epidemic," *Foreign Policy* 105 (1996): 55–73, at 55.

5 Barbara C. George and Kathleen A. Lacey, "A Coalition of Industrialized Nations, Developing Nations, Multilateral Development Banks and Nongovernmental Organizations: A Pivotal Complement to Current Anticorruption Initiatives," *Cornell International Law Journal* 33, no. 3 (2000): 547–592, at 592; Ioannis N. Androulakis, *Die Globalisierung der Korruptionsbekämpfung: Eine Untersuchung zur Entstehung, zum Inhalt und zu den Auswirkungen des internationalen Korruptionsstrafrechts unter Berücksichtigung der sozialökonomischen Hintergründe* (Baden-Baden: Nomos, 2007), 220–224.

6 Androulakis, *Die Globalisierung der Korruptionsbekämpfung*, 221–224; Glynn, Kobrin, and Naím, "The Globalization of Corruption," 9–12.

7 European Union, "European Commission and Council of Europe Launch 2.4 Million Euro Programme to Fight Corruption and Organised Crime in Central and Eastern Europe," press release, 3 February 1999, http://europa.eu/rapid/press-release_IP-99-72_en.htm; Claire A. Daams, "Regional Initiatives: European Union against Corruption," paper prepared for the 9th International Anti-corruption Conference, Durban, South Africa, 10–15 October 1999, https://perma.cc/7LJ8-CN94; Patrycja Szarek-Mason, *The European Union's Fight against Corruption: The Evolving Policy towards Member States and Candidate Countries* (Cambridge: Cambridge University Press, 2010), 20–21; Leslie Holmes, "International Anti-corruption Regimes and Corruption Levels in European and Eurasian Post-communist State," in *International Anti-corruption Regimes in Europe*, ed. Wolf and Schmidt-Pfister, 25–45.

8 Holger Moroff, "Internationalisierung von Anti-Korruptionsregimen," in *Dimensionen politischer Korruption: Beiträge zum Stand der internationalen Forschung*, ed. Ulrich von Alemann (Wiesbaden: VS Verlag für Sozialwissenschaften, 2005), 444–477, at 455.

9 Arnold J. Heidenheimer and Holger Moroff, "Controlling Business Payoffs to Foreign Officials: The 1998 OECD Anti-bribery Convention," in *Political Corruption: Concepts and Contexts*, ed. Arnold J. Heidenheimer and Michael Johnston (New Brunswick, NJ: Transaction Publishers, 2002), 943–959, at 944–945.

Introduction 19

10 Philip M. Nichols, "Regulating Transnational Bribery in Times of Globalization and Fragmentation," *Yale Journal of International Law* 24 (1999): 257–303; Androulakis, *Die Globalisierung der Korruptionsbekämpfung*, 226.

11 George and Lacey, "A Coalition of Industrialized Nations," 554.

12 See Ha-Joon Chang, "The Hazard of Moral Hazard: Untangling the Asian Crisis," *World Development* 28, no. 4 (2000): 775–788; Linda Y. C. Kim, "Whose 'Model' Failed? Implications of the Asian Economic Crisis," *Washington Quarterly* 21, no. 3 (1998): 25–36.

13 James W. Williams and Margarete E. Beare, "The Business of Bribery: Globalization, Economic Liberalization, and the 'Problem' of Corruption," *Crime, Law and Social Change* 32 (1999): 115–146; Bukovansky, *Corruption is Bad*; Janine R. Wedel, "High Priests and the Gospel of Anti-corruption," *Challenge* 58, no. 1 (2015): 4–22.

14 Jennifer L. McCoy and Heather Heckel, "The Emergence of a Global Anti-corruption Norm," *International Politics* 38, no. 1 (2001): 65–90, at 69.

15 Androulakis, *Die Globalisierung der Korruptionsbekämpfung*, 220; Janine R. Wedel, "Rethinking Corruption in an Age of Ambiguity," *Annual Review of Law and Social Science* 8, no. 1 (2012): 453–498, at 460.

16 Moroff, "Internationalisierung von Anti-Korruptionsregimen," 450; Lori Ann Wanlin, "The Gap between Promise and Practice in the Global Fight against Corruption," *Asper Review of International Business and Trade Law* 6 (2006): 209–240, at 229–232.

17 Margot Cleveland, Christopher M. Favo, Thomas J. Frecka, and Charles L. Owens, "Trends in the International Fight against Bribery and Corruption," *Journal of Business Ethics* 90, no. S2 (2009): 199–244, at 202–203; David Metcalfe, "The OECD Agreement to Criminalize Bribery: A Negotiation Analytic Perspective," *International Negotiation* 5 (2000): 129–155, at 132–135.

18 Kenneth W. Abbott and Duncan Snidal, "Values and Interests: International Legalization in the Fight against Corruption," *Journal of Legal Studies* 31, no. S1 (2002): 141–177, at 162; McCoy and Heckel, "The Emergence of a Global Anti-corruption Norm," 72.

19 George and Lacey, "A Coalition of Industrialized Nations," 560–563; Abbott and Snidal, "Values and Interests."

20 Androulakis, *Die Globalisierung der Korruptionsbekämpfung*, 353–355.

21 Katzarova has traced the development of US ideas and their impact on the anti-corruption agenda in admirable detail: Elitza Katzarova, "From Global Problems to International Norms: What Does the Social Construction of a Global Corruption Problem Tell Us about the Emergence of an International Anti-corruption Norm," *Crime, Law and Social Change* 31, no. 1 (2017): 299–313; Elitza Katzarova, *The Social Construction of Global Corruption: From Utopia to Neoliberalism* (Basingstoke: Palgrave Macmillan, 2019).

22 Lucy Koechlin, *Corruption as an Empty Signifier: Politics and Political Order in Africa* (Leiden and Boston, MA: Brill, 2013), ch. 1; Sarah O'Byrne, "'There is Nothing More Important than Corruption': The Rise and Implementation of a New Development Agenda" (doctoral dissertation, Johns Hopkins University, 2012), 52–53; Stephen P. Riley, "The Political Economy of Anti-corruption Strategies in Africa,"

20 *Introduction*

European Journal of Development Research 10, no. 1 (1998): 129–159, at 132; McCoy and Heckel, "The Emergence of a Global Anti-corruption Norm," 73.

23 Paolo Mauro, "Corruption and Growth," *Quarterly Journal of Economics* 110, no. 3 (1995): 681–712; Paolo Mauro, *The Effects of Corruption on Growth, Investment, and Government Expenditure* (Washington, DC: International Monetary Fund, 1996), https://ssrn.com/abstract=882994; Paolo Mauro, *The Persistence of Corruption and Slow Economic Growth* (Washington, DC: International Monetary Fund, 2004), www.imf.org/External/Pubs/FT/staffp/2004/01/pdf/mauro.pdf.

24 Duane Windsor and Kathleen A. Getz, "Multilateral Cooperation to Combat Corruption: Normative Regimes Despite Mixed Motives and Diverse Values," *Cornell International Law Journal* 33, no. 3 (2000): 731–772, at 756–762.

25 Wedel, "Rethinking Corruption in an Age of Ambiguity," 463; John Brademas and Fritz Heimann, "Tackling International Corruption: No Longer Taboo," *Foreign Affairs* 77, no. 5 (1998): 17–22, at 20; Sandholtz and Gray, "International Integration and National Corruption," 770.

26 James D. Wolfensohn, "'People and Development': Annual Meetings Address by James D. Wolfensohn, President, The World Bank," 1 October 1996, http://go.worldbank.org/PUC5BB8060.

27 Heidenheimer and Moroff, "Controlling Business Payoffs to Foreign Officials: The 1998 OECD Anti-bribery Convention," 945; Sandholtz and Gray, "International Integration and National Corruption," 769–770.

28 Catherine Weaver, *Hypocrisy Trap: The World Bank and the Poverty of Reform* (Princeton, NJ: Princeton University Press, 2008).

29 Bukovansky, *Corruption is Bad*, 9–11; Barbara C. George, Kathleen A. Lacey, and Jutta Birmele, "On the Threshold of the Adoption of Global Antibribery Legislation: A Critical Analysis of Current Domestic and International Efforts toward the Reduction of Business Corruption," *Vanderbilt Journal of Transnational Law* 32, no. 1 (1999): 1–37, at 24–25.

30 Mlada Bukovansky, "The Hollowness of Anti-corruption Discourse," *Review of International Political Economy* 13, no. 2 (2006): 181–209, at 192–193.

31 Sampson, "The Anti-corruption Industry," 274.

32 Peter Eigen, "A Coalition to Combat Corruption: TI, EITI, and Civil Society," in *Corruption, Global Security, and World Order*, ed. Robert I. Rotberg (Washington, DC: Brookings Institution Press, 2009), 416–429, at 421–423; Luís de Sousa, "TI in Search of a Constituency: The Institutionalization and Franchising of the Global Anti-corruption Doctrine," in *Governments, NGOs and Anti-corruption*, ed. de Sousa, Larmour, and Hindess, 186–208.

33 Eigen, "A Coalition to Combat Corruption," 419; Abbott and Snidal, "Values and Interests," 165.

34 McCoy and Heckel, "The Emergence of a Global Anti-corruption Norm," 76.

35 Cited in Wedel, "High Priests and the Gospel of Anti-corruption," 16.

36 Bukovansky, *Corruption is Bad*, 12; Julie Bajolle, *The Origins and Motivations of the Current Emphasis on Corruption: The Case of Transparency International* (working paper, 2005), http://hussonet.free.fr/bajolle.pdf.

Introduction   21

37 Heidenheimer and Moroff, "Controlling Business Payoffs to Foreign Officials," 948.
38 Hongying Wang and James N. Rosenau, "Transparency International and Corruption as an Issue of Global Governance," *Global Governance* 7, no. 1 (2001): 25–49, at 40; Eigen, "A Coalition to Combat Corruption," 421; Bukovansky, *Corruption is Bad*, 16; Nancy Zucker Boswell, "Emerging Consensus on Controlling Corruption," *University of Pennsylvania Journal of International Economic Law* 18, no. 4 (1997): 1165–1176, at 1173–1175; Bruce Zagaris and Shaila Lakhani Ohri, "The Emergence of an International Enforcement Regime on Transnational Corruption in the Americas," *Law and Policy in International Business* 30, no. 1 (1999): 53–93, at 86–89.
39 E.g., Abbott and Snidal, "Values and Interests"; Kolawole Olaniyan, "The African Union Convention on Preventing and Combating Corruption: A Critical Appraisal," *African Human Rights Law Journal* 4, no. 1 (2004): 74–92; Philippa Webb, "The United Nations Convention Against Corruption: Global Achievement or Missed Opportunity?," *Journal of International Economic Law* 8, no. 1 (2005): 191–229; Antonio Argandoña, "The United Nations Convention Against Corruption and its Impact on International Companies," *Journal of Business Ethics* 74, no. 4 (2007): 481–496; Mathis Lohaus, "Ahead of the Curve: The OAS as a Pioneer of International Anti-corruption Efforts," in *Governance Transfer by Regional Organizations: Patching Together a Global Script*, ed. Tanja A. Börzel and Vera van Hüllen (Houndmills: Palgrave Macmillan, 2015), 159–176.
40 Thomas R. Snider and Won Kidane, "Combating Corruption through International Law in Africa: A Comparative Analysis," *Cornell International Law Journal* 40 (2007): 691–748; Jan Wouters, Cedric Ryngaert, and Ann Sofie Cloots, "The International Legal Framework against Corruption: Achievements and Challenges," *Melbourne Journal of International Law* 14, no. 1 (2013): 1–76; Marco Arnone and Leonardo S. Borlini, *Corruption: Economic Analysis and International Law* (Cheltenham: Edward Elgar Publishing, 2014); Cecily Rose, *International Anti-corruption Norms: Their Creation and Influence on Domestic Legal Systems* (Oxford: Oxford University Press, 2015).
41 Summit of the Americas (1994), *First Summit of the Americas: Declaration of Principles*, www.summit-americas.org/i_summit/i_summit_dec_en.pdf.
42 United Nations, *United Nations Conventions Against Corruption* (2003), https://www.unodc.org/pdf/crime/convention_corruption/signing/Convention-e.pdf.
43 Kenneth W. Abbott, Robert O. Keohane, Andrew Moravcsik, Anne-Marie Slaughter, and Duncan Snidal, "The Concept of Legalization," *International Organization* 54, no. 3 (2000): 17–35.
44 Fabrizio Gilardi, "Transnational Diffusion: Norms, Ideas, and Policies," in *Handbook of International Relations*, 2nd ed., ed. Walter Carlsnaes, Thomas Risse, and Beth A. Simmons (London: SAGE, 2013), 453–478, at 454–457.
45 Tanja A. Börzel and Thomas Risse, "From Europeanisation to Diffusion: Introduction," *West European Politics* 35, no. 1 (2012): 1–19.
46 Tanja A. Börzel and Thomas Risse, "Introduction," in *The Oxford Handbook of Comparative Regionalism*, ed. Tanja A. Börzel and Thomas Risse

22   *Introduction*

(Oxford: Oxford University Press, 2016), 3–15; Tanja A. Börzel and Vera van Hüllen, ed., *Governance Transfer by Regional Organizations: Patching Together a Global Script* (Houndmills: Palgrave Macmillan, 2015).

47 John W. Meyer and Brian Rowan, "Institutionalized Organizations: Formal Structure as Myth and Ceremony," *American Journal of Sociology* 83, no. 2 (1977): 340–363; John W. Meyer, Gili S. Drori, and Hokyu Hwang, "World Society and the Proliferation of Formal Organization," in *Globalization and Organization: World Society and Organizational Change*, ed. Gili S. Drori, John W. Meyer, and Hokyu Hwang (Oxford: Oxford University Press, 2006).

48 Beth A. Simmons, Frank Dobbin, and Geoffrey Garrett, "Introduction: The International Diffusion of Liberalism," *International Organization* 60, no. 4 (2006): 781–810; Börzel and Risse, "From Europeanisation to Diffusion."

49 E.g., Oona A. Hathaway, "Between Power and Principle: An Integrated Theory of International Law," *University of Chicago Law Review* 72, no. 2 (2005): 469–536; Jack L. Goldsmith and Eric A. Posner, "Moral and Legal Rhetoric in International Relations: A Rational Choice Perspective," *Journal of Legal Studies* 31, no. S1 (2002): 115–139.

50 Cited in John Hatchard, *Combating Corruption: Legal Approaches to Supporting Good Governance and Integrity in Africa* (Cheltenham: Edward Elgar Publishing, 2014), 13.

51 Transparency International, "What is Corruption?," 2018, www.transparency.org/what-is-corruption/.

52 Sarah Bracking, "Political Development and Corruption: Why 'Right Here, Right Now!'?," in *Corruption and Development: The Anti-corruption Campaigns*, ed. Sarah Bracking (Houndmills: Palgrave Macmillan, 2007), 3–27, at 4–17; Bukovansky, "The Hollowness of Anti-corruption Discourse"; Jacquelin Coolidge and Susan Rose-Ackerman, "Kleptocracy and Reform in African Regimes: Theory and Examples," in *Corruption and Development in Africa: Lessons from Country Case-studies*, ed. Kempe Ronald Hope and Bornwell C. Chikulo (Basingstoke and New York: Macmillan and St. Martin's Press, 1999), 57–86; Carl J. Friedrich, "Corruption Concepts in Historical Perspective," in *Political Corruption*, ed. Heidenheimer and Johnston, 15–23; John Gardiner, "Defining Corruption," in *Political Corruption*, ed. Heidenheimer and Johnston, 25–40; Arnold J. Heidenheimer and Michael Johnston, "Introduction to Part I," in *Political Corruption*, ed. Heidenheimer and Johnston, 3–14; Michael Johnston, "Keeping the Answers, Changing the Questions: Corruption Definitions Revisited," in *Dimensionen politischer Korruption: Beiträge zum Stand der internationalen Forschung*, ed. Ulrich von Alemann (Wiesbaden: VS Verlag für Sozialwissenschaften, 2005), 61–76; Oskar Kurer, "Corruption: An Alternative Approach to Its Definition and Measurement," *Political Studies* 53, no. 1 (2005): 222–239; Oskar Kurer, "Definitions of Corruption," in *Routledge Handbook of Political Corruption*, ed. Paul M. Heywood (London and New York: Routledge, 2015), 30–41; Mark Philp, "Conceptualizing Political Corruption," in *Political Corruption*, ed. Heidenheimer and Johnston, 41–57; Laura S. Underkuffler, "Defining Corruption: Implications for Action," in *Corruption, Global Security, and World Order*, ed. Rotberg, 27–46.

Introduction 23

53 Tina Søreide, "Democracy's Shortcomings in Anti-corruption," in *Anti-Corruption Policy: Can International Actors Play a Constructive Role?*, ed. Susan Rose-Ackerman and Paul D. Carrington (Durham, NC: Carolina Academic Press, 2013), 129–147, at 135; Kevin E. Davis, "The Prospects for Anti-corruption Law: Optimists versus Skeptics," *Hague Journal on the Rule of Law* 4, no. 02 (2012): 319–336, at 325.

54 Edgardo Buscaglia, "On Best and not so Good Practices for Addressing High-level Corruption Worldwide: An Empirical Assessment," in *International Handbook on the Economics of Corruption*, vol. 2, ed. Susan Rose-Ackerman and Tina Søreide (Cheltenham: Edward Elgar Publishing, 2011), 453–477; Alina Mungiu-Pippidi et al., *Contextual Choices in Fighting Corruption: Lessons Learned: Report 4/2011: Study* (Oslo: Norwegian Agency for Development Cooperation, 2011), https://papers.ssrn.com/sol3/papers.cfm?abstract_id=2042021; Alina Mungiu-Pippidi, *Quantitative Report on Causes of Performance and Stagnation in the Global Fight against Corruption* (Berlin: ANTICORRP Consortium, 2014), www.againstcorruption.eu/wp-content/uploads/2015/12/MS2-Quantitative-report-on-causes-of-performance-and-stagnation-in-the-global-fight-against-corruption 1.pdf.

55 Lucinda A. Low, Sarah R. Lamoree, and John London, "The 'Demand Side' of Transnational Bribery and Corruption: Why Leveling the Playing Field on the Supply Side Isn't Enough," *Fordham Law Review* 84, no. 2 (2015): 563–599, at 580.

56 Hatchard, *Combating Corruption*, 33.

57 Rose, *International Anti-corruption Norms*, 63–95.

58 Susan Rose-Ackerman, "Introduction: The Role of International Actors in Fighting Corruption," in *Anti-Corruption Policy*, ed. Rose-Ackerman and Carrington, 3–38, at 22–25.

59 David Chaikin and J. C. Sharman, *Corruption and Money Laundering: A Symbiotic Relationship* (Basingstoke: Palgrave Macmillan, 2009), 36–37; H. Richard Friman, ed., *The Politics of Leverage in International Relations: Name, Shame, and Sanction* (Houndmills: Palgrave Macmillan, 2015).

60 Alina Mungiu-Pippidi, *The Quest for Good Governance: How Societies Develop Control of Corruption* (Cambridge: Cambridge University Press, 2015), 210, 224.

61 Fritz Heimann and Gillian Dell, *Progress Report 2010: Enforcement of the OECD Anti-bribery Convention* (Berlin: Transparency International, 2010), http://files.transparency.org/content/download/255/1024/file/2010_OECDProgressReport_EN.pdf; Fritz Heimann, Gillian Dell, and Kelly McCarthy, *Progress Report 2011: Enforcement of the OECD Anti-bribery Convention* (Berlin: Transparency International, 2011), http://files.transparency.org/content/download/102/411/file/2011_OECDReport_EN.pdf; Fritz Heimann, Gillian Dell, and Gabor Bathory, *UN Convention Against Corruption: Progress Report 2013* (Berlin: Transparency International, 2013), http://files.transparency.org/content/download/699/3003/file/2013_UNCACProgressReport_EN.pdf; Fritz Heimann, Ádám Földes, and Sophia Coles, *Exporting Corruption: Progress Report 2015: Assessing Enforcement of the OECD Convention on Combating Foreign Bribery* (Berlin: Transparency International, 2015), http://files.transparency.org/content/download/1923/12702/file/2015_ExportingCorruption_OOECDProgressRepor_EN.pdf.

24 *Introduction*

62 Anja P. Jakobi, *Common Goods and Evils? The Formation of Global Crime Governance* (Oxford: Oxford University Press, 2013), 145–148; Mungiu-Pippidi, *The Quest for Good Governance*, 190–192.
63 Davis, "The Prospects for Anti-corruption Law: Optimists versus Skeptics," 323.
64 Phone interview with US government official, June 2013.
65 Mungiu-Pippidi, *The Quest for Good Governance*, 207.

1 The argument
Diffusion and signaling motives

- **The diffusion of international agreements**
- **Agency in international organizations**
- **Signaling motives as a scope condition**
- **The effects of different audiences**
- **Alternative explanations**
- **Conclusion**

How can similarities and differences between international organizations' approaches to anti-corruption be explained? Fundamentally, this concerns the difference between opting in and opting out. Why do some organizations, such as the Council of Europe and the African Union, become active while others, such as ASEAN, fail to adopt any binding anti-corruption agreements? Moreover, my theoretical framework addresses variation among the agreements that have been reached. A quick glance at these agreements reveals vast differences in the number of issues they address. In addition, it is striking that some documents largely avoid obligatory language, whereas others frequently use terms like "shall" to indicate binding commitments. Consequently, my goal is to explain which elements of anti-corruption are addressed (the scope of agreements) and how the documents are drafted in terms of obligatory language and follow-up mechanisms (their legal design).

My main argument is that international anti-corruption agreements result from interdependent decision-making. Given the mushrooming of international agreements over a short timescale, a plausible account of their development needs to explore connections between them. This is in line with theories of diffusion, which emphasize several mechanisms of direct and indirect influence between units of analysis. My model focuses on the agency of those involved in IO decision-making. While member states always have the final say over international

26 *The argument*

agreements, non-state actors, such as civil society and international bureaucrats, must be considered, too. Ultimately, I argue that both the negotiation process and the contents of each international agreement are shaped by the member states' desire to signal their anti-corruption commitment to various audiences. Signaling motives thus serve as scope conditions for diffusion—moderating its effects and explaining why some organizations resist the trend.

The diffusion of international agreements

Anti-corruption arrived swiftly on the political agenda of international organizations during the 1990s and 2000s. Previous research has described how various actors—national governments, international organizations, transnational activists—contributed to this development. This is why a diffusion perspective offers the most plausible starting point to explain patterns in international anti-corruption agreements. Diffusion is defined as a process of interdependent decision-making: change in one unit of observation increases the likelihood of change in another. Typically, this assumes a chronological sequence, but interdependence can also apply in cases of simultaneous or anticipatory decisions.[1]

First, we need to explore how international organizations influence one another. Despite some variation in the labels used, the literature on diffusion commonly identifies four mechanisms: coercion, competition, learning, and emulation.[2] These categories provide a succinct typology. However, a framework that clearly distinguishes between *active* and *indirect* mechanisms of diffusion offers additional precision. In this way, researchers can spell out the roles played by the *senders* of policies or ideas, on the one hand, and the *recipients*, on the other (see Table 1.1).

To analyze the evolution of international anti-corruption agreements, I draw on the diffusion framework outlined by Börzel and Risse.[3] Actors can actively influence decision-making in several ways. The most extreme of these is *coercion*, which requires legal authority or force. This seems irrelevant for relationships between international organizations. Next, there is the *manipulation of utility calculation* through incentives and capacity-building. In this case, an actor provides resources or rewards to incentivize an international organization's adoption of a particular policy. Of course, incentives can be negative, too: for instance, when resources are withheld as a bargaining tool. Decisions can also be influenced by the anticipation of future rewards. *Socialization and persuasion*—the third type of active influence—deviate from a pure logic of consequences. In this scenario, the sender will

The argument   27

Table 1.1 Mechanisms of diffusion[4]

	Social mechanism	*Actions*
Active	Coercion	Sender: Authority, legal force
	Manipulation of utility calculation	Sender: Incentives, capacity-building
	Socialization, persuasion	Sender: Normative pressure, reasoning
Indirect	Competition	Recipient: Functional emulation
	Lesson-drawing	Recipient: Functional emulation
	Mimicry	Recipient: Normative emulation

use normative arguments and reasoning to elicit a response. For instance, to promote a norm or a policy, senders could appeal to ethical concerns, social appropriateness, or higher social status.

Diffusion does not rest solely on agents actively trying to influence others because their actions may also have indirect effects, serving as reference models. For instance, one organization might emulate another because the two institutions are in *competition* for resources. In this logic, adaption and innovation are useful strategies to catch up or at least avoid falling behind. The second example of indirect influence, *lesson-drawing*, is a form of rationalist learning. It is triggered by the desire to address a policy problem, coupled with the impulse to look outwards for potential answers. In the purest form of this logic, international organizations gather information on their peers' policies, update their beliefs on the basis of the new information, then adopt what they perceive as best practice. However, learning is likely to be constrained by resources and bounded rationality. In the face of limited time and resources, decision-makers will not "proactively scan the international environment" but rather opt for geographic or temporal proximity when choosing a reference model.[5] In other words, they tend to be biased towards models that are readily available, and also overestimate how representative these models are.[6] The final indirect mechanism is *mimicry*. In this case, international organizations copy the behavior of others on the basis of their perceived legitimacy. Instead of searching for a functional solution, actors who follow this logic will select a reference model according to the legitimacy and/or prestige of its originators. Normative emulation thus emphasizes the social status of the actors who are associated with an idea.

Having established the various mechanisms of diffusion, the remainder of this chapter addresses two more pillars of the theoretical

28 *The argument*

argument. First, who are the agents of IO decision-making and diffusion? Since this book analyzes international agreements, it makes sense to treat states as primary actors. After all, member-state representatives have the final say when it comes to drafting, negotiating, and adopting international anti-corruption agreements. This is in line with much of the literature on decision-making in international organizations. However, the roles played by non-state actors should not be overlooked. Activists and civil society are important pieces of the puzzle. As discussed in the Introduction, norm entrepreneurs such as Transparency International were crucial in placing corruption on the global agenda. Therefore, when analyzing the design of agreements, it is essential to pay due attention to transnational activists.[7] Additionally, recent scholarship on decision-making in IOs has revealed that authority is often delegated to international bureaucrats and experts. I will discuss these different various forms of agency in the next section.

Second, under which scope conditions do diffusion processes occur? This has become a pressing issue in recent diffusion research. Some authors focus on dense relationships as a prerequisite. For instance, Duina and Lenz refer to "network ties," which they measure through overlaps in membership and the existence of close ties with "pioneer" organizations.[8] In addition, they suggest that adoption becomes more likely over time, as a concept spreads throughout the population. This is akin to the norm life cycle proposed by Finnemore and Sikkink, who argue that legitimation and appropriateness become the key drivers of diffusion once a tipping point has been reached.[9] Other researchers have suggested conditions based on actor characteristics, such as regime type or power asymmetry relative to the sender, the medium through which diffusion takes place, or the properties of the idea in question.[10] As the subject of this book is the adoption of international anti-corruption agreements within a relatively short period of time, most of these potential scope conditions are constant across the cases. Therefore, I focus on member states' signaling motives as scope conditions for diffusion (see below).

Agency in international organizations

At least implicitly, the design of agreements within international organizations has usually been studied from a strict principal-agent perspective. In this view, states are the principal decision-makers, and the agency of organizations is limited to fulfilling these principals' wishes. More recently, however, researchers studying IO decision-making have started to explore the bureaucratic politics of these bodies. Scholars

The argument 29

who adhere to a rationalist principal-agent framework as well as those who favor a constructivist perspective have suggested a more nuanced picture in which delegation does not guarantee that the agents will follow the mandate they receive to the letter. Applying the notion of "agency slack," the principal-agent literature discusses how IO bureaucracies' behavior can be at odds with the wishes of the principals.[11]

Under certain conditions, IO bureaucrats can become actors in their own right:

> When the agent pool is small or agents possess significant expertise, agents can lobby principals for more authority and resources, negotiate with principals the terms of their contracts, and even utilize their resources and knowledge to influence principals' preferences or strategies.[12]

Consequently, IO bureaucrats can have autonomous influence over the design of formal international agreements. Barnett and Finnemore consider several types of IO autonomy, ranked by the degree to which they are at odds with state preferences. Two of their conjectures are particularly relevant for this study. First, IOs can act when member states are indifferent because they have little knowledge or unclear preferences about the subject matter. Second, "IOs may build alliances with publics, nongovernmental organizations, other IOs, and other states to protect policies from powerful states that oppose them."[13]

Summarizing their findings on bureaucratic politics in the context of IOs expanding or changing their mandates, Barnett and Finnemore emphasize the potential for "creative agency" by international bureaucrats. In "periods of rapid global change" or when dealing with "unsettled states" with significant uncertainty, IO staffers are likely to consider innovative proposals. In such circumstances, they may develop and introduce their own policy ideas. In addition, or alternatively, bureaucrats are likely to act as coalition-builders and seek alliances with like-minded NGOs, other IOs, or other states.[14]

When studying the negotiation and adoption of new agreements in the context of international organizations, it thus makes sense to consider the role of IO bureaucracies. Yet, this might not capture the whole picture of the delegation of authority to actors other than official government delegates. Even in a formally intergovernmental setting, there can be "attenuated delegation," where "the powers being exercised are several steps removed from member states' control."[15]

30   *The argument*

This holds true even for the seemingly intergovernmental process of treaty negotiation, which, in practice, frequently involves non-state actors, such as staff who are employed by the international organization itself. These staffers are supposed to play a facilitating role, but they are also likely to pursue bureaucratic self-interest and/or other agendas that are not necessarily aligned with the principals' views. Even when an issue is not explicitly delegated to an IO body, negotiations may be influenced by actors other than member states' delegates. In addition, treaty negotiations may involve accredited external participants, such as experts and civil society representatives. Such actors sometimes play roles during ad hoc conferences, but their involvement is more frequently institutionalized within the structures of international organizations. Thus, "each government ultimately decides whether it will be bound, but by accepting the active participation of non-state actors, they have tacitly delegated some law-making power to them."[16]

Recent work on the access of non-governmental organizations to international organizations is instructive in this regard.[17] According to survey results, NGOs felt they had more influence over decision-making in the United Nations and other international organizations when they were given greater access. Additionally, they were more successful when they used the strategy of supplying information that was valuable to governments, as opposed to making claims based on popular mobilization. However, Tallberg and colleagues identify less influence in "policy areas associated with Westphalian sovereignty, where states are known to be very anxious about their control, which may leave fewer opportunities for NGOs to contribute information that shapes political outcomes."[18] This suggests potential resistance to NGO influence during international negotiations to the extent that anti-corruption is seen as a sensitive issue. Nevertheless, notwithstanding member states' skepticism, civil society input is often well received by IO bureaucrats as NGOs can provide detailed information, additional resources, and legitimacy.[19]

To summarize, international bureaucracies and non-governmental organizations may both carry significant weight in IO decision-making. These political processes are not adequately captured by concise models of intergovernmental policymaking. This is why it is imperative to analyze the influence of non-state actors when attempting to explain variation in outcomes. Simultaneously, as the remainder of this chapter will explain, member states remain crucial because their motives serve as a scope condition for the diffusion processes that shape international agreements.

Signaling motives as a scope condition

Organizations vary in the extent to which they are susceptible to active diffusion influences and the extent to which they seek to emulate others. In light of the primacy of member states in IO decision-making, their motives to develop anti-corruption agreements are the most plausible scope condition. Drawing on the literature on treaty commitments, I argue that international anti-corruption agreements are best understood as a form of signaling.[20] By designing and adopting agreements, member states signal that they are committed to curbing corrupt practices at home and fighting transnational corruption alongside their IO partners.

Hyde uses this approach to explain why states routinely invite observers to monitor their elections even when those elections are sure to be undemocratic.[21] And there are many other situations in which states wish to signal their congruence with some desirable characteristics that others value but they themselves cannot necessarily observe directly. For instance, to increase their chances of acquiring foreign aid, trade, or investment, states are motivated to signal their adherence to the standards that the granters of such benefits demand.[22] Hathaway incorporates the notion of signaling into the "collateral consequences" of treaty commitment. These "arise from the anticipated reactions of individuals, states, and organizations to the state's decision to commit to a treaty and then to abide or not to abide by its terms," irrespective of the costs and benefits that stem directly from the treaty's legal framework.[23]

In fact, these collateral consequences might be beneficial even for states that clearly fail to comply with the treaty after committing to it. First, when international actors find it difficult to gather information on implementation, they often accept the simple act of commitment as a substitute. Second, even if outsiders know that implementation is weak, they might reward a signatory state's supposed good intentions in the hope that either the current government will improve its practice or a successor will prove more active. Third, "some of the transnational actors that exert pressure on states to commit to treaties [may] care little about whether the country actually complies with those commitments"; rather, they are merely seeking clearance to do business with the country in question.[24] States with relatively poor reputations thus have much to gain from committing to an anti-corruption treaty, comparable to the benefits of joining an esteemed economic cooperation organization.[25] If their signal is taken sufficiently seriously to provide at least marginal benefits, they will profit. Even if they fail to

32　*The argument*

comply and their inactivity is criticized, their reputational loss will be minor as "those that possess a poor reputation have a shorter distance to fall."[26]

The signaling logic has been applied to account for the legal design of international agreements. Marcoux and Urpelainen argue that some seemingly binding international agreements might in fact incorporate "non-compliance by design."[27] In their model, government decision-making is not exclusively driven by payoffs and problems with international cooperation. Instead, they focus on domestic and international audiences. A government will agree to design a treaty with the characteristics of hard law because it expects audience benefits from doing so, even when the costs of compliance are excessive. States that are unwilling or unable to comply with a treaty might still agree to mandatory language if they assume there will be little enforcement. Such disingenuous commitments are especially likely when states know that it will be impossible to prove non-compliance for a significant period of time, as this will allow them to enjoy reputational benefits in the interim. In the long run, however, the adoption of moribund hard law is "likely to create frustration, especially among constituencies that supported 'genuine' hard law."[28]

In their work on policy diffusion, Elkins and Simmons suggest a similar connection between the motive to adopt a policy and the likely outcomes. They point out that states might adopt a policy because of the "ancillary benefits associated with the adoption of the institution" rather than due to any appreciation of the policy's inherent merits.[29] These benefits may include reputational gains from adhering to a cultural norm or advantages in the competition for scarce resources, such as capital or loans. If such ancillary benefits are the primary motives to adopt a policy, Elkins and Simmons predict suboptimal outcomes, as the design of the policy does not reflect rational learning, and the "level of commitment and internalization" is relatively low.[30]

These arguments about collateral consequences, ancillary benefits, audience costs, and reputational benefits all point in a similar direction. While Elkins and Simmons do not use the term "signaling," their study illustrates how this logic is compatible with diffusion arguments.

The effects of different audiences

By adopting an anti-corruption agreement within the framework of an IO, member states can address a variety of audiences: domestic constituents; other member states; and external actors. This has important implications.

The argument 33

First, let us consider domestic audiences. International agreements are meant to show constituents that a government is serious about fighting corruption. Anti-corruption norms are closely connected to issues of democracy, the rule of law, and respect for human rights. Thus, we might expect signaling to domestic audiences to be of paramount importance when governments need democratic legitimation. There are multiple reasons to link anti-corruption to democracies. The transnational campaign of the 1990s that pressured leaders to address the issue of corruption relied on civil society and public opinion, both of which enjoy more freedom and leverage in democratic regimes. Furthermore, high-level corruption scandals were widely publicized at the time, increasing the salience of the issue, particularly in democracies. These scandals led to successful electoral campaigns based on anti-corruption promises, which resulted in the new governments seeking to signal their credibility after entering office. Newly established democratic governments are particularly likely to use international agreements to signal their commitment to reform, and indeed to lock in changes to prevent backsliding by their successors.[31] Thus, we may expect the domestic signaling motive to be relevant primarily for democratic governments. In turn, international organizations with more democratic member states should be more likely to adopt binding anti-corruption agreements.

The second signaling motive concerns the other member states within an international organization. Adopting a binding agreement can serve as a signal of commitment within the group. This is particularly useful when member states differ regarding their legal systems or the extent of corruption within their borders. An agreement may serve to harmonize legislation to address negative externalities from corrupt practices, such as foreign bribery. Moreover, it may signal intent regarding future implementation and cooperation: for example, on the provision of mutual legal assistance in anti-corruption efforts. In addition to increasing the likelihood that a binding agreement will be adopted, domestic and intra-group signaling motives have implications for the design of such agreements. If an agreement serves as a signal to domestic or intra-group audiences, I believe there is a good chance that there will be a trade-off between its scope and its legal design. This is congruent with assumptions within the rationalist–functionalist model of decision-making: as they consider the costs of future compliance, states try to achieve a balance between the breadth of their commitments and their level of obligation.[32]

Because both the domestic audience and other states in the organization are likely to notice non-compliance, it is sensible for member

34 *The argument*

states to be cautious. Therefore, we may expect them to include optional clauses and leave room for exceptions to mitigate criticism in the event of non-compliance. At the same time, when the agreement is designed as a signal among IO member states, it usually involves the delegation of follow-up tasks to a newly created body or forum. Such follow-up mechanisms may aid with monitoring compliance with key provisions and thereby increase the strength of the signal. The intra-group signaling motive thus corresponds to credible commitments in the rationalist–functionalist perspective.[33] The prevalence of this motive in any given organization cannot be deduced from members' characteristics, such as regime type, as the importance of signaling within the group depends on the interactions among member states. If several members anticipate benefits from intra-group cooperation on corruption issues, they will set the agenda and bargain with the others to reach an agreement. Evidence of the intra-group signaling motive can thus be gathered by studying agenda-setting and negotiation.

The third type of signal is sent to external audiences. By adopting anti-corruption agreements, member states indicate their adherence to the global trend towards norms of good governance. Anti-corruption is a particularly plausible case for this mechanism since reforms in this sector have been heavily promoted by international actors since the mid-1990s. States looking to improve their reputations can do so by showing external audiences that they take anti-corruption seriously. These are the "collateral consequences of treaty membership."[34] We may expect countries that rely on development cooperation to adopt anti-corruption policies in order to fulfill donor expectations. International agreements may be part of broader efforts to transform policy and behavior, although skeptics may suspect that they are actually disingenuous displays of goodwill that are specifically designed to relieve the pressure to implement substantial changes at the domestic level.[35] Either way, it is reasonable to assume that organizations with member states that receive a great deal of development assistance are most likely to adopt binding international anti-corruption agreements.

If the audience for the signal is external, member states must consider the collateral consequences when drafting agreements. This will probably lead to fewer trade-offs between scope and legal obligations, as the main impulse is simply to signal good intentions rather than balance commitments against the costs associated with non-compliance. In such circumstances, designing international anti-corruption treaties is akin to the cheap talk and window-dressing that are often evident in international law.[36] This is not to say that the resulting documents are invariably inconsequential, but, at the drafting stage, member-state

The argument 35

negotiators are certainly more likely to aim for agreements that *appear* highly ambitious, rather than discuss trade-offs over concerns about future compliance.[37] Enforcement mechanisms are also less of a priority because member states have no need for peer review, given that the agreement does not comprise credible commitments to one another. Moreover, there might be reluctance to establish a follow-up mechanism as this could provide outsiders with grounds for criticism in cases of non-compliance.[38] Overall, then, we might expect IO member states that are motivated by external signaling to negotiate agreements that *seem* impressive in both scope and obligation, with implementation taking a back seat.[39]

When international organizations negotiate agreements, both direct and indirect mechanisms of diffusion may influence the process. Some combinations of signaling motives and diffusion mechanisms seem especially likely. Powerful states, other international organizations, and donor agencies might provide incentives or capacity-building to the organization, moving the utility calculation in favor of a stronger commitment to anti-corruption in line with the influencers' preferences. If an agreement is primarily designed to address intra-group audiences, it will tend to draw on suggestions from agenda-setting member states. By contrast, outsiders will be more influential when agreements are motivated by external signaling. Active influences may also take the form of persuasion and normative pressure. States that seek to signal to domestic democratic constituents should be most amenable to these influences because domestic norm entrepreneurs in democratic regimes will be able to address IO decision-makers directly. Moreover, arguments made by transnational civil society are likely to resonate most strongly with democratically elected governments that must take public opinion into account.

Then there are indirect influences through competition, lesson-drawing, and mimicry. Competition among international organizations plays a role primarily when agreements are motivated by signaling to an external audience. When organizations compete for resources distributed by development partners, they will be motivated to adopt a strong signal whenever their competitors do so. Lesson-drawing is based on learning from best practice and attempts to search for and evaluate existing models, albeit under the constraints of bounded rationality.[40] Such learning is likely to occur in organizations whose member states are motivated by intra-group signaling. After all, this motive implies that the solution to any problem must be based on functional usefulness and feasibility, because the actors care about goal attainment and their future ability to comply. Normative emulation or mimicry, by contrast,

36 *The argument*

refers to a scenario in which a reference model is chosen because of its perceived legitimacy. There is no evaluation of options; rather, a choice is made solely on the basis of status. Mimicry presumably plays a greater role in agreements drafted by member states that are likely to benefit from collateral consequences. Organizations that wish to signal congruence with external audiences' standards and norms may mimic the approaches chosen by prestigious role models.

Alternative explanations

There are two alternative ways to account for the similarities and differences among international anti-corruption agreements. The first is the rationalist–functionalist view of international regimes for cooperation. Proponents of rational design argue that "states use international institutions to further their own goals, and they design institutions accordingly."[41] Rational outcomes depend on the configuration of actors, the nature of the issue area, and/or the type of cooperation problem. While my argument draws on similar factors, particularly in the case of intra-group signaling, the assumption of functional problem-solving stands in contrast to the diverse mechanisms of diffusion. Simply put, I believe that the "eruption" of anti-corruption agreements over a short period of time strongly suggests that many actors influenced one another. Therefore, to do justice to the process that led to these agreements, we need an explanatory model based on interdependence rather than individual rational choice.

Setting aside the process, could the outcomes be explained with a more concise model? Nadelmann's concept of "prohibition regimes" broadens the regime logic by incorporating moral entrepreneurs, who lobby their own and foreign governments first to create and then to comply with the desired international regime.[42] Yet, this also lays bare the limitations of the rationalist–functionalist approach. Anti-corruption is loaded with ethical and moral concerns. Even if one does not expect such claims to shape decision-makers' beliefs directly, they should not be ignored entirely, given their salience in political negotiations. Moreover, large portions of the anti-corruption agreements concern the reform of domestic political systems. These aspects do not promise immediate benefits from cooperation; they do not involve opportunities for reciprocity or retaliation. The rationale for designing such agreements goes far beyond narrow functional payoffs, which is why I consider a wider range of motives.[43]

The second alternative explanation is much closer to my diffusion argument. At the macro level, the spread of international anti-corruption

The argument 37

agreements is compatible with the World Society Approach (WSA). This model predicts isomorphism across cases, meaning that outcomes take similar shapes due to structural conditions: "social structure is ontologically prior to and generative of agents."[44] When a policy objective and the related toolbox spread across the globe, the WSA interprets this as the manifestation of a shared script of rationality and modernity.[45] Isomorphism thus offers a baseline explanation as to why many instances of anti-corruption agreements exist. Indeed, Jakobi provides a highly persuasive account of how corruption and other "evils" have made their way onto the agendas of numerous IOs.[46]

Yet, the structural lens of the WSA becomes problematic with respect to smaller-scale differences among IOs—the very issues that motivated this study. The assumption that a general quest for legitimacy drives international organizations glosses over variation associated with different aspects of anti-corruption policy and different actors.[47] Moreover, how can we know which norms and ideas are in line with world culture? WSA scholars emphasize modern bureaucratic problem-solving, together with a focus on individual rights.[48] Kim and Sharman, for instance, argue that certain aspects of anti-corruption gained prominence due to their congruence with basic notions of modernity.[49] Yet, my findings contradict their central empirical claim that prosecuting corrupt heads of state is more prevalent in international agreements than institutional reforms at the national level. As Finnemore puts it, the "picture painted by institutionalist studies is one in which world culture marches effortlessly and facelessly across the globe."[50] My research questions require more nuance, so I emphasize the agents and mechanisms of diffusion.

Conclusion

My goal is to explain why international agreements to combat corruption not only share many features but also display significant differences. With this aim in mind, my approach has been informed by the empirical and theoretical literature in two significant ways. First, it seems that international organizations influence one another with respect to their choices about the adoption and design of anti-corruption agreements. Previous research on the emergence of anti-corruption on the international agenda suggests that decision-making was at least indirectly connected. Second, as this book investigates differentiation among international organizations within a single historical context and issue area, I decided to focus on the agency of IO member states, international bureaucrats, and civil society, rather than structure.

38 The argument

Figure 1.1 presents the different elements of my theoretical model. International anti-corruption agreements, as measured by the dimensions scope and legal design, are products of diffusion processes. Diffusion can operate through a variety of active and indirect mechanisms involving government delegates, international bureaucrats, and other non-state actors. The signaling motives of member states act as scope conditions, and thereby also shape the results. Intuitively, one might assume that certain mechanisms and agents will be associated with specific signaling motives. I will revisit these heuristic assumptions in Chapter 5.

For both active and indirect modes of diffusion, an IO's decision-making process is of paramount importance. Drafting and negotiating agreements can take place in very different settings: ad hoc or institutionalized; informal or formal; one-off or iterative; with or without input from IO bureaucrats; strictly intergovernmental or open to outsiders. A crucial component is the involvement of actors other than member states.[51] Legal or subject-matter experts may be asked to contribute, which opens the door for lesson-drawing or emulation facilitated by them. The same is true for IO bureaucrats, who might be tasked with preparatory work that shapes outcomes. In addition, when norm entrepreneurs and activists are involved in the drafting and negotiations, they can influence decision-making. I am unable to evaluate the circumstances of negotiations and drafting in Chapter 2, but I will do so in Chapters 3 and 4.

Notwithstanding the potential for diffusion through various mechanisms, I do not expect ever more ambitious anti-corruption agreements to emerge. My baseline assumption is that governments are wary of making strong commitments, because their benefits and costs are often uncertain. After all, international agreements curtail sovereignty and can go against the interests of powerful domestic actors, such as when corrupt officials are prosecuted. Adopting international

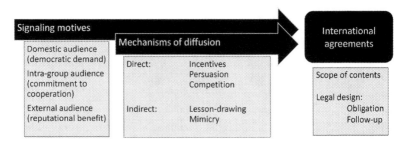

Figure 1.1 Theoretical model

The argument 39

agreements also opens the door for criticism in the event of poor implementation. Thus, I have specified scope conditions to portray how states "negotiate international law in the shadow of domestic and international political pressures."[52] When it comes to international anti-corruption agreements, the signaling motives of member states moderate the effects of diffusion. First, organizations with insufficient signaling motives avoid adopting binding agreements. Second, both the scope and the legal design of agreements are influenced by the relative importance of domestic, intra-group, or external audiences.

Notes

1 Erin R. Graham, Charles R. Shipan, and Craig Volden, "The Diffusion of Policy Diffusion Research in Political Science," *British Journal of Political Science* 43, no. 3 (2013): 673–701, at 675, n.9.
2 Graham, Shipan, and Volden, "The Diffusion of Policy Diffusion Research in Political Science," 690; Beth A. Simmons, Frank Dobbin, and Geoffrey Garrett, "Introduction: The International Diffusion of Liberalism," *International Organization* 60, no. 4 (2006): 781–810.
3 Tanja A. Börzel and Thomas Risse, "From Europeanisation to Diffusion: Introduction," *West European Politics* 35, no. 1 (2012): 1–19.
4 Based on Börzel and Risse, "From Europeanisation to Diffusion: Introduction."
5 Kurt Weyland, *Bounded Rationality and Policy Diffusion: Social Sector Reform in Latin America* (Princeton, NJ: Princeton University Press, 2007), 6.
6 Fabrizio Gilardi, "Transnational Diffusion: Norms, Ideas, and Policies," in *Handbook of International Relations*, 2nd ed., ed. Walter Carlsnaes, Thomas Risse, and Beth A. Simmons (London: SAGE, 2013), 453–478, at 465–466; Zachary Elkins and Beth A. Simmons, "On Waves, Clusters, and Diffusion: A Conceptual Framework," *Annals of the American Academy of Political and Social Science* 598, no. 1 (2005): 33–51, at 43–45; Weyland, *Bounded Rationality and Policy Diffusion*, 7–8.
7 Margaret E. Keck and Kathryn Sikkink, *Activists beyond Borders: Advocacy Networks in International Politics* (Ithaca, NY: Cornell University Press, 1998); Thomas Risse, Stephen C. Ropp, and Kathryn Sikkink, eds., *The Power of Human Rights: International Norms and Domestic Change* (Cambridge: Cambridge University Press, 1999); Thomas Risse, "Transnational Actors and World Politics," in *Handbook of International Relations*, 2nd ed., ed. Carlsnaes, Risse, and Simmons, 426–453.
8 Francesco Duina and Tobias Lenz, "Regionalism and Diffusion Revisited: From Final Design towards Stages of Decision-making," *Review of International Studies* 42, no. 4 (2016): 773–797.
9 Martha Finnemore and Kathryn Sikkink, "International Norm Dynamics and Political Change," *International Organization* 52, no. 4 (1998): 887–917, at 902–904; Elkins and Simmons, "On Waves, Clusters, and Diffusion," 39–41.
10 Tanja A. Börzel and Thomas Risse, "When Europeanisation Meets Diffusion: Exploring New Territory," *West European Politics* 35, no. 1 (2012): 192–207, at 198–204; Etel Solingen, "Of Dominoes and Firewalls: The

40 *The argument*

Domestic, Regional, and Global Politics of International Diffusion," *International Studies Quarterly* 56, no. 4 (2012): 631–644, at 640–641.

11 Michael N. Barnett and Martha Finnemore, "The Politics, Power, and Pathologies of International Organizations," *International Organization* 53, no. 4 (1999): 699–732; Michael N. Barnett and Martha Finnemore, *Rules for the World: International Organizations in Global Politics* (Ithaca, NY: Cornell University Press, 2004).

12 Darren G. Hawkins, David A. Lake, Daniel L. Nielson, and Michael J. Tierney, "Delegation under Anarchy: States, International Organizations, and Principal-Agent Theory," in *Delegation and Agency in International Organizations*, ed. Darren G. Hawkins, David A. Lake, Daniel L. Nielson, and Michael J. Tierney (Cambridge: Cambridge University Press, 2006), 3–38, at 31.

13 Barnett and Finnemore, *Rules for the World*, 28.

14 Barnett and Finnemore, *Rules for the World*, 162.

15 Ian Johnstone, "Law-making by International Organizations: Perspectives from IL/IR Theory," in *Interdisciplinary Perspectives on International Law and International Relations: The State of the Art*, ed. Jeffrey L. Dunoff and Mark A. Pollack (Cambridge: Cambridge University Press, 2013), 266–292, at 268.

16 Johnstone, "Law-making by International Organizations," 271.

17 Jonas Tallberg, Thomas Sommerer, Theresa Squatrito, and Christer Jönsson, *The Opening up of International Organizations: Transnational Access in Global Governance* (Cambridge: Cambridge University Press, 2013); Jonas Tallberg, Lisa M. Dellmuth, Hans Agné, and Andreas Duit, "NGO Influence in International Organizations: Information, Access, and Exchange," *British Journal of Political Science* 48, no. 1 (2018): 213–238.

18 Tallberg, Dellmuth, Agné, and Duit, "NGO Influence in International Organizations," 233.

19 Peter J. Spiro, "Nongovernmental Organizations in International Relations (Theory)," in *Interdisciplinary Perspectives on International Law and International Relations*, ed. Dunoff and Pollack, 223–243, at 233.

20 Jack L. Goldsmith and Eric A. Posner, "Moral and Legal Rhetoric in International Relations: A Rational Choice Perspective," *Journal of Legal Studies* 31, no. S1 (2002): 115–139.

21 Susan D. Hyde, "Catch Us if You Can: Election Monitoring and International Norm Diffusion," *American Journal of Political Science* 55, no. 2 (2011): 356–369.

22 Hyde, "Catch Us if You Can," 366–367.

23 Oona A. Hathaway, "Between Power and Principle: An Integrated Theory of International Law," *University of Chicago Law Review* 72, no. 2 (2005): 469–536, at 492.

24 Hathaway, "Between Power and Principle," 507–508.

25 Julia Gray, *The Company States Keep: International Economic Organizations and Investor Perceptions* (Cambridge: Cambridge University Press, 2013).

26 Hathaway, "Between Power and Principle," 510; Rachel Brewster, "Reputation in International Relations and International Law Theory," in *Interdisciplinary Perspectives on International Law and International Relations*, ed. Dunoff and Pollack, 524–543.

The argument 41

27 Christopher Marcoux and Johannes Urpelainen, "Non-compliance by Design: Moribund Hard Law in International Institutions," *Review of International Organizations* 8, no. 2 (2013): 163–191, at 164.
28 Marcoux and Urpelainen, "Non-compliance by Design," 188.
29 Elkins and Simmons, "On Waves, Clusters, and Diffusion," 47.
30 Elkins and Simmons, "On Waves, Clusters, and Diffusion," 46–48.
31 Andrew Moravcsik, "The Origins of Human Rights Regimes: Democratic Delegation in Postwar Europe," *International Organization* 51, no. 4 (2000): 217–252; Daniel Berliner and Aaron Erlich, "Competing for Transparency: Political Competition and Institutional Reform in Mexican States," *American Political Science Review* 109, no. 1 (2015): 110–128, at 110.
32 Barbara Koremenos, "Contracting around International Uncertainty," *American Political Science Review* 99, no. 4 (2005): 549–565; Andrew T. Guzman, *How International Law Works: A Rational Choice Theory* (Oxford: Oxford University Press, 2008), 138–141.
33 Emilie M. Hafner-Burton, David G. Victor, and Yonatan Lupu, "Political Science Research on International Law: The State of the Field," *American Journal of International Law* 106 (2012): 47–97, at 75–77; Gregory Shaffer and Mark A. Pollack, "Hard and Soft Law," in *Interdisciplinary Perspectives on International Law and International Relations*, ed. Dunoff and Pollack, 197–222.
34 Hathaway, "Between Power and Principle."
35 Tiyanjana Maluwa, "Ratification of African Union Treaties by Member States: Law, Policy and Practice," *Melbourne Journal of International Law* 13 (2012): 1–49, at 9–13.
36 Goldsmith and Posner, "Moral and Legal Rhetoric in International Relations"; Hathaway, "Between Power and Principle."
37 Similar concerns have been raised about the ability of external actors to promote anti-corruption reforms at the national level (and indeed whether such behavior is legitimate): Kevin E. Davis, "The Prospects for Anti-corruption Law: Optimists versus Skeptics," *Hague Journal on the Rule of Law* 4, no. 2 (2012): 319–336, at 333–336.
38 Hyde, "Catch Us if You Can."
39 Others have pointed to this link between external motives and functionally suboptimal results: Elkins and Simmons, "On Waves, Clusters, and Diffusion," 46–48; Anja Jetschke and Tobias Lenz, "Does Regionalism Diffuse? A New Research Agenda for the Study of Regional Organizations," *Journal of European Public Policy* 20, no. 4 (2013): 626–637, at 633.
40 Weyland, *Bounded Rationality and Policy Diffusion*.
41 Barbara Koremenos, Charles Lipson, and Duncan Snidal, "The Rational Design of International Institutions," *International Organization* 55, no. 4 (2001): 761–799, at 762.
42 Ethan A. Nadelmann, "Global Prohibition Regimes: The Evolution of Norms in International Society," *International Organization* 44, no. 4 (1990): 479–526; Kathleen A. Getz, "The Effectiveness of Global Prohibition Regimes: Corruption and the Antibribery Convention," *Business and Society* 45, no. 3 (2006): 254–281.
43 Anti-corruption and human rights raise similar questions in this respect. See Oona A. Hathaway, "The Costs of Commitment," *Stanford Law Review* 55, no. 5 (2003): 1821–1862; Oona A. Hathaway, "Why Do

42 *The argument*

Countries Commit to Human Rights Treaties?," *Journal of Conflict Resolution* 51, no. 4 (2007): 588–621.

44 Martha Finnemore, "Norms, Culture, and World Politics: Insights from Sociology's Institutionalism," *International Organization* 50, no. 2 (1996): 325–347, at 333.

45 Gili S. Drori, John W. Meyer, and Hokyu Hwang, "Foreword," in *Globalization and Organization. World Society and Organizational Change*, ed. Gili S. Drori, John W. Meyer, and Hokyu Hwang (Oxford: Oxford University Press, 2006); John W. Meyer, "Globalization. Theory and Trends," *International Journal of Comparative Sociology* 48, no. 4 (2007): 261–273.

46 Anja P. Jakobi, *Common Goods and Evils? The Formation of Global Crime Governance* (Oxford: Oxford University Press, 2013).

47 Consider two examples. First, while members of one organization might discuss corruption in the context of regime change and expanding membership, in different circumstances they might be motivated by their relationships with actors from other regions. Second, harmonizing criminal laws to curb certain practices of foreign bribery is very different from committing to broad reforms of domestic governance.

48 Finnemore, "Norms, Culture, and World Politics," 331–333.

49 Hun Joon Kim and J. C. Sharman, "Accounts and Accountability: Corruption, Human Rights, and Individual Accountability Norms," *International Organization* 68, no. 2 (2014): 417–448, at 439.

50 Finnemore, "Norms, Culture, and World Politics," 339.

51 Johnstone, "Law-making by International Organizations."

52 Marcoux and Urpelainen, "Non-compliance by Design," 164.

2 International anti-corruption agreements in comparison

- **Mapping the global landscape of anti-corruption**
- **Summary: first movers, laggards, outliers**
- **Comparing the scope and legal design of the agreements**
- **How do ideas spread? Evidence of diffusion processes**
- **Conclusion**

How much do international and regional organizations resemble one another in their approaches to anti-corruption? And what explains the similarities and differences among them? This chapter deals with these questions from a comparative perspective. First, I discuss how an increasing number of IOs have adopted anti-corruption agreements over time, but also show that a few outliers resist this trend. To account for this pattern, I address signaling motives as scope conditions for diffusion. Second, I compare the scope and legal design of these agreements. To analyze the scope, I map which elements of prevention, criminalization, jurisdiction, domestic enforcement, and international enforcement each document addresses. With respect to legal design, I address obligation and delegation: which provisions are designed to be legally binding; and what type of follow-up mechanism—if any—does each treaty establish? Finally, I explore whether sections of agreements have been copied verbatim from one case to another.

Mapping the global landscape of anti-corruption

Almost all states today have ratified at least one binding international agreement to combat corruption. Indeed, at the time of writing, a total of 186 states had ratified the UN Convention Against Corruption, making it the most widely ratified document in this sphere.[1] Many countries are parties to other agreements, too. Of course, this does not automatically translate into compliance with legal standards, let alone

44   *Agreements in comparison*

total eradication of the various practices that have been labeled "corruption." However, it is indicative of a strong trend over the last two decades. In 1995, not a single binding international agreement against corruption was available for ratification. Since then, regional and other international organizations have drafted numerous documents for adoption and ratification, sometimes bolstered by follow-up mechanisms. The rest of this chapter discusses the mushrooming of these international agreements in various regions and notes that they were adopted at different points in time. In addition, some organizations are outliers that have not yet adopted any binding agreement.

I have focused on a group of regional organizations that are considered relatively active in terms of promoting and protecting governance norms at the domestic level.[2] In a sense, this makes them likely to embrace anti-corruption treaties. They are all multi-purpose, geographically contiguous entities, and all of the world's main regions are represented among them. The UN and the OECD are also included because of their high salience in the fight against corruption. Given the geographic and political diversity of the organizations studied, I consider them to be a sufficiently representative sample. That said, an even more comprehensive sample would be desirable.[3]

Council of Europe, European Union, and OECD

The Council of Europe's efforts to address corruption can be traced back to a summit in Malta in 1994, at which a working group on the issue was created.[4] In 1999, the COE adopted two conventions—one focusing on criminal law, the other on civil law—to which non-members may accede. In addition, it adopted the "Twenty Guiding Principles" (1997), the Council of Ministers' recommendations on codes of conduct for public officials (2000), a recommendation on political party and campaign funding (2003), and an additional protocol extending the range of the criminal-law convention (also 2003). Compliance with the conventions and guiding principles is monitored by a peer-review mechanism called the "Group of States against Corruption" (GRECO). All reports are confidential, but summaries may be published. In addition, GRECO's Statutory Committee has the power to issue public statements if states are passive and achieve unsatisfactory results. While no such public statement has been issued yet, GRECO published "ad hoc reports" in response to legislative changes in Poland and in Romania in 2018.[5]

The European Union has adopted several documents that are binding for member states. Two protocols to the Convention on the

Agreements in comparison 45

Protection of the European Communities' Financial Interests are concerned with criminalizing both active and passive public-sector bribery, making legal persons liable, and requiring states to ensure there are sanctions. The 1997 Convention on the Fight Against Corruption addresses the same issues, but it is no longer limited to potential damage to EU finances. The criminalization focus was extended with two Council decisions from 1998 and 2003 that criminalize both active and passive bribery in the private sector.

The EU's focus has traditionally been on corruption within the organization itself. With its vast budget and thousands of staff who are potential targets for bribes and embezzlement, the Commission's priorities have been different from those of other organizations.[6] Notably, in 1999, when under the leadership of Jacques Santer, it was heavily criticized because of alleged corruption and collectively resigned.[7] Consequently, after Romano Prodi replaced Santer, the Commission established the European Anti-Fraud Office (OLAF), which was mandated to safeguard the integrity of the EU budget. A second focal point has been corruption in accession countries: rather than regulating the domestic affairs of its members, the EU has demanded governance reforms from neighboring countries that wish to join the organization.[8]

Indeed, arguably, the European Union is relatively weak when it comes to ensuring that its member states conform to good-governance norms.[9] Regarding follow-up, there is no peer-review mechanism, and the European Commission was unable to initiate enforcement action while corruption belonged to the so-called "third pillar" of the European Union. However, the legal situation changed with the conclusion of the Treaty of Lisbon's transition period at the end of 2014.[10] Based on a 2011 Commission decision to start collecting data, the first "Anti-corruption Report," published in February 2014, contains assessments of country-level implementation.[11] The Commission collected and published information on how many corruption cases were prosecuted in domestic courts in 2016, but also scrapped the Anti-corruption Report.[12] This suggests some ongoing uncertainty about its role in anti-corruption monitoring among member states.

Overall, the provisions in the EU conventions are difficult to assess with the analytical toolkit that is used in this book. The organization is unique in its degree of political and legal integration, and its regulations contain a wide array of provisions on issues such as public procurement, the regulation of business transactions, and cooperation in criminal matters.[13] Thus, some of the matters that are omitted in the documents that specifically address corruption are covered in other

46 *Agreements in comparison*

pieces of EU legislation. Unfortunately, though, I am unable to analyze these statutes due to the limited scope of this book.

The OECD adopted a convention on transnational bribery in 1997.[14] However, this Convention on Combating Bribery of Foreign Public Officials in International Business Transactions has a very narrow focus. At its core, it bans the payment of bribes to foreigners, which means that prevention and criminalization are to the fore. Since 1997, several "recommendations" on related issues have followed, broadening the OECD's approach to include public officials' conduct (1998), conflict of interest (2003), public procurement and public-sector transparency (2008), and, most recently, transparency in lobbying (2010). Monitoring states' compliance with the convention— but not the supplementary recommendations—is undertaken by the Working Group on Bribery, which has been in existence since 1994.[15] Its guidelines for peer review were established on the basis of the 1997 Revised Recommendations of the Council on Combating Bribery in International Business Transactions, then updated in 2009.[16]

Organization of American States and sub-regions

The Organization of American States covers North America, the Caribbean, Central America, and South America. In July 1975, its Permanent Council issued a resolution urging member states to ban bribery by "transnational enterprises."[17] Five months later, the UN issued a similar resolution.[18] In 1996, the OAS was again in the vanguard when creating the Inter-American Convention Against Corruption (IACAC)—the world's first binding anti-corruption agreement.[19] While the IACAC did not include a follow-up mechanism when it was adopted, member states subsequently created a peer-review mechanism called MESICIC at the first Conference of the States Parties in 2001.[20] Over time, the Secretariat has published model laws covering the preventive measures listed in the treaty.

By contrast, the South American regional organization MERCO- SUR, with Brazil and Argentina as its most important member states, has not adopted any broad, binding anti-corruption agreement. In 2002, the organization's meeting of interior ministers adopted a short resolution on fighting corrupt practices in the border regions, but this contained no specific governance standards or other self-commitments. Eight years later, MERCOSUR heads of state adopted a declaration that referred to the ongoing fight against corruption and urged members to implement the OAS and the UN conventions.

The Andean Community, like MERCOSUR, has not adopted a binding anti-corruption agreement. However, in 2007 an "action plan" that referenced the OAS and UN conventions suggested improving domestic governance and international cooperation. Finally, the Caribbean Community, whose 15 members are also members of the OAS, has not adopted any anti-corruption agreements.

The African Union and sub-regions

In 2003, the AU adopted its Convention on Combating Corruption. This introduced good governance and human rights as additional goals for anti-corruption, and covered a wide range of other issues. As a follow-up mechanism, the AU created an independent Advisory Board consisting of 11 experts rather than government delegates,[21] but this subsequently came under considerable criticism (see Chapter 4).

The continental AU was not the first African organization to address corruption. In 2001, ECOWAS adopted a binding Protocol on the Fight Against Corruption. However, follow-up was very weak and the protocol was not implemented in practice. Indeed, it did not enter into force until 2015, six years after ECOWAS members had established a network of national anti-corruption agencies.[22]

The SADC also adopted a Protocol Against Corruption in 2001. This entered into force in 2005 following ratification by a sufficient number of member states, but the planned creation of a regional program for implementation has since been delayed multiple times. Regional anti-corruption agencies were connected via the Southern African Forum Against Corruption (SAFAC), which was established in 2001.[23] However, at the time of writing, the formal follow-up procedure, as envisioned in the protocol, had not been established, and SAFAC no longer had an active website.

In contrast to ECOWAS and SADC, the East African Community (EAC) has not adopted a binding anti-corruption document since its re-establishment in 2000. A draft document includes some binding commitments, but as yet the member states have not signed it.[24] Negotiations were continuing at the time of writing (see Chapter 4).

United Nations Convention Against Corruption

As early as 1975, the UN condemned bribery in a non-binding document.[25] However, it was almost three decades before it adopted an agreement containing binding obligations for member states. The UN Convention Against Corruption—which is sometimes called the

48   *Agreements in comparison*

Merida Convention due to the location of the signing conference—was adopted in 2003 and entered into force two years later. UNCAC stands out because it is very comprehensive and contains precise and detailed wording on several issues. However, it contains "no fewer than a dozen different levels of implementation obligations ... from hard (mandatory requirements) to very soft,"[26] which has led legal experts to criticize its complexity and enforceability.[27]

UNCAC established a Conference of States Parties and suggested that an "appropriate mechanism or body to assist in the effective implementation of the Convention" should be created.[28] This clause was finally implemented at the Third Conference of the Parties, held in Doha in 2009, with the creation of the Implementation Review Group (IRG).[29] Procedurally, the IRG relies on desk reviews with optional on-site visits. Experts are asked to consider material from other peer reviews, and only executive summaries of the resulting reports are published. The peer review's potential impact thus seems limited in comparison with other cases.[30] This echoes earlier concerns that copying the OECD model of peer review might be "unrealistic" because of the much larger and more diverse UN membership.[31] On the other hand, UNCAC enjoys almost universal support in terms of signatures and ratifications. Consequently, its provisions affect many more states than those of the previously discussed regional agreements, most of which preceded the UN effort by several years.

League of Arab States, ASEAN, and others

In 2010, the League of Arab States adopted the Arab Anti-corruption Convention through its Council of Ministers of the Interior. Analyzing this document in detail is difficult because the official English translation is unreliable, and very few secondary sources discuss it. While it draws heavily on the UN convention,[32] the drafters have added the caveat "that the description of acts of corruption, criminalized by the present Convention, is subject to the laws of the State Party."[33] The document's ratification status remained unclear at the time of writing.

In 2004, several member states of the Association of South-East Asian Nations (ASEAN) adopted a memorandum of understanding that addressed cooperation between national anti-corruption agencies. More members have subsequently adopted the memorandum, but ASEAN still seems reluctant to draft a more far-reaching anti-corruption agreement.[34] For instance, the organization's 2009 Political–Security Community Blueprint mentions corruption but contains no clauses on states' obligations at the domestic level.[35] Rather, it simply urges all

Agreements in comparison 49

members to adopt the memorandum of understanding and ratify any treaties they have previously signed. Interestingly, the parallel Economic Community Blueprint does not even mention corruption.

Two other anti-corruption initiatives in the Asian region deserve mention. However, both are strongly driven and indeed financed by non-Asian countries. The first is the Asian Development Bank and OECD's Anti-Corruption Initiative for Asia and the Pacific, which boasts 31 members, including all of the ASEAN member states, with the exception of Brunei, Laos, and Myanmar. A clear example of North–South cooperation, the language is centered on capacity-building rather than legal commitments. Since 2006, the initiative has published "thematic reviews" on three topics.[36] Its 2001 Action Plan lists a number of issues to be addressed as "legally non-binding principles and standards towards policy reform which participating governments ... voluntarily commit to implement."[37] Thus, the initiative is explicitly non-binding and best characterized as a supporting instrument for UNCAC, reflecting members' sovereignty concerns: "As a result, although there is a great deal of expertise and advice on offer, the pressure for countries to implement common standards and live up to their commitment is weaker."[38]

The second initiative is Asia–Pacific Economic Cooperation (APEC), which brings together 21 Pacific Rim countries. This forum adopted non-binding declarations on fighting corruption after lobbying from the United States, Chile, and South Korea in 2004.[39] It created a Working Group on Transparency and Corruption, and in 2014 endorsed a Chinese initiative to establish an information exchange among anti-corruption agencies.[40]

Summary: first movers, laggards, outliers

International organizations in different parts of the world vary in their approaches to anti-corruption. A total of nine international organizations, two of which (UN and OECD) span several regions, have adopted binding anti-corruption agreements. Among the regional organizations, those in Europe and Africa show the highest density of treaties, with both macro-regional (AU, COE) and sub-regional (EU, ECOWAS, SADC) bodies drafting agreements. The League of Arab States finally followed suit after a significant delay. Africa already has an overlapping patchwork of regional agreements, and the EAC is currently discussing the adoption of another agreement. In the Americas, by contrast, there is one continental treaty (OAS), while the sub-regional organizations (MERCOSUR, CAN, CARICOM)

50 *Agreements in comparison*

have refrained from drafting individual binding agreements. Finally, Asia is an outlier, as neither ASEAN nor other regional organizations have adopted binding agreements.

As Table 2.1 indicates, the OAS, OECD, and European organizations were pioneers in the field of binding anti-corruption agreements. Between 1996 and 1999, a total of five agreements were adopted in the OAS, OECD, EU, and COE. A second wave occurred shortly afterwards in Africa, when the ECOWAS, SADC, and AU adopted their agreements. A few months later, negotiations over the UN

Table 2.1 Binding anti-corruption agreements

Document	Organization	Adoption	Entry into force	Parties
Inter-American Convention Against Corruption	OAS	1996	1997	34 (97%)
Convention on the Fight Against Corruption Involving Officials of the European Communities or Officials of Member States of the European Union	EU	1997	2005	27 (97%)
Convention on Combating Bribery of Foreign Public Officials in International Business Transactions	OECD	1997	1999	44 (100+%)
Criminal Law Convention on Corruption	COE	1999	2002	48 (100+%)
Civil Law Convention on Corruption	COE	1999	2003	35 (72+%)
Protocol Against Corruption	SADC	2001	2005	13 (87%)
Protocol on the Fight Against Corruption	ECOWAS	2001	2015	10 (67%)
Convention on Preventing and Combating Corruption	AU	2003	2006	37 (70%)
Convention Against Corruption	UN	2003	2005	186 (96%)
Arab Convention to Fight Corruption	LAS	2010	n/a	n/a

Sources: Respective organizations' websites.

Notes: The percentage in the final column shows the proportion of (full) member states that have ratified the agreement, with + indicating that non-members have also ratified.

Agreements in comparison 51

Convention Against Corruption concluded. The Arab League was a significant laggard as it did not adopt its Convention to Fight Corruption until 2010. There is considerable variation in member states' ratification of these agreements. Ratification rates are above 90 percent for the OAS convention, the COE criminal law convention, the OECD convention, and, most notably, the UN convention, with its very wide and diverse audience. The EU is a special case because it almost always requires new members to ratify the whole *acquis communautaire*, with Malta the sole exception. With respect to the SADC protocol, 87 percent of member states have now ratified the agreement. The COE civil law convention, the AU convention, and the ECOWAS protocol have been less successful, with ratification rates of around 70 percent. There is no reliable information about the ratification or otherwise of the Arab convention.

Accounting for leaders and laggards

While some international organizations have adopted at least one binding anti-corruption agreement, others have not. How may we explain this variation? Explaining whether a regional organization adopts a binding agreement is akin to identifying scope conditions for diffusion processes. To allow for the spread of ideas, an organization must first fulfill the necessary conditions to reach a binding agreement. We may expect the decision to adopt or reject binding anti-corruption agreements to be conditioned by signaling motives. Agreements can serve as signals to political constituents at home (domestic), commitments among the members of an international organization (intragroup), or signals to third parties, such as development partners (external). In this section, I present statistics to explore the influence of these scope conditions for diffusion. I do not employ inferential statistical models for two reasons. First, the number of cases is very small, as I survey just 14 organizations. Second, I am not attempting to build a fully fledged explanatory model; rather, my intention is to probe the plausibility of scope conditions for the subsequent analysis.

The domestic signaling hypothesis leads to the assumption that organizations formed by relatively democratic states should be inclined to tackle corruption. Constituents in such states are likely to care about corruption and may put pressure on their elected leaders to tackle it. Additionally, civil society groups have more opportunities to lobby for anti-corruption in democracies. There are several datasets on domestic regime types, with Polity IV and Freedom House two of the most

52 *Agreements in comparison*

widely used. To avoid gaps in the data and biases with either of these, I rely on the combined score provided by the Quality of Government project.[41]

The intra-group signaling motivation presents an analytical challenge at this point. Members have a motive to signal to one another when there are asymmetries between them that lead to a subset of states lobbying the others. Alternatively, there is the potential for mutually beneficial cooperation based on specific anti-corruption issues. However, assessing these motives requires information on the negotiation processes themselves, rather than "dataset observations," such as information on regime type.[42] Thus, while I address the implications of intra-group signaling in the following sections, I omit them from this stage of the analysis.

When it comes to signaling to external audiences, the crucial variable is the inflow of development aid. This is because the global anti-corruption agenda is tightly linked to development cooperation. Countries that receive a great deal of foreign aid thus have a strong motive to signal their good-governance credentials to the external audience of bilateral and multilateral development actors. My information on aid flows once again comes from the Quality of Government project, which in turn draws on the World Bank's World Development Indicators.[43] For the following analysis, I use data on official development aid for member states in each organization.

What could be alternative explanations? From a functionalist perspective, agreements may be expected if corruption poses a policy problem. In other words, when states have a problem with corruption, international measures should form part of problem-solving efforts. Alternatively, it could be that relatively high levels of corruption among member states are counterproductive, since entering into agreements would expose the extent of the problem. One way to operationalize corruption levels is the World Bank's measure of control of corruption. Notwithstanding a number of methodological challenges,[44] I choose this indicator—which is based on multiple sources—as a reasonable approximation of corruption levels. Time-series data were accessed through the Quality of Government dataset.[45] A related notion concerns wealth and state capacity: reaching agreements to tackle corruption should be less challenging when more resources are available. Data come from the World Bank's World Development Indicators that are included in the Quality of Government dataset.[46]

Data on these factors take the form of per-country time series spanning the years 1995 to 2012. I chose this starting point because the middle of the 1990s marked the beginning of the global trend towards

Agreements in comparison 53

anti-corruption agreements, and it was when better data started to become available. To adapt this country-level data to the level of analysis that is appropriate for my research question, I added information on the memberships of various regional organizations to the Quality of Government dataset. For both democracy and aid, this leads to values for each organization based on the average values for the respective member states. Having converted country-level time-series data to group-level time-series data, I then calculated the average value for the whole period. This reduces each organization to a single data point per variable, allowing for easy appraisal of patterns.

Democracy and development aid as conditions favoring binding agreements

To capture the conditions under which organizations adopt binding anti-corruption agreements, Figure 2.1 plots the levels of democratic governance against the inflows of foreign aid. At first glance, there is no clear pattern, and positive and negative outcomes are scattered across the board. Yet, if we take the relationships between cases into account, the findings become clearer. The four early adopters (EU, OECD, COE, OAS) are clustered in the top left. All of them have a

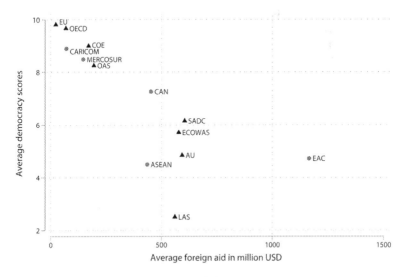

Figure 2.1 Democracy and foreign aid inflows
Note: Triangles indicate organizations that have adopted binding agreements; circles indicate those that have not.

54 *Agreements in comparison*

high proportion of democracies among their memberships, while inflows of development aid are very low. As hypothesized, then, democratic regimes seem to be eager to adopt anti-corruption agreements.

To explain why none of the Central and Latin American sub-regional organizations (CARICOM, MERCOSUR, CAN) has adopted a binding agreement, despite their relatively democratic memberships, consider that all of the members of these IOs are parties to the 1996 OAS convention. As mentioned earlier, the sub-regional groupings in the Americas appear to defer to the OAS in the field of anti-corruption (see Chapter 3 for further details).

A second cluster is evident in the center of the figure: the member states of the SADC, ECOWAS, and the AU all have medium levels of democratic governance and relatively high aid inflows. All three of these organizations adopted agreements in the second wave, after the year 2000. But why do the sub-regional organizations in Western and Southern Africa duplicate the continental anti-corruption efforts? The answer may be linked simply to institutional inertia, with the large and very diverse AU taking longer to reach an agreement than the smaller sub-groups. In addition, however, the AU suffers from a relatively poor ratification record, and the sub-regional agreements are still being ratified by new member states. It thus appears that the drafting of seemingly redundant agreements reflects a conscious decision by member states. Further evidence for this is provided by the fact that the East African Community is currently in the process of creating yet another sub-regional anti-corruption agreement, even though its member states are also members of the African Union and the United Nations, both of which have long-since adopted far-reaching conventions. I will address this pattern of seemingly deliberate duplication in Chapter 4.

The EAC, together with ASEAN and the LAS, constitutes the third part of the distribution. Given their positions in the scatter plot, it seems misguided to speak of a "cluster," since the three organizations differ in their positioning in terms of democracy, incoming aid, and the outcome variable. At the time of writing, neither ASEAN nor the EAC had committed to a binding agreement, whereas the Arab League did in 2010. However, all three could be viewed as either laggards or opt-outs in the global trend of anti-corruption agreements. ASEAN, with its low to medium levels of both democracy and incoming aid, has never adopted a binding agreement, and this holds true for the whole Asian macro region, which engages in the global anti-corruption movement solely in non-binding forums such as the OECD–ADB and APEC.

Besides opting out, there is the outcome of delayed adoption. The East African Community, with very large aid inflows but a low democracy rating, is a laggard in comparison with the other African cases. Its negotiations about an anti-corruption protocol have been ongoing for many years. The Arab League, which has the lowest democracy rating and low to medium aid inflows, is in the unique position of adopting a regional convention at an extremely late date, long after the global UN convention had been widely ratified.

Table 2.2 summarizes the findings on scope conditions and the results in terms of pioneers, laggards, and opt-outs. Neither functional necessity (which would suggest a correlation with member states' domestic ability to control corruption) nor state capacity (as indicated by member states' wealth) provides a more convincing explanation of these patterns (see Appendix 2).

In sum, two characteristics at the level of member states are associated with adopting binding anti-corruption agreements. The first is regime type. All of the organizations with relatively democratic memberships have adopted agreements with the exception of those in Central and Latin America, whose member states are also members of the OAS. In contrast, the three organizations with the lowest democracy scores have either not adopted binding agreements or, in the case of the Arab League, have done so after a significant delay. The non-adopters

Table 2.2 Conditions under which agreements have been adopted

	Europe and North America	Central and Latin America	North Africa and the Middle East	Sub-Saharan Africa	South-East Asia
Democracy levels	High	High	Low	Medium	Low/ Medium
Development aid	Low	Low	Medium	High	Low/ Medium
Domestic ability to curb corruption	High	Medium/ Low	Low	Low	Low
Wealth (GDP per capita)	High	Medium/ Low	Medium	Low	Medium
Binding agreements	Yes: COE, EU, OECD 1997–1999	Yes: OAS 1996	Yes: LAS 2010	Yes: ECOWAS, SADC, AU 2001–2003	No

56 *Agreements in comparison*

among the regional organizations under investigation confirm this explanation, as they share the characteristic of low democracy ratings. It seems that, under these circumstances, reservations about sovereignty paired with high levels of autonomy for government leaders that do not face competitive elections convince member states to resist the global trend. There was a shift from this position in the Arab League in 2010, although the extent to which its convention will be implemented remains unclear. Might ASEAN similarly transition from its long-term opt-out position and eventually adopt some form of binding agreement? After all, it has been argued that this organization has changed course on the sensitive issue of human rights over recent years.[47] Nevertheless, it also has a history of upholding the concept of non-interference much more "stubbornly" than other regional organizations.[48]

The second factor is the magnitude of incoming foreign aid. It is difficult to assess if aid inflows can be considered a necessary condition for adopting an agreement at medium levels of democracy, since there is no comparison case of a somewhat democratic organization with no incoming aid. However, aid inflows may be one reason why sub-regional organizations in Africa have adopted agreements despite the activities of the AU, whereas in the Americas the top-level organization (OAS) remains the sole actor in the field. The regional organizations in question are funded to a significant extent by non-members; moreover, they represent member states that receive a great deal of foreign aid.

One final point of discussion concerns the European and OECD initiatives. At first sight, there appears to be significant overlap here, as in the African context, because the COE shares many member states with both the European Union and the OECD. However, these organizations focused on different aspects of anti-corruption when setting up their agreements. Therefore, any overlap can be explained by functional differentiation.

Comparing the scope and legal design of the agreements

How do international agreements differ in terms of scope and legal design, and what explains this variation? Logically, the greatest possible difference between two organizations is when one adopts a binding, broad treaty while the other makes no attempt even to draft an anti-corruption document. Yet, the variation between individual cases is often much more nuanced than this. I describe this potential variation along two dimensions: the scope of anti-corruption efforts; and their legal design.

Agreements in comparison 57

The scope of international anti-corruption agreements

Scope concerns the policies, standards, and ideas that constitute the substance of each agreement. This is consistent with the descriptive elements of the "rational design of international institutions" framework, which conceptualized the substance of international institutions under the heading "Scope."[49] Both political science and legal studies researchers have explicitly compared the various anti-corruption agreements.[50] Drawing on these works, I categorize the aspects of my scope dimension in a way that reflects their function and proximity to policy objectives (see Table 2.3). This leads to five categories, each of which contains multiple elements:

- preventive measures (17);
- criminalization (12);
- jurisdiction (7);
- domestic enforcement (13); and
- international cooperation (8).

Prevention is a broad category that includes all provisions aimed at reducing opportunities for acts of corruption, and thus the likelihood of incidents. Preventive measures fall into five sub-categories, the first of which is concerned with public officials. Many agreements suggest adopting codes of conduct and providing training to ensure that public officials are aware of legal and ethical standards. Another preventive provision aimed at public officials is to make them disclose their personal finances, which can act as a deterrent to potential bribe-takers. The second sub-category is concerned with public processes. Agreements often contain clauses that urge signatory states to ensure integrity in the processes of hiring, procurement, and accounting. Third, prevention is addressed in the form of measures to increase transparency. This can mean ensuring citizens' access to information. Transparency with respect to political (party) funding is another issue. Some agreements also suggest that civil society and the media should be supported with a view to increasing transparency. Raising public awareness is the last of the transparency-related typical provisions. The fourth sub-category concerns the private sector. Agreements typically call for prevention through clear accounting rules; abolishing tax benefits related to bribery is another typical provision. Fifth, there are usually clauses on corruption-related institutions. Signatory states are often asked to set up specialized agencies to combat corruption and ensure that government agencies cooperate in this area. The work of the judiciary must be protected, given its role in deterring corruption.

58 *Agreements in comparison*

Table 2.3 The scope of international anti-corruption agreements

Prevention				
Public officials	*Public processes*	*Transparency*	*Private sector*	*Institutions*
Codes of conduct	Hiring	Access to information	Accounting	Special agencies
Personal finances	Procurement	Political funding	Tax deductibility	Agency cooperation
Training	Accounting	Civil society		Protect judiciary
		Media		False claims
		Public awareness		
Criminalization				
Public-sector bribes	*Public-sector abuse*	*Related offenses*	*Private sector*	*Transnational bribes*
Active/ passive	Abuse of office	Complicity	Active/ passive	National officials
Trading in influence	Embezzlement	Money laundering	Embezzlement	International officials
	Illicit enrichment	Obstruct justice		
Jurisdiction				
Extraterritoriality	*Limits*			
Citizens abroad	Double jeopardy			
Effect on state	Consult if overlap			
Effect on citizens				
National officials				
Related offenses				

Agreements in comparison 59

Domestic enforcement

Sanctions	Protection	Suspects' rights	Civil law
Criminal sanctions	Whistleblowers	Statute of limitations	Void if corrupt
Civil sanctions	Witnesses	Fair trial	Right to void
Legal persons liable	Victims	Limits to immunity	Private right to act
Confiscation			

International cooperation

Legal assistance	Law enforcement	Assets
Mutual legal assistance	Technical cooperation	Trace and freeze
No bank secrecy	Special techniques	Return
Extradition	Single authority	

Finally, some agreements include sections on discouraging false claims in the context of corruption investigations.

Criminalization is crucial given that anti-corruption agreements revolve around regulating undesirable behavior. This category includes all provisions that describe which forms of behavior constitute corruption and therefore should be outlawed. As with prevention, it may be divided into five sub-categories. The first concerns public-sector bribery, with the payment and the solicitation of bribes (active and passive bribery) both outlawed. A related offense is trading in influence, which refers to officials meddling in decision-making that is not formally under their authority, such as within a different department. The definition usually includes offers to pay for informal influence as well as solicitation by officials (active and passive). Second, criminalization often includes abuse of public office without a quid pro quo exchange between bribe-payer and bribe-taker, such as when officials gain advantages for themselves. Relatedly, the embezzlement or diversion of public funds may be banned. Finally, the concept of illicit enrichment comes under this sub-category. This concerns any increase in assets that cannot be reasonably explained on the basis of official income. The third sub-category comprises offenses related to corruption, such as acting as an accomplice or accessory. Money laundering also falls

60 *Agreements in comparison*

into this sub-category, as it can be used to transfer the proceeds of corruption. The same is true for obstruction of justice. The fourth sub-category is private-sector corruption, including active as well as passive bribery and embezzlement or misappropriation. Finally, there is bribery outside of the domestic legal context: besides outlawing active and passive bribery involving foreign public officials, agreements may extend the ban to international civil servants.

Jurisdiction refers to all provisions that determine the reach of the agreement's rules. States typically have jurisdiction within their own territory. Therefore, to capture the variation among agreements, I focus on two sub-categories of clauses: those that establish extraterritorial jurisdiction on the basis of various factors; and those that impose limits on jurisdiction. In some circumstances, jurisdiction may be extended to citizens outside of the national territory. Further, according to the effects-based approach, states are given jurisdiction whenever an instance of corruption affects their national interest or their citizens. Another criterion to extend jurisdiction is whether a national public official was involved in the corruption. Finally, states can claim jurisdiction over offenses abroad that are linked to domestic corruption. With respect to limiting jurisdiction, two provisions are typical. Double jeopardy—or *ne bis in idem*—clauses stipulate that nobody may be tried twice for the same crime. Relatedly, agreements may include a clause urging states to consult with one another in the event of overlapping investigations.

Domestic enforcement is an umbrella term for all provisions designed to increase compliance with the penal and preventive aspects covered in the agreements. This is an important addition to criminalization, since an agreement with no procedural standards would allow for massive variations in how signatories deal with corruption. Provisions in this area are grouped into four sub-categories. The first concerns sanctions. For instance, agreements may stipulate that criminal sanctions for corrupt practices must include prison sentences, and that civil or administrative sanctions must be available, too. Another typical provision establishes the liability of legal persons. Additionally, an agreement may include a clause that urges states to trace and then confiscate the proceeds of corruption. The second sub-category relates to judicial proceedings, and specifically the protection of whistleblowers, witnesses, and victims. Similarly, the third sub-category addresses the rights of suspects in judicial proceedings. Agreements often insist on respect for a statute of limitations, guarantee a fair trial, and outline limits to immunity for members of the legislature or other officials. The fourth sub-category covers civil law. Corrupt contracts may be declared void, and those that are affected by corrupt behavior can be made

Agreements in comparison 61

voidable to give damaged parties a way out. Finally, an agreement may contain a clause that establishes a private right to action in cases of corruption, explicitly enabling private actors to seek civil-law redress.

The final category—*international cooperation*—is the only one that does not address domestic standards in signatory states. Instead, as the title implies, it contains clauses that regulate interactions among signatories to the agreement. These provisions are grouped into three sub-categories. The first regulates legal assistance among parties to the agreement. In addition to clauses relating to mutual legal assistance in general, many documents contain a declaration that bank secrecy should not be an obstacle to cooperation. Moreover, agreements often urge member states to extradite offenders in corruption cases, with varying degrees of detail.[51] The second sub-category deals with cooperation among law-enforcement agencies, especially the technical aspects of cooperation, such as the exchange of information. In addition, special investigative techniques are often elaborated. Finally, agreements may include clauses on tracing and seizing assets, so proceeds of corruption that have been transferred to a foreign country can be frozen through a process of legal assistance. In addition, there may be provisions about the repatriation of assets to the state where the corruption occurred.

Legal design as measured by obligation and delegation

While scope addresses *what* is covered in anti-corruption agreements, legal design captures *how* this is done. At the most basic level, the decisive question is whether an international organization decides to adopt an anti-corruption document that contains legally binding language. However, if such a document is tabled, there is still room for variation. To map commonalities and differences in legal design, I borrow the notions of obligation and delegation from the "legalization" framework (see Table 2.4).[52] In their introduction to this analytical toolkit, Abbott *et al.* define obligation as follows:

> Obligation means that states or other actors are bound by a rule or commitment or by a set of rules or commitments. Specifically, it means that they are legally bound by a rule or commitment in the sense that their behavior thereunder is subject to scrutiny under the general rules, procedures, and discourse of international law, and often of domestic law as well.[53]

To capture the degree of obligation, Abbott *et al.* propose six levels in descending order. Empirically, it is sensible to condense these into just

62 Agreements in comparison

Table 2.4 Degrees of legalization[54]

Obligation	Precision	Delegation
	(higher legalization)	
-Unconditional obligation, legally binding language	-Determinate rules, narrow issues of interpretation	-Binding regulations and centralized enforcement
-Implicit conditions on obligation	-Substantial but limited issues of interpretation	-Binding regulations with consent or opt-out
-Reservations, contingent obligations, escape clauses	-Broad areas of discretion	-Decentralized enforcement legitimated by rules
-Hortatory obligations	-"Standards" that are meaningful only with reference to specific situations	-Coordination standards
-Recommendations and guidelines		-Monitoring and publicity
-Explicit negation of intent to be legally bound	-Impossible to determine whether conduct complies	-Confidential monitoring
		-Normative statements
		-Forum for negotiations
	(lower legalization)	

two levels to indicate whether a clause is mandatory or not. Non-binding clauses typically come in two forms: permissive or optional. The former qualify the obligation by means of an escape clause or contingency, such as compatibility with domestic law, whereas the latter are clearly hortatory or aspirational. Of course, obligation can vary across the different scope elements, so I assess whether each of the 57 issues listed above is addressed in a mandatory or a non-binding manner. This assessment is based on the language used in the agreements, with phrases such as "shall" (obligatory), "subject to domestic laws ... shall" (permissive), and "endeavor to" (hortatory) serving as indicators of the degree of obligation.

Additionally, I determine whether the monitoring of compliance is delegated to follow-up bodies. According to Abbott *et al.*, delegation describes the extent to which "third parties have been granted authority to implement, interpret, and apply the rules; to resolve disputes; and (possibly) to make further rules."[55] With respect to anti-corruption agreements, the crucial questions are whether they include monitoring mechanisms and the extent to which these involve publicity. Higher levels of delegation do not occur empirically. Analyzing the follow-up clauses codified in agreements provides information about the degree of delegation. Contrary to obligation, delegation does not vary issue by issue; rather, it is consistent throughout the whole agreement. Nevertheless, delegation is closely linked to obligation: mandatory

Agreements in comparison 63

commitments are severely weakened when there is no monitoring, and a monitoring mechanism that detects non-compliance with non-binding provisions will be less consequential. This mutually reinforcing effect of obligation and delegation is why Marcoux and Urpelainen suggest that the existence of a monitoring mechanism is the minimum "threshold for identifying hard law."[56]

Follow-up provisions in anti-corruption agreements are designed to regulate future interactions among signatories with respect to the agreement itself (see Table 2.5). Besides exchanging information, an implicit goal of such provisions is to increase compliance. On the basis of the principle of peer review, member states evaluate one another's implementation of the agreement. Such monitoring increases the costs of non-compliance because the other parties are able to gain access to information and react accordingly.[57] A measure of the strength of these mechanisms is whether reports are published or remain secret. If they are publicly accessible, this increases the reputational costs for those with negative assessments because anti-corruption activists and the general public have full knowledge of their poor performance.[58] Alternatively, some agreements contain a clause stating that only a summary or a consensus-based report will be published. Provisions on peer review may also include clauses to mandate on-site visits as well as statements on whether civil society actors will participate in the assessments.

In addition to obligation and delegation, the legalization framework refers to precision (see Table 2.4). The degree of precision is characterized by the extent to which there is room for interpretation regarding an issue. As Abbott *et al.* point out, "imprecision is not generally the result of a failure of legal draftsmanship, but a deliberate choice given the circumstances of domestic and international politics."[59] Here, the legalization framework presents a continuum from precise rules to hazy statements that might be so vague that parties do not know whether they are complying. In anti-corruption agreements, however, virtually all of the language leaves some room for interpretation, with most clauses resembling the notion of relatively vague

Table 2.5 Elements of delegation (monitoring and follow-up)

Peer review
- Publish full reports
- Summary reports
- On-site visits
- Civil society involvement

64 *Agreements in comparison*

"standards." Consequently, I refrain from coding the degree of precision and concentrate solely on obligation and delegation.

Scope and legal design by organization

Table 2.6 provides a comprehensive mapping of the scope covered by each organization. To this end, I track all 57 elements of the scope of issues for each agreement, plus the provisions relating to follow-up mechanisms. Every row represents issues according to the legend that precedes the table. Therefore, it is possible to track the precise contents of each document by reading the cells from left to right. In the case of public officials, for instance, the first row indicates how each organization addresses codes of conduct, personal finances, and provisions on training. The two circles and one dash in the top-left cell show that the OAS addresses the first two of these, but not the third.

Additionally, the table depicts the documents' legal design by indicating which clauses are legally binding for member states. Full circles indicate that an issue is addressed in mandatory terms, whereas unfilled circles indicate non-binding clauses. Finally, the table shows whether the scope has been widened by supplementary documents: for example, the OECD addresses prevention of corruption among public officials in additional recommendations. This is indicated by the gray shading for those items in the top cell. At a glance, the table thus shows how many aspects are covered in each category; at the more detailed level, it allows to track differences between cases.

Prevention

- "Public officials" = codes of conduct; personal finances; training
- "Public process" = hiring; procurement; accounting
- "Transparency" = access to information; political funding; civil society; media; public awareness
- "Private sector" = accounting rules; tax deductibility
- "Institutions" = creation of anti-corruption agency; cooperation among agencies; protection of judiciary; discourage false claims

Criminalization

- "Public bribery" = public bribery (active and passive); trading in influence
- "Public abuse" = abuse; embezzlement; illicit enrichment
- "Related offenses" = complicity; money laundering; obstruction of justice

Agreements in comparison 65

- "Private sector" = Private-sector bribery (active and/or passive); embezzlement
- "Transnational" = Transnational bribery; bribery of international officials

Jurisdiction

- "Extraterritoriality" = own citizen; effect on state; effect on citizen; involves official; related offense abroad
- "Limits" = double jeopardy; consult if overlap

Domestic enforcement

- "Sanctions" = criminal (including prison); civil on top of criminal; liability of legal persons; confiscation of proceeds
- "Protection" = whistleblowers; witnesses; victims
- "Suspects" = statute of limitations; fair trial; limits to immunity
- "Civil law" = voiding corrupt contracts; making contracts voidable if affected by corruption; establishing private right to action

International cooperation

- "Legal assistance" = mutual legal assistance; no bank secrecy; extradition
- "Law enforcement" = Technical cooperation; special techniques; designated central authority
- "Assets" = freezing/seizure; repatriation

Delegation/follow-up

- "Peer review" = publish full report; publish at least a summary or a consensus-based full report; on-site visits; civil society involved

Table 2.6 illustrates that pioneer regional organizations adopted relatively narrow agreements. While the OAS was the only one to address preventive measures early on, its agreement contains shortcomings regarding domestic enforcement. It is the other way round in the COE conventions: while they are very strong on domestic enforcement and international cooperation, their criminalization provisions focus on bribery to the exclusion of other corrupt behavior. Preventive measures for the public sector are also absent from these conventions. The most obvious example of narrow scope yet highly obligatory design is the OECD convention, with its exclusive focus on transnational bribery. Rather than including prevention and banning a broad range of corruption offenses, the member states agreed on a binding set of standards aimed at regulating the behavior of traders and investors abroad.

Table 2.6 Scope, obligation, and delegation in comparison

	OAS	EU	OECD	COE	ECO	SADC	AU	UN	LAS
Prevention									
Public officials	○○-	—	○○○	◉-	●●-	●-	●●●	●○○	○○●
Public processes	○○○	—	-◉-	-◉-	●●●	●●●	●●●	○○●	-●○
Transparency	-○-	——	◉◉-	-◉-○○	-●●-	●-●●●	●-●●●	○○○-○	●○-
Private sector	○○	-	●○	●○	●-	●●	—	○●	●-
Institutions	○—	—	—	●●—	●-	●-●	●-●	○○○-	●●○-
Criminalization									
Public bribery	●○	●-	—	●○	●●	●●	●●	●○	○○
Public abuse	●○○	—	—	—	-●○	●●-	●●○	○●○	○○○
Related offenses	●●-	●●-	●-	●●-	●○-	●●-	●●-	○○●	○○-
Private sector	-	●-	—	○-	●-	●-	●-	○○	○○
Transnational	○-	-	●-	●●	●-	○-	—	●●	○○
Jurisdiction									
Extraterritoriality	○——	●-●-	○——	○—○-	●——	●——	●●-	○○-○○	●●●-●
Limits	-	●●	-●	-	-●	●-	●-	-●	-●
Domestic enforcement									
Sanctions	——	●●●●	●○○●●	●-●●	●●●●	—●	—●	-○●○	-○○-
Protection	○—	—	◉-	●●-	●●●	●-	●●-	○●●	●●●
Suspects	—	—	●-	●-◉	—	—	-●○	●-○	—○
Civil law	—	—	—	●●●	—	—	—	-○●	-○●

	OAS	EU	OECD	COE	ECO	SADC	AU	UN	LAS
			International cooperation						
Legal assistance	●●●	●-●	●●●	●●●	●●●	●●●	●●●	●●●	●●●
Law enforcement	●-○	—	▣-●	●○●	●○●	●-●	●-●	○○●	○○●
Assets	○○	—	—	●-	○○	○○	●○	○○	○○
			Delegation/follow-up						
Peer review	○●▣▣	——	●●●○	-○●-	——	——	——	-▣○-	——

Notes: Filled circles indicate mandatory provisions; unfilled circles indicate non-binding provisions; dashes indicate omissions; gray shading indicates when scope has been widened by subsequent documents. The legend preceding the table indicates which marker corresponds to which provision (left to right in the table).

68 Agreements in comparison

Of course, this focus on just one aspect of criminalization means that all of the document's procedural provisions are similarly limited to this single issue. Likewise, the European Union's agreement is narrow, addressing only a few issues in each scope category. In contrast, the OAS and the African agreements cover a great deal of ground in terms of preventive measures and criminalization, although the OAS and SADC hardly mention enforcement. UNCAC and the more recent Arab League convention also adopt a broad, holistic approach. As one legal scholar put it in an early analysis of anti-corruption agreements, "beyond the core crime of bribery in the International Conventions, the approaches to corruption diverge."[60]

That said, the European organizations and the OECD have subsequently widened the scope of their narrow core agreements by adopting additional documents that display a more holistic approach to anti-corruption, leading to a different overall picture (see Appendix 1). The Council of Europe addresses prevention by means of less obligatory but still peer-reviewed additional texts, most importantly its "Twenty Guiding Principles." A similar expansion has occurred in the OECD: for instance, since the adoption of its relatively narrow anti-bribery convention, it has published recommendations on preventive measures in the public sector that go far beyond the original tight focus. As a side-effect, the proportion

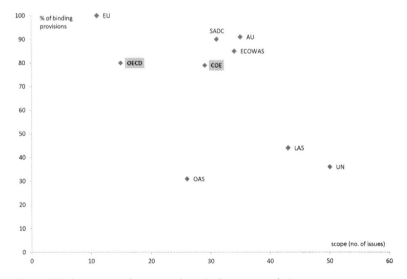

Figure 2.2 Agreements in comparison (only core treaties)
Note: Gray shading indicates that an agreement contains a peer-review mechanism.

Agreements in comparison 69

of binding provisions in the OECD's and COE's anti-corruption agreements has decreased, reducing the average degree of obligation (compare Figures 2.2 and 2.3). In contrast, none of the African organizations has changed either the scope or the legal design of its agreement.

To what extent is there a trade-off between broad scope and the use of obligatory language? UNCAC is the prime example of reducing the level of obligation in order to achieve consensus over broader scope. Most of the provisions in this agreement, despite being broad and detailed, are hedged by making them either permissive or optional. The OAS convention also contains a very small set of mandatory core obligations alongside many optional clauses, while the additions to the European conventions are similarly non-binding. By contrast, the SADC, ECOWAS, and AU agreements all contain many obligatory preventive measures. Indeed, in the 30–40 issues they address, 80 percent of the clauses use mandatory language.

There is also considerable variation among the agreements with respect to follow-up mechanisms. Four organizations apply the concept of peer review, which will be conducted in rounds that change their thematic focus over time. The OECD and the COE included these procedures from the start, whereas the OAS added a follow-up mechanism a few years after its anti-corruption convention entered

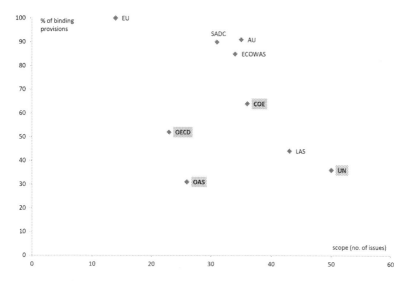

Figure 2.3 Agreements in comparison (including additional documents)
Note: Gray shading indicates that an agreement contains a peer-review mechanism.

70　*Agreements in comparison*

into force. The same is true for the United Nations. While scope and obligation have remained unchanged in both of the latter cases, the introduction of delegation has certainly strengthened both agreements. All of the follow-up mechanisms rely on questionnaires, country delegates acting as reviewers, and coordination by secretariats, but there are some important differences. The OECD's mechanism is quite strict, as it includes on-site visits, and no member state can block the publication of a negative evaluation. The Council of Europe's GRECO is less transparent, but it does adhere to well-established internal procedures and has long conducted on-site visits. By contrast, the OAS introduced on-site visits quite recently, and its reports, which tend to be non-confrontational, are published only after consultation with the plenum.[61] Finally, the UN's follow-up mechanism seems to be even weaker, as its reports are not published in full and on-site visits are optional.

The African and Arab League agreements all allude to the establishment of follow-up mechanisms, but as yet there has been very little, if any, practical progress in this direction. The African Union's independent "Advisory Board," which consists of eleven experts, is an interesting innovation.[62] Yet, it was many years before it was convened for the first time, and ever since it has focused on establishing its own procedural rules and collecting information from member states. Thus, it seems unlikely to undertake a fully fledged supervisory role any time soon, particularly given its internal problems (see Chapter 4). Meanwhile, it seems that SADC and ECOWAS have made no effort to establish the follow-up procedures set out in their protocols.[63] Finally, the Arab League's convention merely alludes to a conference of parties, rather than a more ambitious follow-up mechanism, and there is no evidence that even this has been organized as yet, so it seems highly unlikely that a rigorous peer review will be conducted in the near future.

Between enforcement cooperation and illusionary giants

Thus far, we have seen that three of the pioneer organizations—the OECD, EU, and COE—focused on criminalization and enforcement, addressing only a relatively narrow set of bribery offenses in mandatory terms. The OECD and COE have both established strong peer-review mechanisms, whereas the EU agreement does not include a corruption-focused peer review. However, the latter organization's deep political and legal integration is a functional equivalent. This approach may be labeled "enforcement cooperation": a number of states adopt an agreement that combines narrow scope, high obligation, and delegation to some form of peer-review mechanism.

Agreements in comparison 71

This behavior is in line with the intra-group signaling motive, where states negotiate on the basis of their expected ability to comply while also taking measures to foster implementation. As discussed in the Introduction, in the European cases this motive was linked to harmonizing rule of law and governance standards in old and new member states, given the enlargement of the organizations after the end of the Cold War.[64] In the OAS, US leadership and a coalition of Latin American governments possessed a similar motive as they wished to harmonize laws and ensure cross-border cooperation.[65] Finally, members of the OECD were motivated to assure one another of their willingness to cooperate following strong pressure from the United States to internationalize its rules against foreign bribery.[66]

In contrast, ECOWAS, SADC, and the AU have adopted agreements that combine broad scope with a high degree of obligation. However, they are all stymied by a lack of meaningful delegation because they have failed to establish strong peer-review or other powerful follow-up mechanisms. I label these agreements "illusionary giants."[67] From afar, they appear to be broad and deep commitments, but closer examination reveals that they are actually rather weak. This finding corresponds to the logic of signaling to external audiences. All of the African organizations, which are composed of countries with high aid inflows that have a motive for external signaling, have adopted broad and seemingly binding documents. Their strong focus on prevention issues is in line with donor expectations under conditions of limited rule of law and state capacity.[68] Follow-up is absent because there is no intra-group demand for it; moreover, it could prove to be counterproductive by providing information about non-compliance to various audiences.

Empirically, organizations do not perfectly conform to these ideal types. For instance, the OECD and the COE have both widened the scope of their agreements in other documents, with the former addressing subjects other than the core issue of transnational bribery and the latter suggesting preventive measures in its non-binding "Twenty Guiding Principles" (which actually preceded the core conventions by two years). The key difference is that the OECD's peer review focuses exclusively on the original convention, whereas the COE's GRECO mechanism also subjects the non-binding elements to peer review.

The OAS agreement and UNCAC lie somewhere between enforcement cooperation and illusionary giants. The latter seems to reflect a compromise across many issue areas. In terms of scope, it is the most comprehensive of all the anti-corruption agreements, but low levels of obligation for most of its provisions have allowed reluctant member

72 *Agreements in comparison*

states to make few changes. On the other hand, the UN's recent adoption of a follow-up mechanism may have an effect. While this mechanism is relatively weak in comparison with others, its adoption suggests that intra-group signaling motives are starting to play a significant role. Indeed, the UN peer review is unique in its emphasis on technical assistance in exchange for monitoring.[69] Years before UNCAC was drafted, the OAS was a pioneer in the anti-corruption field. Its agreement, which is broader in scope than those of the other early adopters, features a mixture of binding and non-binding provisions; moreover, member states agreed to create a follow-up mechanism a few years after adoption.

I label these agreements "compromises plus peer review." Obligation varies across the scope elements, reflecting concerns about sovereignty and compliance costs, and they contain follow-up mechanisms with varying degrees of strength and transparency. The OAS, COE, and UN all fall into this category, whereas the OECD remains closer to enforcement cooperation. The group is less homogeneous than the others, but united by the combination of varying obligation and peer-review mechanism.

One organization—the League of Arab States—does not fit within any of the aforementioned groups. In terms of scope and design, the LAS drafted an agreement that is too weak in obligation to be an illusionary giant, too broad and non-binding to be classed as enforcement cooperation, and lacks the follow-up procedures that would turn it into a compromise. Moreover, given the lack of information regarding its implementation, it seems it will remain uncategorizable for some time to come.

To conclude, the various international and regional organizations share many elements. At the same time, analyzing their scope, obligation, and delegation reveals significant differentiation. While contingencies and idiosyncratic factors certainly have an impact on the development of these agreements, member states' signaling motives shape the outcomes. The cases investigated here may be placed in one of three groups: organizations that are motivated by signaling to domestic and intra-group audiences fall into the enforcement cooperation and compromise-plus categories, while those that wish to send messages to external audiences have adopted agreements that may be termed illusionary giants.

How do ideas spread? Evidence of diffusion processes

Having introduced the agreements and discussed and analyzed general patterns in their scope and legal design, what may be said about

Agreements in comparison 73

similarities in their details? In the literature on anti-corruption agreements, researchers sometimes point out that an agreement was modeled—at least partially—on an earlier convention or protocol. For instance, Androulakis writes that the OAS convention "obviously served as a model" for the SADC protocol.[70] In Chapters 3 and 4, I analyze the extent to which the OAS and AU conventions were drafted on the basis of reference models. At this point, however, it is worth discussing the incidence of shared provisions in all of the agreements under investigation.

A relatively straightforward way to assess the extent of diffusion is to compare the texts of international agreements. When such analyses have been undertaken in studies of preferential trade agreements, they have revealed a high baseline of explicit *copying and pasting* across these documents.[71] Given the highly technical nature of trade agreements and the specialized trade-law environment in which they are drafted, it should come as no surprise that the documents frequently share "boilerplates" and follow "templates."[72]

By contrast, the field of anti-corruption covers broader standards of political behavior in addition to technical standard-setting, so it is logical to assume that there will be a somewhat lower baseline of copying and pasting across the agreements. This is because, while IO member states are sure to be under the influence of diffusion mechanisms when drafting their agreements, they will also tailor the wording of those agreements very carefully on the basis of their individual signaling motives. When many provisions are copied verbatim (or when they are not identical but still very similar in terms of content and meaning), this indicates that an international organization has been strongly influenced by another's decision-making. Here, I focus on the previously discussed 57 substantive issues, so instances of copying are captured only within the agreements' meaningful content. Analysis of the incidence of verbatim copying throughout the documents would generate many more false positives, due to the prevalence of the type of boilerplate language that also occurs in preferential trade agreements.

Short descriptions of the clauses in the anti-corruption agreements may be found in the online appendix that accompanies this book.[73] As I have coded 57 issues across five categories of scope (prevention, criminalization, jurisdiction, domestic enforcement, and international cooperation) for nine organizations, a total of 513 individual values might have been observed. As shown in the previous section, however, not every organization covers every issue. Taking this into account, we are left with 291 opportunities for a uniquely worded anti-corruption provision.

74 *Agreements in comparison*

In this analysis, I counted only perfect copies and those in which a few minor words were changed. If the provision on a specific issue is identical in three treaties, I counted this as one original and two copies. On this basis, I found 72 instances of provision copying (see Table 2.7). In other words, almost a quarter of the clauses across all nine agreements seem to have been copied verbatim. The Organization of American States features most often as a reference model, as it provides the source material for 11.3 percent of the clauses across all of the agreements. Provisions from the COE, EU, and UN conventions are copied roughly half as frequently. However, all of the copies of the latter's provisions are found in a single document—the LAS convention—as it is the only agreement that was adopted after UNCAC. The OECD convention is very rarely copied.

To reiterate, these findings are by no means exhaustive and they cannot account for more subtle diffusion. Indeed, by design, the numbers presented here may be expected to *underestimate* the prevalence of diffusion. First, drafters may draw on an agreement but then choose not to copy it verbatim. Second, and more importantly, many provisions are very similar in meaning without quite reaching the level of word-for-word copy and paste. Nevertheless, roughly a quarter of the provisions that could be direct copies *are* direct copies, which lends strong support to the hypothesis that the drafters of anti-corruption agreements have been systematically influenced by reference models.

Observable implications regarding diffusion processes

Simply learning that outcomes have converged does not provide a complete picture of diffusion processes. In general, the convergence of outcomes suggests that diffusion did occur. Yet, observing the former is

Table 2.7 Observed frequency of copying and pasting in nine anti-corruption agreements

	Number	*Percentage**
Provisions that are copies of any others	72	24.8
Copies of OAS provisions	33	11.3
Copies of COE and EU provisions	20	6.9
Copies of OECD provisions	2	0.7
Copies of UNCAC provisions	17	5.8
Unique AU, SADC, and ECOWAS provisions	7	2.4

Note: * Percentage of the total number (291) of potentially unique provisions.

Agreements in comparison 75

neither necessary nor sufficient for diagnosis of the latter. For the hypothesis that one case serves as a reference model for another based on normative considerations (emulation), convergence should be indicative of diffusion. This is because one cannot claim that emulation took place if the results do not look similar. For the hypothesis that one case becomes a reference model through a process of rational learning, convergence also suggests that there might have been a diffusion process. But in this case it is not a "hoop test" that has to be passed.[74] For instance, actors might have engaged in rational learning and then decided not to copy what they discovered in their research. This is why a hypothesis on rational learning should not be rejected solely on the basis of the ultimate absence of convergence.

Therefore, in the two case studies that follow, I will search for procedural evidence. For each diffusion mechanism, it makes sense to consider the observable implications that help to diagnose its presence or absence.[75] First, consider the active influences theorized in Chapter 1: incentives and capacity-building, on the one hand; normative pressure, on the other. To diagnose these mechanisms of diffusion, there should be evidence that the sender attempted to influence the recipient's decision-making.

For the case of incentives, we may expect to find evidence of external actors providing or promising material benefits or negative consequences tied to an outcome. Similarly, capacity-building should leave a trace that is analogous to positive incentives. Evidence for this mechanism could come in the form of invitations to seminars or events, memoranda of understanding or other agreements to provide resources, or perhaps written evidence of sanctions or other negative incentives that are tied to the issue of anti-corruption. That said, we are unlikely to find a "smoking gun," such as an agreement that explicitly ties funding to a specific outcome or threatens withdrawal of support. Nevertheless, there might be circumstantial evidence, such as documents that profess support for an initiative but fail to demand specific outcomes, which would still suggest at least implicit expectations.

Normative pressure and attempts at persuasion are traceable if governmental or non-governmental norm entrepreneurs express normative arguments in favor of anti-corruption in writing. These arguments may be advanced either directly (by stressing that corruption should be addressed because of its negative effects) or indirectly (by mentioning that other actors have become active in the anti-corruption field). In the absence of a definitive paper trail, there may be secondary evidence in the form of attendance lists showing that activists participated in meetings or protocols, minutes, or attendees' statements.

76 *Agreements in comparison*

Second, consider the different indirect diffusion influences: competition, lesson-drawing, and emulation. To support the notion that competition prompted an international organization to address corruption and then design its treaty on the basis of another organization's document, there should be evidence that the two organizations were in competition for the same resources. An indicator of this may be the extent to which the drafters of a document made statements about which cases they took into consideration. Such evidence may be found in the official records of negotiations, internal documents, early drafts of international agreements, reports or memoirs written by key participants, or oral statements. Alternatively, explicit links to earlier agreements may be embedded in the treaty itself or other official documents adopted by the organization. This can occur, for instance, when an agreement's preamble references another document, or when a clause states that one organization wishes to cooperate with another.

Lesson-drawing should be characterized by systematic efforts to determine best practices through analysis of reference models. As noted above, however, this does not necessarily lead to convergence of outcomes. Evidence for lesson-drawing would usually comprise a paper trail of records of meetings with representatives from other organizations, expert presentations, or the drafting of working documents by the organization's own officials that systematically analyze the benefits and weaknesses of alternative options.

Finally, a reference model that is named and explicitly linked with a positive value judgement would provide evidence of mimicry (normative emulation). A more normatively motivated mode of emulation should be characterized by a combination of convergence in outcomes, explicit positive public statements about another organization, and no evidence that alternative options were even considered. That said, it is difficult to distinguish learning from mimicry as they are often observationally equivalent.

Conclusion

This comparative chapter has addressed several aspects of my principal research question. Scope conditions were applied to explain why just nine out of fourteen organizations under investigation adopted binding anti-corruption agreements. Organizations adopt such conventions only if they have a sufficient signaling motive, which may be geared towards domestic, intra-group, or external audiences. Operationalized as average levels of democracy and average inflows of development aid,

Agreements in comparison 77

these factors are congruent with the distinction between organizations that have adopted binding agreements and those that have not.

Focusing on those organizations with binding agreements, I then addressed the scope and legal design of their anti-corruption documents. These may be characterized as enforcement cooperation, compromises plus peer review, or illusionary giants. The first group consists of agreements adopted by the OECD and the EU, which combine narrow scope with high obligation and follow-up. The second comprises the agreements of the COE, OAS, and UN, which have broad scope with varying levels of obligation per issue, plus some form of peer-review mechanism. Finally, the agreements of SADC, ECOWAS, and the AU comprise the illusionary giants group. At first sight, these documents appear to be strong due to their broad scope and high degree of obligation, but the lack of meaningful follow-up mechanisms is a significant limitation. My findings regarding scope and legal design correspond to the expected effects of signaling motives. Organizations that are driven by domestic and intra-group signaling appear in the first two groups, whereas the illusionary giants are clearly linked to the motive of external signaling.

I then briefly analyzed the precise wording of the agreements in order to explore the plausibility of the assumption that the negotiation and drafting of anti-corruption agreements is best viewed through the lens of diffusion. I found significant evidence in support of this notion as roughly a quarter of the provisions in the agreements were directly copied from others. Of course, this also means that no agreement has ever been copied in its entirety. Hence, while the anti-corruption documents share many characteristics, there is still considerable variation among them. This points to differentiated diffusion between the cases.

Thus far, it has been impossible to assess the processes behind the drafting of these agreements, let alone the underlying diffusion processes. Therefore, over the next two chapters, I shift from a macro perspective to detailed case studies. In Chapter 3, I analyze the Organization of American States—a pioneer in the field of binding anti-corruption agreements that was motivated by domestic and intra-group signaling. Chapter 4 then considers the African Union—the foremost example of diffusion in a context of signaling to external audiences.

Notes

1 UNODC, *UNCAC Signature and Ratification Status*, 2018, www.unodc. org/unodc/en/corruption/ratification-status.html.

78 *Agreements in comparison*

2 Tanja A. Börzel and Vera van Hüllen, eds., *Governance Transfer by Regional Organizations: Patching Together a Global Script* (Houndmills: Palgrave Macmillan, 2015).

3 E.g., Diana Panke and Sören Stapel, "Exploring Overlapping Regionalism," *Journal of International Relations and Development* 21, no. 3 (2018): 635–662; Tobias Lenz, Jeanine Bezuijen, Liesbet Hooghe, and Gary Marks, *Patterns of International Organization: Task Specific vs. General Purpose* (Florence: European University Institute, Robert Schuman Centre for Advanced Studies, 2014), http://cadmus.eui.eu/bitstream/handle/1814/34050 /RSCAS_2014_128.pdf?sequence=1&isAllowed=y.

4 Wayne Sandholtz and Mark M. Gray, "International Integration and National Corruption," *International Organization* 57, no. 4 (2003): 761–800, at 773; Anja P. Jakobi, *Common Goods and Evils? The Formation of Global Crime Governance* (Oxford: Oxford University Press, 2013), 148–149.

5 Jan Wouters, Cedric Ryngaert, and Ann Sofie Cloots, "The International Legal Framework against Corruption: Achievements and Challenges," *Melbourne Journal of International Law* 14, no. 1 (2013): 1–76, at 22–23; GRECO, *Ad Hoc Procedures (Rule 34)* (Brussels: Council of Europe, 2018), www.coe.int/en/web/greco/ad-hoc-procedure-rule-34-.

6 Anja P. Jakobi, "The Changing Global Norm of Anti-corruption: From Bad Business to Bad Government," *Zeitschrift für Vergleichende Politikwissenschaft* 7, no. S1 (2013): 243–264, at 251–252.

7 Barbara C. George and Kathleen A. Lacey, "A Coalition of Industrialized Nations, Developing Nations, Multilateral Development Banks and Nongovernmental Organizations: A Pivotal Complement to Current Anticorruption Initiatives," *Cornell International Law Journal* 33, no. 3 (2000): 547–592, at 567.

8 Tanja A. Börzel, Yasemin Pamuk, and Andreas Stahn, "Fighting Corruption Abroad: The EU's Good Governance Export," in *International Anticorruption Regimes in Europe: Between Corruption, Integration, and Culture*, ed. Sebastian Wolf and Diana Schmidt-Pfister (Baden-Baden: Nomos, 2010), 47–68.

9 Vera van Hüllen and Tanja A. Börzel, "Why Being Democratic Is Just Not Enough: The EU's Governance Transfer," in *Governance Transfer by Regional Organizations*, ed. Börzel and van Hüllen, 227–241.

10 European Commission, *Communication from the Commission to the European Parliament, the Council and the European Economic and Social Committee: Fighting Corruption in the EU*, COM(2011) 308 final (Brussels: European Commission, 2011), https://eur-lex.europa.eu/LexUriServ/LexUriServ.do?uri=COM:2011:0308:FIN:EN:PDF.

11 European Commission, *Decision of 6.6.2011: Establishing an EU Anti-corruption Reporting Mechanism for Periodic Assessment*, C(2011) 3673 final (Brussels: European Commission, 2011), https://ec.europa.eu/home-affairs/ sites/homeaffairs/files/e-library/docs/pdf/com_decision_c%282011%29_3673 _final_en_en.pdf; European Commission, *Report from the Commission to the Council and the European Parliament: EU Anti-corruption Report*, COM(2014) 38 final (Brussels: European Commission, 2014), https:// eur-lex.europa.eu/legal-content/EN/TXT/?uri=COM:2014:0038:FIN.

12 European Commission, *Collection of Official Data on Corruption Offences* (Brussels: European Commission, 2016), http://ec.europa.eu/dgs/home-affa

Agreements in comparison 79

irs/what-we-do/policies/organized-crime-and-human-trafficking/corruption/docs/official_corruption_statistics_2011_2013_jan16_en.pdf; Nikolaj Nielsen, "EU Commission Drops Anti-corruption Report," *EUobserver*, 2 February 2017.

13 Marco Arnone and Leonardo S. Borlini, *Corruption: Economic Analysis and International Law* (Cheltenham: Edward Elgar Publishing, 2014), 229–244.

14 Kenneth W. Abbott and Duncan Snidal, "Values and Interests: International Legalization in the Fight against Corruption," *Journal of Legal Studies* 31, no. S1 (2002): 141–177; Arnold J. Heidenheimer and Holger Moroff, "Controlling Business Payoffs to Foreign Officials: The 1998 OECD Anti-bribery Convention," in *Political Corruption: Concepts and Contexts*, ed. Arnold J. Heidenheimer and Michael Johnston (New Brunswick, NJ: Transaction Publishers, 2002), 943–959.

15 OECD, *Convention on Combating Bribery of Foreign Public Officials in International Business Transactions and Related Documents*, DAFFE/IME/BR(97)20 (Paris: OECD, 1998), 8, www.oecd.org/site/adboecdanti-corruptioninitiative/39360623.pdf.

16 OECD, *Convention on Combating Bribery of Foreign Public Officials in International Business Transactions and Related Documents* (Paris: OECD, 2011), 20ff., www.oecd.org/daf/anti-bribery/ConvCombatBribery_ENG.pdf.

17 OAS, *Permanent Council Resolution CP/Res. 154 (167/75): Behavior of Transnational Enterprises Operating in the Region and Need for a Code of Conduct to be Observed by Such Enterprises*, reprinted in: *American Society of International Law, International Legal Materials* 14, no. 5 (1975): 1326–1328.

18 Ioannis N. Androulakis, *Die Globalisierung der Korruptionsbekämpfung: Eine Untersuchung zur Entstehung, zum Inhalt und zu den Auswirkungen des internationalen Korruptionsstrafrechts unter Berücksichtigung der sozialökonomischen Hintergründe* (Baden-Baden: Nomos, 2007), 189.

19 Mathis Lohaus, "Ahead of the Curve: The OAS as a Pioneer of International Anti-corruption Efforts," in *Governance Transfer by Regional Organizations*, ed. Börzel and van Hüllen, 159–176.

20 Mathis Lohaus, *Governance Transfer by the Organization of American States (OAS): A B2 Case Study Report* (Berlin: Collaborative Research Center (SFB) 700, 2014), http://edoc.vifapol.de/opus/volltexte/2015/5742/pdf/SFB_Governance_Working_Paper_49.pdf.

21 African Union, *Convention on Preventing and Combating Corruption* (Maputo: African Union, 2003), Article 22, https://perma.cc/2G42-SXW7.

22 Christof Hartmann, *Governance Transfer by the Economic Community of West African States (ECOWAS)* (Berlin: Collaborative Research Center (SFB) 700, 2013), 44, http://edoc.vifapol.de/opus/volltexte/2015/5740/pdf/SFB_Governance_Working_Paper_47.pdf.

23 SADC, *Southern African Forum Against Corruption: Constitution* (Gaborone: SADC SAFAC, 2001); SADC, *The Southern African Forum Against Corruption (SAFAC): Introduction Prepared by Dr. Edward G. Hoseah, SAFAC Chairman* (Gaborone: SADC SAFAC, 2005), www.pccb.go.tz/wp-content/uploads/2017/04/SAFAC.pdf.

24 Fred Oluoch, "Regional Agencies Seek More Powers to Fight Corruption," *East African*, 28 June 2014.

25 Androulakis, *Die Globalisierung der Korruptionsbekämpfung*, 189.

26 Arnone and Borlini, *Corruption*, 258.

80 *Agreements in comparison*

27 For a detailed analysis and critique, see: Peter W. Schroth, "The United Nations Convention against Doing Anything Serious about Corruption," *Journal of Legal Studies in Business* 12, no. 2 (2005): 1–22.

28 United Nations, *United Nations Conventions Against Corruption* (2003), Article 63 (7), www.unodc.org/pdf/crime/convention_corruption/signing/Convention-e.pdf.

29 Matti Joutsen, "The United Nations Convention Against Corruption," in *Handbook of Global Research and Practice in Corruption*, ed. Adam Graycar and Russell Smith (Cheltenham: Edward Elgar Publishing, 2011), 303–318, at 311–315; Matti Joutsen and Adam Graycar, "When Experts and Diplomats Agree: Negotiating Peer Review of the UN Convention Against Corruption," *Global Governance* 18 (2012): 425–439.

30 Wouters, Ryngaert, and Cloots, "The International Legal Framework against Corruption," 16–17; Jakobi, *Common Goods and Evils?*, 154.

31 David Chaikin and J. C. Sharman, *Corruption and Money Laundering: A Symbiotic Relationship* (Basingstoke: Palgrave Macmillan, 2009), 42.

32 Cecily Rose, *International Anti-corruption Norms: Their Creation and Influence on Domestic Legal Systems* (Oxford: Oxford University Press, 2015), 119.

33 League of Arab States, *Arab Anti-corruption Convention* (Cairo: League of Arab States, 2010), Article 4.

34 Jiangyu Wang, "ASEAN Struggles in Anti-corruption Fight," *Global Times*, 9 August 2012.

35 ASEAN, *ASEAN Political–Security Community Blueprint* (Jakarta: ASEAN Secretariat, 2009), https://perma.cc/Y3LW-8B4D.

36 ADB/OECD Initiative, *Supporting the Fight against Corruption in Asia and the Pacific: The ADB/OECD Anti-corruption Initiative*, January 2015, www.oecd.org/site/adboecdanti-corruptioninitiative/ADB-OECD-Initiative-Information-Sheet.pdf.

37 ADB/OECD Initiative, *Anti-corruption Action Plan for Asia and the Pacific* (Tokyo: ADB/OECD, 2001).

38 Chaikin and Sharman, *Corruption and Money Laundering*, 46–47.

39 APEC, *APEC Course of Action on Fighting Corruption and Ensuring Transparency*, 2004/AMM/033rev2 Agenda Item: XII (Santiago, Chile: APEC, 2004); APEC, *Santiago Commitment to Fight Corruption and Ensure Transparency*, 2004/AMM/032rev1 Agenda Item: XII (Santiago, Chile: APEC, 2004).

40 APEC, *Beijing Declaration on Fighting Corruption: Annex H to the Joint Ministerial Statement at the 26th APEC Ministerial Meeting* (Beijing: APEC, 2014), www.mofa.go.jp/mofaj/files/000059616.pdf.

41 Axel Hadenius and Jan Teorell, *Assessing Alternative Indices of Democracy: IPSA Committee on Concepts and Methods*, working paper, 2005, https://perma.cc/J95M-7FR3; Jan Teorell *et al., The Quality of Government Dataset*, Version 20Dec13 (Gothenburg: Quality of Government Institute, University of Gothenburg, 2013), www.qog.pol.gu.se.

42 David Collier, Henry E. Brady, and Jason Seawright, "Sources of Leverage in Causal Inference: Toward an Alternative View of Methodology," in *Rethinking Social Inquiry: Diverse Tools, Shared Standards*, 2nd ed., ed. Henry E. Brady and David Collier (Guilford, CT: Rowman & Littlefield, 2010), 161–199.

Agreements in comparison 81

43 World Bank, *World Development Indicators (WDI)*, 2013, http://data. worldbank.org/data-catalog/world-development-indicators; Teorell *et al.*, *The Quality of Government Dataset.*

44 Nathaniel Heller, "Defining and Measuring Corruption: Where Have We Come From, Where Are We Now, and What Matters for the Future?," in *Corruption, Global Security, and World Order*, ed. Robert I. Rotberg (Washington, DC: Brookings Institution Press, 2009), 47–65; Paul M. Heywood and Jonathan Rose, "'Close but no Cigar': The Measurement of Corruption," *Journal of Public Policy* 34, no. 3 (2014): 507–529.

45 Daniel Kaufmann, Art Kraay, and Massimo Mastruzzi, *Worldwide Governance Indicators*, 2013, http://info.worldbank.org/governance/wgi/index. aspx#home; Teorell et al., *The Quality of Government Dataset.*

46 World Bank, *World Development Indicators (WDI)*; Teorell *et al., The Quality of Government Dataset.*

47 Anja Jetschke, "Why Create a Regional Human Rights Regime? The ASEAN Intergovernmental Commission for Human Rights," in *Governance Transfer by Regional Organizations*, ed. Börzel and van Hüllen, 107–124.

48 Brooke Coe, "Sovereignty Regimes and the Norm of Noninterference in the Global South: Regional and Temporal Variation," *Global Governance* 21, no. 2 (2015): 275–298.

49 Barbara Koremenos, Charles Lipson, and Duncan Snidal, "The Rational Design of International Institutions," *International Organization* 55, no. 4 (2001): 761–799.

50 Androulakis, *Die Globalisierung der Korruptionsbekämpfung*; Arnone and Borlini, *Corruption*; Indira Carr, "Fighting Corruption through Regional and International Conventions: A Satisfactory Solution?," *European Journal of Crime, Criminal Law and Criminal Justice* 15, no. 2 (2007): 121–153; David A. Gantz, "Globalizing Sanctions against Foreign Bribery: The Emergence of a New International Legal Consensus," *Northwestern Journal of International Law and Business* 18, no. 2 (1997): 457–497; Peter J. Henning, "Public Corruption: A Comparative Analysis of International Corruption Conventions and United States Law," *Arizona Journal of International and Comparative Law* 18 (2001): 793–865; Anna-Catharina Marsch, *Strukturen der internationalen Korruptionsbekämpfung: Wie wirksam sind internationale Abkommen?* (Marburg: Tectum-Verlag, 2010); Thomas R. Snider and Won Kidane, "Combating Corruption through International Law in Africa: A Comparative Analysis," *Cornell International Law Journal* 40 (2007): 691–748; Philippa Webb, "The United Nations Convention Against Corruption: Global Achievement or Missed Opportunity?," *Journal of International Economic Law* 8, no. 1 (2005): 191–229.

51 Extradition is also addressed in earlier UN (and regional) treaties, most notably the ground-breaking 1988 UN Narcotics Convention. The goal in the more recent generation of documents is to make extradition applicable to corruption offenses.

52 Kenneth W. Abbott, Robert O. Keohane, Andrew Moravcsik, Anne-Marie Slaughter, and Duncan Snidal, "The Concept of Legalization," *International Organization* 54, no. 3 (2000): 17–35.

53 Abbott *et al.*, "The Concept of Legalization," 17.

54 Based on Abbott *et al.*, "The Concept of Legalization."

82 Agreements in comparison

55 Abbott *et al.*, "The Concept of Legalization," 17.
56 Christopher Marcoux and Johannes Urpelainen, "Non-compliance by Design: Moribund Hard Law in International Institutions," *Review of International Organizations* 8, no. 2 (2013): 163–191, at 179.
57 Jonas Tallberg, "Paths to Compliance: Enforcement, Management, and the European Union," *International Organization* 56, no. 3 (2002): 609–643; Charles F. Sabel and Jonathan Zeitlin, "Learning from Difference: The New Architecture of Experimentalist Governance in the EU," *European Law Journal* 14, no. 3 (2008): 271–327; Mark T. Nance, "Naming and Shaming in Financial Regulation: Explaining Variation in the Financial Action Task Force on Money Laundering," in *The Politics of Leverage in International Relations: Name, Shame, and Sanction*, ed. H. Richard Friman (Houndmills: Palgrave Macmillan, 2015), 123–142.
58 Chaikin and Sharman, *Corruption and Money Laundering*, 37.
59 Abbott *et al.*, "The Concept of Legalization," 31.
60 Henning, "Public Corruption," 864.
61 Interview with OAS official, Washington, DC, May 2013.
62 African Union, *Convention on Preventing and Combating Corruption*, Article 22.
63 Wouters, Ryngaert, and Cloots, "The International Legal Framework against Corruption," 26–27.
64 Claire A. Daams, "Regional Initiatives: European Union against Corruption," paper prepared for the 9th International Anti-corruption Conference, Durban, South Africa, 10–15 October 1999, https://perma.cc/7LJ8-CN94; Leslie Holmes, "International Anti-corruption Regimes and Corruption Levels in European and Eurasian Post-communist States," in *International Anti-corruption Regimes in Europe*, ed. Wolf and Schmidt-Pfister, 25–45; Holger Moroff, "Internationalisierung von Anti-Korruptionsregimen," in *Dimensionen politischer Korruption: Beiträge zum Stand der internationalen Forschung*, ed. Ulrich von Alemann (Wiesbaden: VS Verlag für Sozialwissenschaften, 2005), 444–477; Patrycja Szarek-Mason, *The European Union's Fight against Corruption: The Evolving Policy towards Member States and Candidate Countries* (Cambridge: Cambridge University Press, 2010).
65 Lohaus, "Ahead of the Curve"; see also Chapter 4.
66 George and Lacey, "A Coalition of Industrialized Nations"; Abbott and Snidal, "Values and Interests."
67 The term "illusionary giant" comes from Michael Ende's novel *Jim Button* (1960), which features a character who seems gigantic from afar but is revealed to be of normal size as the protagonists approach him.
68 Sarah Bracking, "Political Development and Corruption: Why 'Right Here, Right Now!'?," in *Corruption and Development: The Anti-corruption Campaigns*, ed. Sarah Bracking (Houndmills: Palgrave Macmillan, 2007), 3–27; Stephen P. Riley, "Western Policies and African Realities: The New Anti-corruption Agenda," in *Corruption and Development in Africa: Lessons from Country Case-Studies*, ed. Kempe Ronald Hope, Sr. and Bornwell C. Chikulo (Basingstoke and New York: Macmillan and St. Martin's Press, 1999), 137–158.
69 Joutsen and Graycar, "When Experts and Diplomats Agree."
70 Androulakis, *Die Globalisierung der Korruptionsbekämpfung*, 338; my translation.

Agreements in comparison 83

71 Todd Allee and Manfred Elsig, "Are the Contents of International Treaties Copied-and-Pasted? Unique Evidence from Preferential Trade Agreements," paper prepared for the Annual Meeting of the American Political Science Association, San Francisco, 3–6 September 2015; Soo Yeon Kim, *The Language of Institutional Design: Text Similarity in Preferential Trade Agreements*, working paper, 2015.

72 Allee and Elsig, *Are the Contents of International Treaties Copied-and-Pasted?*, 21.

73 I have collated the raw material in an online appendix, available at https://lohaus.org/corruptionconsensus/.

74 David Collier, "Understanding Process Tracing," *PS: Political Science and Politics* 44, no. 4 (2011): 823–830, at 825.

75 Judith Kelley, "Assessing the Complex Evolution of Norms: The Rise of International Election Monitoring," *International Organization* 62, no. 2 (2008): 221–255, at 232–236; Collier, "Understanding Process Tracing"; John Gerring, *Social Science Methodology: A Unified Framework* (Cambridge: Cambridge University Press, 2012); Derek Beach and Rasmus Brun Pedersen, *Process-tracing Methods: Foundations and Guidelines* (Ann Arbor: University of Michigan Press, 2013).

3 Organization of American States
Activist governments and domestic reference models

- **History, design, and implementation**
- **Motivations and drivers**
- **Tracing the drafts over time**
- **Evidence of diffusion**
- **Conclusion**

The OAS was the first international organization to adopt a binding anti-corruption agreement. In this chapter, I will discuss the history of this agreement and the factors that motivated member states to signal their commitment to the fight against corruption. To investigate the role of diffusion mechanisms in shaping results at the regional level, I present in-depth evidence on the document's drafting process, showing the extent to which decision-makers in the OAS drew on reference models from within and outside the Americas.

History, design, and implementation

The Inter-American Convention Against Corruption was signed in Caracas, Venezuela, on 29 March 1996. Its roots can be traced to December 1994, when all 34 states from the Americas, with the exception of Cuba, met in Miami for the First Summit of the Americas. This initiative was based on an invitation by the US government, which was the main proponent of creating a Free-Trade Area of the Americas (FTAA). The summit failed to deliver a comprehensive free-trade agreement, but it did result in a short "Declaration of Principles" that defined four goals: strengthening democracy; promoting free trade and economic integration; eradicating poverty and discrimination; sustainable development and conservation. One of several items under the first of these aims stated: "Effective democracy requires a comprehensive attack on corruption as a factor of social disintegration and

Organization of American States 85

distortion of the economic system that undermines the legitimacy of political institutions."[1]

The summit also adopted a "Plan of Action" that linked the four main goals to 23 specific issues. Item five on this list announced that states would address corruption both domestically and through contact with other international actors. It also specifically called for the OAS to develop a hemispheric approach. This mandate was taken up by the OAS's Working Group on Probity and Public Ethics, which had been initiated by the General Assembly six months earlier.[2] Over the course of the next year, the Working Group held several meetings in Washington, DC. The Venezuelan government produced a first draft convention, a second was proposed by the head of the Working Group, and input from other OAS bodies then resulted in a third. Finally, at the end of the Working Group's deliberations, a fourth draft convention was submitted.

This final draft was the product of extensive preparatory meetings and served as a starting point for a "Specialized Conference," which was held in Caracas in March 1996. It was here that the document was finalized and adopted as the Inter-American Convention Against Corruption. The Latin American members of the OAS with civil-law systems were quick to sign and ratify, whereas the United States, Canada, and Caribbean island states with common-law systems took longer. The IACAC entered into force on 6 March 1997—30 days after the deposition of the second instrument of ratification. All OAS member states, with the exception of Cuba, whose membership was suspended for many decades, have now ratified the convention. This makes it the most successful OAS treaty in terms of ratification.[3]

In addition to the IACAC itself, the OAS has pursued several other anti-corruption initiatives. In 1997, the organization's General Assembly adopted the "Inter-American Program for Cooperation in the Fight Against Corruption,"[4] which calls for measures to be adopted in four areas. In the legal area, states decided to gather information on existing national laws, work on definitions of different aspects of corruption, and propose drafts for new laws, codes of conduct, and publicity efforts. The document also specifies the need for coordination of and support for relevant national institutions. At the international level, the OAS aims to cooperate with the United Nations, the Council of Europe, and other international organizations. Finally, the program addresses civil society, specifically the media and professional organizations that could support anti-corruption efforts. In 1999, the OAS Working Group on Probity and Public Ethics was "reactivated" and tasked with implementing this program.[5]

86 Organization of American States

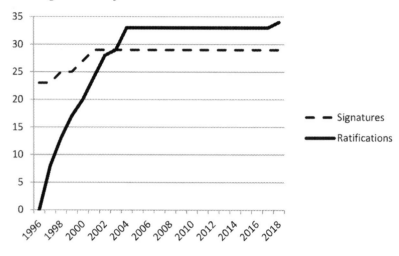

Figure 3.1 Signing and ratification of the OAS convention
Source: Based on OAS data.

Multiple intergovernmental conferences have been held since the adoption of the IACAC. In May 2001, the 17 states that had ratified the treaty by that point met in Buenos Aires. Their goal was to establish a follow-up mechanism for the IACAC in accordance with deliberations that had been ongoing since 1999. A proposal for the mechanism's design was developed by the Working Group and a meeting of experts in March 2001. Following the conference in Buenos Aires, the General Assembly acknowledged the creation of a "Mechanism for Follow-up of Implementation of the Inter-American Convention Against Corruption" (MESICIC) in June 2001.[6] In July 2004, the parties to the IACAC met in Managua, Nicaragua, and approved a further declaration of their commitment.[7]

After the creation of MESICIC, OAS member states convened four Conferences of States Parties within the mechanism's framework. The first took place at the OAS headquarters in Washington, DC, and addressed the role of the secretariat, funding for the mechanism, and other organizational issues.[8] At the second conference, which was held in 2006, an updated version of the Program of Cooperation to Fight Corruption was adopted.[9] The subsequent conferences in Brasilia (in December 2010) and Washington (in December 2015) discussed progress and organizational matters.[10] In addition, the OAS held two "Conferences on the Progress and Challenges in Hemispheric Cooperation against Corruption" in Lima, Peru (in 2010), and Cali, Colombia (in 2011). As indicated by the title, these meetings focused

Organization of American States 87

on the exchange of best practice and technical discussions on challenges with implementation.

In parallel to these conferences and the documents adopted by the OAS's decision-making bodies, MESICIC has remained active ever since its creation. It consists of two bodies: the aforementioned Conference of States Parties, which is tasked with general decision-making, and the Committee of Experts, which deals with technical analysis and the drafting of recommendations. Each party to the treaty appoints an expert, while administrative assistance is provided by the OAS General Secretariat. The review process is organized in rounds that last for several years. Member-state compliance with particular aspects of the convention is assessed through peer review, with the Committee of Experts deciding which provisions are reviewed in each round.

During the course of each round, member states first report on their progress by answering a questionnaire. Their responses are then collated in a report by the Technical Secretariat, a subsidiary of the OAS Secretariat for Legal Affairs in Washington. In 2013, each of the six researchers in the Technical Secretariat was responsible for approximately two country reports per year, in addition to their other tasks.[11] Next, the first draft of each country's report is sent to two committee members who act as lead reviewers for that country. At least one of them must be from a state with a similar legal tradition as the one under review to ensure familiarity with the peculiarities of either common or civil law. After the reviewers have commented on the draft report, the state under review is given the opportunity to comment. The Technical Secretariat then prepares a revised draft and circulates it to all members of the Committee of Experts. Additional information may be supplied by civil society representatives, who are invited to give verbal presentations to the committee as long as they have filed written reports on compliance in advance. In 2011, the procedural rules were amended to allow for on-site visits if the countries under review consented.[12]

All of the reports are finalized in a plenary session of the Committee of Experts, which may introduce modifications in light of this final discussion. Each report has to be adopted by the committee "preferably pursuant to a consensus decision."[13] While the procedural rules suggest that consensus on the final wording is preferable but not mandatory, in practice the reports have always avoided harsh criticism. For instance, a report on the very first session of the committee notes that delegates insisted on amendment of the first reports because they deemed them "inappropriate in tone."[14] The final country reports are published on the OAS website, including both an assessment of the status quo and recommendations for improvements.

88 *Organization of American States*

Four of these review rounds had been completed by the time of writing. Each had a thematic focus, covering the implementation of a subset of provisions contained within the IACAC. In addition, the reports address the states' level of compliance with earlier rounds' recommendations. At the conclusion of each round, the OAS has published a "Hemispheric Report" that outlines general trends and presents some descriptive statistics.[15] These reports do not, however, rank or even directly compare member states. The fifth round of reviews had been launched at the time of writing.

To summarize, the OAS convention was adopted after a very short period of deliberations and it has since been ratified by virtually all of the organization's member states. A peer-review mechanism was added in 2001, became operational shortly thereafter, and has since published four sets of reports on compliance. Judging from these reports and the frequency of regional conferences, the OAS's anti-corruption efforts enjoy significant political and administrative support.

Motivations and drivers

What were the driving forces behind the adoption and design of the OAS convention? Arguably, the 1994 Summit of the Americas represents a significant turning point in the discourse about anti-corruption at the OAS. Following this summit, the US government worked in tandem with a group of Latin American countries to establish a regional convention.

The Summit of the Americas as a turning point

In 1990, the Chilean government suggested that the OAS should put ethics and corruption on its agenda. Guerzovich and de Michele offer a twofold explanation for why this initial effort failed: first, respect for sovereignty and the principle of non-intervention prevailed; second, opponents argued that regional initiatives could have unintended consequences, because "drawing attention to the links between corruption and political and governing processes could delegitimize very fragile democratization dynamics in the hemisphere."[16]

However, four years later, the Summit of the Americas in Miami marked a turning point for anti-corruption in the OAS. Formally, such meetings are not part of the OAS structure. Yet, according to the OAS website, most of its mandates over recent years have resulted from summits, for which the organization provides technical and administrative support. Thus, it appears that the summits have become the de

Organization of American States 89

facto forum for agenda-setting, as they frequently generate plans of action for the OAS and its individual member states. Indeed, the General Assembly's official decisions often directly reference summit outcomes before translating the latter into the formal and legal context of the OAS. Moreover, a dedicated committee at the OAS—the Summit Implementation Review Group—is tasked with supervising follow-up, while the member states' foreign ministers "meet periodically in order to establish a more specific agenda on the various issues."[17]

The United States has always been the largest contributor to the OAS budget and it is particularly active in orchestrating Inter-American summits and initiatives. The first Summit of the Americas, in 1994, was a case in point. Although the goal of creating a FTAA was not reached, the OAS was revived as a by-product of attempts to intensify regional integration. After a long period of paralysis and neglect by heads of state, not least due to discontent with the way in which the US government had used the OAS to promote its foreign policy agenda, the summit succeeded in attracting attention and drafted a range of new mandates for the organization.[18] Notably, the United States was not only the formal host but also hosted preparatory meetings to create momentum.[19]

Around this time, in a contribution to a policy symposium, the director of the OAS's Department of Legal Cooperation and Information pointed out that his organization had been prioritizing anti-corruption in the context of promoting democracy since the start of the decade. Indeed, several OAS documents had previously mentioned the term "corruption" alongside "democracy promotion" and "state modernization." Yet, according to Garcia-Gonzalez, the summit should still be regarded as a turning point:

> [W]ithout a doubt, the Summit process of the Heads of States and of Governments of the Americas introduced with great vigour the treatment of this issue on a hemispherical level. In fact, the first Summit, held in Miami in December of 1994, targeted the issue for the first time. On this occasion, the Heads of States and of Governments acknowledged that this problem was of a multilateral nature and, aware of that, they committed themselves to negotiate within the OAS framework, a hemispherical accord.[20]

US goals: internationalization of the FCPA and extradition

The US government ensured that the Summit of the Americas put corruption high on the regional agenda. The meetings of the OAS

90   *Organization of American States*

Working Group on Probity and Public Ethics prior to the adoption of the IACAC were also held in Washington, DC, once again at the invitation of the United States. Furthermore, US delegates met with several Latin American leaders to gauge their reactions to the proposals and to lobby for the plan in the run-up to the Summit of the Americas.[21] In an interview with the *Washington Post* after the 1996 Specialized Conference in Caracas, one US official summarized his government's role in simple terms: "We wrote it, and we convinced everyone in the hemisphere to adopt it."[22] This statement was aimed at the US audience, so it could be dismissed as hyperbole. Yet, the evidence suggests that the United States did indeed provide substantial leadership in the field of anti-corruption. So, what motivated the US government to put corruption on the agenda and push for a hemispheric treaty? First, it wished to internationalize its own rules against foreign bribery, codified in the 1977 Foreign Corrupt Practices Act (FCPA). Second, anti-corruption was linked to crime-fighting and security goals.

In the Introduction, I discussed the US government's unique motivation to level the playing field regarding transnational bribery. Business groups were putting pressure on the Clinton administration to mitigate their disadvantages in international trade and investment. They argued that foreign competitors could hand out bribes to secure contracts while the FCPA prohibited them from doing the same. Watering down US laws on corruption was unconscionable, so the strategy was to bind competing exporters to the same norms through international standard-setting. As mentioned earlier, the OECD—an elite club of powerful economies and the biggest exporters in the world—seemed the natural forum in which to address this issue. Yet, it was the OAS that took the lead. Why was this the case?

By banning the acceptance of bribes and raising the salience of anti-corruption, the IACAC would make it more difficult for corrupt enterprises to gain an unfair competitive advantage when exporting to or investing in OAS member states. More importantly, though, the US government faced very strong opposition to its anti-corruption proposals within the OECD, whereas the OAS offered an opportunity to "create a precedent for the internationalization of the FCPA."[23] In contrast to the OECD, very few multinational corporations that were in direct competition with US businesses were based in the rest of the Americas, so outlawing the supply side of bribery would have little practical impact. Yet, the OAS convention did set a precedent for the introduction of US legal standards into international law. The IACAC's provision against transnational bribery thus created "a

Organization of American States 91

geographic and legal bridge from the FCPA to the OECD Convention."[24] It is difficult to judge the extent to which this legal precedent buttressed the US position in the OECD negotiations. That said, the IACAC did at least prove that an international anti-corruption convention was feasible,[25] and the US government certainly used it to "prod the members of the OECD to take similar action."[26]

The United States' fight against drug trafficking also drove its advocacy of an anti-corruption convention, as the IACAC would provide the necessary legal instruments to prosecute traffickers across borders. However, this important goal was not universally welcomed at the time:

> Banking secrecy, the right to political asylum and immunity from extradition are the international fugitive's tried-and-tested defences, sometimes against justice, sometimes against its reverse. The United States' zeal to lay its hand on foreigners whom it accuses of drug-trafficking is a sore point with Latin governments, though some have in fact given way.[27]

This agenda is mirrored in the IACAC's preamble, which mentions "organized crime" and "proceeds generated by illicit narcotics trafficking" in addition to the importance of anti-corruption for democratic governance. From a US perspective, the desire to establish a ban on foreign bribery in international law combined with the need for regional cross-border cooperation to counteract drug trafficking provided clear incentives to secure an agreement. As a result, the OAS convention is the only document of its kind to mention narcotics explicitly.[28]

Latin America: signals to regional and domestic audiences

That said, the OAS anti-corruption agenda was not driven by US interests alone. For instance, Venezuelan President Rafael Caldera played a particularly important role as he not only hosted the decisive final conference at which the document was approved but has also been hailed as the initial driver of the whole project.[29] In a meeting with a US delegate prior to the 1994 Summit of the Americas, he promised Venezuelan support for the internationalization of the FCPA in exchange for US support on his priority of facilitating extraditions.[30] Three other Latin American governments were also advocating for a regional agreement: Chile had introduced new ethics legislation and was seeking to export it; Honduras wanted to tackle military

92 *Organization of American States*

corruption; and Ecuador's vice-president was a strong supporter of the local chapter of Transparency International.[31] Thus, the agenda-setting and lobbying were shared among a coalition of at least five states.

In the build-up to the 1994 Summit of the Americas, US negotiators frequently met with delegates from the Venezuelan, Honduran, Chilean, and Ecuadorian embassies in Washington, and these states were later joined by Argentina and Colombia in promoting the convention among Latin American countries.[32] For several Latin American governments, adopting an anti-corruption agreement promised smoother extradition and the prosecution of former public officials and private individuals who had fled the country.[33] For instance, Caldera was motivated by the fact that large-scale corruption had recently bankrupted several Venezuelan banks. He sought to create a means to punish the perpetrators and gain access to the funds they had transferred to other countries.[34] This desire for tougher rules was shared by a number of other Latin American leaders who were similarly motivated by their inability to seize either wrongdoers or their ill-gotten gains.

Broader changes during the 1990s contributed to the growing anti-corruption coalition among governments in the Americas. The end of the Cold War and the subsequent democratization of Latin America provided a stimulus for international cooperation and legalization. This coincided with increasing trade and foreign direct investment as well as growing interest in emerging markets in Latin America and elsewhere.[35] Economic globalization and international anti-corruption efforts are intrinsically linked because investment and trade flows create more situations in which corruption becomes a transnational phenomenon. Consequently, this leads to competitive pressures within capital-importing countries. Governments across Latin America hoped to make their markets attractive for investors and wanted to encourage multinational corporations to do business with them. Their intention was to send a credible signal to attract foreign direct investment as well as bids on public procurement tenders by committing themselves to "more transparency and more objective and predictable conditions in contracting."[36] These developments formed part of broader attempts at public-sector reform in Latin American countries.[37]

In addition to the inherently international tasks of regulating transnational business and helping with criminal investigations, the proponents of the IACAC appreciated its value as a signal to domestic audiences. Like the logic of locking in democratic reforms, anti-corruption commitments allow policy-makers to constrain the activities of their successors and peers. For the relatively new Latin American democracies, signing the IACAC meant fulfilling election promises. For example, Caldera and his Honduran counterpart, Carlos Reina, had both campaigned on anti-corruption platforms.[38] In addition, pledging to combat corruption pulled the rug from under the supporters of military dictatorships:

> For decades, proponents of military rule had often called for a "strong hand against corruption" as one of several justifications for the creation and continuation of military governments. Thus, upon the widespread reemergence of civilian rule over the course of the 1980s, the new democratic regimes had to have a credible anticorruption position to become stronger. A regional legal instrument could force their pledge and send a strong signal about their commitment.[39]

Worries about the destabilizing effects of corruption were shared by elements within the US government, where officials warned of the rise of autocratic populists in the wake of scandals in Latin America.[40] For Latin American governments, committing to the IACAC thus served as a twofold signal to domestic constituencies and third parties: specifically, it delivered on campaign promises; more generally, it was designed to increase confidence in relatively new democratic governments' ability to curb corrupt practices.

Sub-regional initiatives

Multiple regional organizations across Latin America aim to foster economic integration and political cooperation among their respective member states.[41] The first of these, founded as the Andean Pact in 1969 and renamed the Andean Community (CAN) in 1996, currently comprises Bolivia, Colombia, Ecuador, and Peru as full members. Next was the Caribbean Community—CARICOM—which was established in 1973 and mainly consists of the Caribbean island states. It currently has 15 full members. MERCOSUR, founded in 1991, comprises Argentina, Brazil, Uruguay, Paraguay, and Venezuela (since 2006, although suspended at the time of writing). All of these Latin American sub-regional organizations have been active in terms of setting standards of governance for their member states in the areas of human rights, democracy, and the rule of law.[42] Yet, as mentioned in Chapter 2, none of them has developed a binding anti-corruption agreement.

The Andean Community is the most active in terms of issuing anti-corruption declarations. For instance, in 1999, the Andean Presidential

94   *Organization of American States*

Council stated its intention to ratify and implement the OAS convention. Furthermore, it promised to establish two mechanisms regarding public procurement: first, a register of companies that violated procurement regulations would be used to disqualify such enterprises from future contracts for up to 10 years; second, from 2002 onwards, no contracts would be awarded to multinationals based in OECD member countries that had not ratified that organization's convention.[43] I have been unable to establish whether these two measures have been implemented.

In 2003, and repeatedly thereafter, the Andean Community's highest official body instructed the Council of Foreign Ministers and several subordinate bodies to draft a plan of action for fighting corruption. An action plan was finally adopted in 2007. It references both the IACAC and the UNCAC and envisages 10 "programs of action" in the fields of: raising public awareness; cooperating with the media; fostering legislative developments in accordance with the IACAC and the UNCAC; increasing public-sector transparency; introducing measures for the private sector; strengthening anti-corruption agencies; dealing with corrupt high-level officials; ensuring that all officials provide statements about their assets; ensuring that public interest is defended in judicial proceedings; and promoting transparent procurement. The action plan lists several issues to be promoted in each of these fields, and the Andean Community's Secretariat and member states are tasked with gathering information on particular subjects.[44] Again, I was unable to establish the extent to which this plan has been implemented, although the absence of a paper trail suggests that little practical progress has been made as yet. Nevertheless, the Andean Community has issued multiple statements in support of the OAS convention, and while its own measures do not amount to binding commitments, they do at least display a willingness to foster implementation.

CARICOM is less active than CAN. One observer criticized the lack of commitment up to 2007, pointing out that regional leaders even avoided using the term "corruption" in official communiqués.[45] This might be related to diplomatic disputes about some Caribbean nations' perceived status as financial havens and their inclusion in the OECD Financial Action Task Force's list of "uncooperative countries." However, anti-money-laundering legislation started to gain a foothold in CARICOM member states during the 2000s, which led the task force to remove all of the Caribbean states from its blacklist.[46] Nevertheless, CARICOM leaders remained reluctant to declare their opposition to corruption, let alone commit themselves to concrete measures to combat it. One 2002 internal report on regional crime and security

Organization of American States 95

issues states, "[D]rug corruption provides Caribbean civil servants with some US$320 million in income annually. This is not an insignificant problem,"[47] and goes on to recommend legislative action against corruption. However, it does not prioritize the issue. I found only one other reference to corruption—a short passage in a plan of action that CARICOM leaders adopted at a joint summit with the Central American Integration System (SICA). This merely suggests that existing agreements should be used to address the issue.[48] Overall, then, CARICOM leaders have made very few attempts to tackle corruption in their regional forum. In contrast to their counterparts in the Andean Community, they seem to see little value in creating sub-regional agreements or even detailed action plans.

In 2002, MERCOSUR adopted an agreement in which the member states made a commitment to prevent and punish acts of corruption along their borders. Therefore, the intention seems to be to tackle smuggling and customs fraud. The agreement borrows the IACAC's definition of "corruption," but adds no substantial provisions. Instead, member states declare that they will coordinate their activities through a special commission and exchange information to fight corruption along their borders.[49] Eight years later, the member states' leaders adopted another declaration that mentions corruption. However, this amounts to little more than a statement of good intentions:

> [Member states reiterate their willingness to] continue to work together to harmonize respective national regulations in the fight against corruption and transnational organized crime by applying the recommendations and guidelines in the framework of the Inter-American Convention, the UN Convention Against Corruption, and the UN Convention Against Transnational Organized Crime.[50]

In sum, MERCOSUR generally defers to the OAS and the UN when it comes to addressing corruption, with the only exception being an agreement on technical cooperation relating to cross-border trade.

Summary: signaling to domestic, intra-group, and external audiences

The United States—the dominant power in the OAS—cooperated with several Latin American governments to set the agenda and lobby for the adoption of a regional anti-corruption treaty. These actors were motivated primarily by a desire to send a signal to domestic and intra-group audiences: both the US government and its Latin American

96 *Organization of American States*

counterparts sought to reach an agreement that would ensure international cooperation in the region, specifically with respect to extradition. Anti-corruption also correlated with the agenda of economic integration and liberalization that was promoted at the Summit of the Americas. Additionally, some Latin American governments were motivated by the need to signal to their domestic constituencies. Corruption scandals had recently brought down several governments, and concerns about public ethics had the potential to undermine the newly established and as yet unproven democratic orders.[51]

It seems that signaling to external audiences was a secondary motivation, less salient than either the domestic or the intra-group dynamic. For the United States, internationalizing its ban on foreign bribery via the OAS meant creating a precedent for the OECD. In that sense, the IACAC also had value as a signal to non-member states. Meanwhile, for the Latin American countries, public commitments to fight corruption had the potential to boost international trade and investment.

Analysis of the sub-regional organizations supports the hypothesis that anti-corruption in the Americas is primarily driven by domestic and regional signaling motives because no regional sub-group has created a parallel structure of binding commitments, which one might expect if they hoped to reap benefits from sending signals to external audiences. Instead, the sub-regional organizations have limited themselves to adopting a few minor policies to complement the overarching OAS framework.

Tracing the drafts over time

Having analyzed the drivers and motivations that prompted member states to negotiate the IACAC, we now turn to the drafting process itself. By the time this got under way, the OAS already had a very long history of addressing corruption. As early as 1975, the Permanent Council adopted a resolution on the conduct of transnational enterprises in the region. Resolution 154 (167/75) noted that transnational businesses ought to operate in accordance with national laws as well as goals for economic and social development. The Permanent Council resolved to conduct a study on possible action and urged member states to exchange information. Moreover, it urged members to outlaw all bribery in transnational business interactions.[52] Comparable to the early anti-corruption efforts at the United Nations, this first initiative was limited to the narrow field of transnational bribery. Moreover, it did not amount to a binding commitment, nor contain concrete language to clarify the provisions to be codified in national laws. It was only at the start of the 1990s that a comprehensive, binding approach began to take shape in the OAS.

Initiatives leading to the Summit of the Americas

Within the OAS framework, General Assembly Resolution 1294, which was adopted in June 1994, established the Working Group on Probity and Public Ethics. This initiative was led by Chile, and that country's legal expert Edmundo Vargas Carreño subsequently became the Working Group's first chairman. In the resolution, the General Assembly pledged to create a body that would study the existing legal frameworks in member states, compile a list of relevant provisions in national laws, and draft a proposal for international cooperation. Furthermore, it asked member states to cooperate by providing any information requested by the Working Group.[53] Over the next few months, the Working Group on Probity and Public Ethics "kept in close contact with the Washington embassy working group [which was organizing the Summit of the Americas], and its working drafts paralleled theirs in most respects."[54]

In September 1994, the Rio Group—a loose coalition of 14 Latin American governments—held a summit in Rio de Janeiro.[55] This meeting's main declaration contained a paragraph linking anti-corruption to the fight against organized crime. Moreover, this theme was repeated in a separate declaration on "coordination of the fight against drug trafficking," in which the heads of state declared their concerns over trafficking and called for the Summit of the Americas to draft an "inter-American convention to combat money laundering."[56]

In the meantime, US diplomats had initiated preparatory meetings for the Summit of the Americas. These had begun in January 1994 with visits to Latin American countries as well as meetings in various embassies in Washington, DC, which houses not just the US government but also the headquarters of the OAS. These informal negotiations resulted in a document known as the "October draft" that included sections reflecting the main concerns of a number of member states: transnational bribery (United States); public procurement (Chile); the link between corruption and democracy (several Latin American countries); liaison with the OECD, rather than merely following that organization's lead, as an early US draft had envisaged; and international cooperation over legal assistance and extradition (Venezuela).[57]

The last preparatory meeting for the summit was held at Airlie House, Virginia, at the end of November 1994. This served as a

98 *Organization of American States*

melting pot in which the Rio Group, the diplomats behind the October draft, and the official OAS Working Group could all scrutinize one another's proposals. One US negotiator reported that the Rio Group—which was under Brazilian leadership—presented the least specific and shortest plan of action, not just on corruption but across all issues. Ultimately, the coalition that had been working towards a strong stance against corruption prevailed:

> The plenary sessions reviewed the US-circulated draft initiative by initiative. On any particular issue, leadership tended to devolve onto those countries with recognized authority and expertise. For example, delegates were aware that certain countries had been working on the anticorruption initiative and deferred to them on that issue. The anticorruption coalition was sufficiently large and representative of the various subregional groups to maintain plenary discussion momentum, discourage dissonance, and even strengthen the paragraphs on corruption.
>
> The US composite draft declaration of principles mentioned corruption only briefly, as one item in a list of propositions to be undertaken to ensure continuing faith in democratic institutions. The anticorruption coalition—primarily Venezuela, Ecuador, Honduras, and Chile, strongly supported by Argentina and Colombia—successfully pressed for a full sentence and then proposed that sentence be set apart as a separate paragraph. The assembly concurred that corruption should be framed as not only undermining the legitimacy of political democracy but also as fostering social disintegration and distorting economic decisions.[58]

After the draft had been broadened to include a Brazilian proposal regarding cooperation in international investigations, "the anticorruption initiative sailed through with little controversy" at Airlie House.[59] A few weeks later, at the summit itself, the heads of government endorsed the final draft and several presidential speeches emphasized the importance of anti-corruption measures. As discussed in the previous section, the fight against corruption also features prominently in the summit declaration. Moreover, the associated plan of action suggests that member states should initiate domestic measures to prevent corrupt practices. Most importantly, its final paragraph declares that governments will develop "a hemispheric approach to acts of corruption in both the public and private sectors that would include extradition and prosecution of individuals so charged."[60] Therefore, it alludes to both prevention and international cooperation. This wording

Organization of American States 99

provided the foundation for a binding and relatively comprehensive anti-corruption effort.

Taking up the mandate from the summit

In December 1994, shortly after the Summit of the Americas, the Venezuelan government presented a first draft resolution, which was disseminated to the Working Group and the other member states.[61] This document contained a total of 14 articles, 10 of which were substantive: (I) definitions; (II) a short note on the scope of the convention; (III) jurisdiction; (IV) offenses, namely active and passive bribery and acting as an accomplice; (V) a commitment to mutual legal assistance; (VI) denying asylum for those accused of corruption; (VII and VIII) extradition, irrespective of nationality; (IX) tracing, seizing, and returning property; (X) dispute settlement among states parties. To summarize, the Venezuelan proposal contained a criminalization clause, some provisions on jurisdiction and related aspects, and several commitments to international cooperation—specifically, extradition and the freezing and return of assets.[62]

The plan of action proposed at the summit then led to an expansion of the Working Group's mandate. At its 25th regular session in July 1995, the General Assembly passed Resolution 1346—on probity and public ethics—which instructed the Working Group to "prepare a draft Inter-American Convention against Corruption, with support from the General Secretariat and on the basis of the proposal submitted by the Government of Venezuela, bearing in mind observations contributed by the governments."[63] Thus, a second draft was prepared by the Working Group's chairman, the Chilean Edmundo Vargas Carreño. This draft generally followed the structure of the Venezuelan proposal, with some additions and amendments. A new article IV was added, which allowed states to deny requests for assistance if they were in the process of trying an individual under their own laws. Meanwhile, article VI (on denying asylum) was dropped and a new article VII was introduced. The latter noted that parties might use earlier treaties and agreements for mutual assistance. The chairman's draft also contained slightly more detailed language on the procedures to be used for cooperation over extradition and asset seizure and recovery.[64]

Juridical Committee draft

Resolution 1346 also instructed the OAS's Juridical Committee, Permanent Council, and General Secretariat to provide their input. The

100 Organization of American States

goal was to produce another draft convention, which would be adopted by a Specialized Conference that Venezuela volunteered to host.[65] The Inter-American Juridical Committee is an expert body that consists of 11 jurists elected by the General Assembly for four-year terms. In response to the General Assembly's request for input, on 31 August 1995 it submitted extensive comments on the Working Group chairman's draft and proposed one of its own.

The Juridical Committee's draft differed from its predecessor in several important respects. The overall emphasis was shifted to the goal of cooperation; clarification was provided on the scope of application, which would be based on territory but also include effects; criminalization was de-emphasized, as it was deemed unnecessary for legal cooperation; and the definition of corruption was narrowed towards quid pro quo exchanges. Taken together, these changes amounted to refocusing the agreement entirely towards legal cooperation, with no requirement that specified acts of corruption must be criminalized in all member states.[66]

The new draft also contained some additional elements. Definitions were provided for "requested" and "requesting" states as well as "property"; a new article stated that simply acquiring property for political purposes was insufficient to make corruption a "political offense," eliminating the potential that this could be used to claim asylum; the issue of transnational bribery was mentioned for the first time; extradition would be granted even in the absence of a bilateral treaty; and, if bank secrecy were lifted, the information would be used only for the intended anti-corruption purpose. Finally, a new article XIV allowed states to deny requests from another state if the latter had violated human rights and democracy.[67]

Overall, then, the Juridical Committee's draft introduced some clarifications and helpful additions regarding the regulation of international cooperation. It deviated from the notion of committing member states to banning corruption in their domestic legislation, focusing instead on facilitating cooperation among them. Thus, its provisions may be classified under the sub-categories of jurisdiction and international cooperation (see Chapter 2). It failed to address prevention, criminalization, domestic enforcement, or follow-up.

Final deliberations in the Working Group and the Specialized Conference

Over the course of the winter of 1995/1996, the Working Group used the Juridical Committee's draft as the main basis for discussions during

Organization of American States 101

three meetings in Washington, DC. Ultimately, these deliberations resulted in a fourth draft that incorporated substantial changes.[68] Most significantly, the innovative concept of suspending cooperation in cases of rights violations was removed. Other aspects were largely retained, such as the provisions on bank secrecy, corruption not being a political crime, and establishing a central authority.

One important addition was the new article III—a non-binding clause that urged states to consider a set of 12 preventive measures. These mainly concerned the public sector and addressed issues such as codes of conduct and requirements to declare assets. The article was based on a US draft coupled with input from Colombia, and it enjoyed the support of Argentina.[69]

The list of acts of corruption largely followed the Juridical Committee's draft, with a few minor changes. In the articles on the convention's purpose and the acts that should be outlawed, the wording again included domestic criminalization. Cooperation was retained as an equally important goal and focal point, but the Juridical Committee's notion of limiting the agreement to international cooperation was dropped. The new article VII, which committed all parties to banning the behavior outlined in article VI, was the core obligation of the treaty.

Moreover, the draft introduced two more clauses related to criminalization. The new article VIII called for states to ban transnational bribery, while article IX introduced the notion of "illicit enrichment," criminalizing any significant increase in an official's assets that could not be explained by legitimate income. Both of these clauses were placed outside of the core criminalization provisions and the level of obligation was lower in both cases, as implementation was conditional on compatibility with domestic legal principles. Article X then asked states to notify the OAS in the event of enacting domestic legislation on either of the two preceding articles.

The new article XI—titled "Progressive development"—was another addition resulting from the Working Group meetings. It declared that "the States Parties view as desirable, and undertake to consider, establishing as offenses under their laws" abuse of public office and embezzlement. The level of obligation was slightly higher than in the purely optional article III (on possible preventive measures), but lower than in the permissive articles on illicit enrichment and transnational bribery. Consequently, article XI comprised much less of an obligation than the provisions on banning the core bribery offenses.

Article XIV, which addressed legal cooperation and technical assistance, expanded on a Juridical Committee proposal that had focused

102 Organization of American States

on requests based on ongoing legal proceedings. The new, broader language permitted requests for legal assistance from prosecutorial and other agencies investigating corruption. Furthermore, it included a paragraph on technical assistance, such as information and intelligence exchange. This broader understanding of assistance was promoted by Argentina, Peru, Venezuela, the United States, and other member states.[70]

Article XV, on assets, was relatively short, as the preceding article already covered property-related proceedings. It contained a commitment to the "widest possible assistance" in tracing, freezing, and forfeiting property. Moreover, following a US proposal, it incorporated language from the UN's drug-trafficking convention, "pursuant to which a state that has cooperated in an investigation on an act of corruption, at the request of another state party, may benefit from the distribution of a portion of the property forfeited as a result of the offense, provided that this distribution is lawful."[71]

Finally, at the Specialized Conference, which was held at the end of March 1996 in Caracas, discussions focused on several issues that had not been finalized during the Working Group's third meeting, two weeks earlier. There were no significant changes to the agreement, although a new article XIX, based on a joint proposal by Peru and Colombia and backed by the United States, was introduced. The original proposal had sought to make the IACAC applicable to events that had occurred prior to its entry into force, but this was strongly contested during negotiations. A compromise was reached that allowed for the provisions on international cooperation to be applied to crimes committed before entry into force, but only if both parties agreed and the non-retroactivity principle of criminal law were maintained.[72]

In accordance with the plan laid out in Resolution 1346, the IACAC was finalized and formally adopted at the Specialized Conference. The resulting treaty covers prevention, criminalization, jurisdiction, and international cooperation, but there is no mention of domestic enforcement, for instance regarding minimum standards for sanctions. Additionally, it does not address delegation to ensure follow-up within the regional organization.

The creation of MESICIC as a follow-up mechanism

After the IACAC was adopted and quickly gained signatures and ratifications, a plan of action was adopted to complement the treaty. The issue of establishing a follow-up mechanism then gradually gained traction.[73] Previously, according to one high-ranking OAS official,

Organization of American States   103

none of the member states had given much thought to creating such a mechanism:

> If the viability of international treaties in this field were disputable during this time, the possibility of creating monitoring mechanisms or instruments for evaluating compliance of the treaties by the states was practically unthinkable ... [The adoption of such mechanisms by the OECD and the Council of Europe later] led to the suggestion of creating a follow-up mechanism for the implementation of the Inter-American Convention against Corruption by the States Parties to it.[74]

In June 1999, the General Assembly approved a US proposal and instructed the Permanent Council to develop measures to encourage ratification and implementation. To this end, the Working Group on Probity and Public Ethics was reactivated. In November, a nongovernmental roundtable was organized by the American University, the Inter-American Bar Association, Washington College of Law, and Transparency International. The goal was to develop recommendations for the Permanent Council on how to address the issue of follow-up. Discussions among 25 officials and legal experts concluded with a recommendation to create a multilateral monitoring mechanism that "should draw on models in the hemisphere and beyond."[75]

The following March, the Working Group held a meeting to discuss, *inter alia*, a follow-up mechanism, which resulted in an endorsement of the roundtable's proposal. This was formalized in June 2000 in the form of Resolution 1723, in which the General Assembly asked the Permanent Council "to analyze existing regional and international follow-up mechanisms with a view to recommending, by the end of the year, the most appropriate model that States Parties could use."[76]

During the second half of 2000, the Working Group met several times at OAS headquarters in Washington, DC. "The principal contributors to the negotiations were Argentina, Canada, Jamaica, the United States, and Mexico, with additional input from Uruguay, Peru, Brazil, and El Salvador."[77] The Working Group presented its assessment in a document dated 13 October 2000, which it forwarded to the Permanent Council. This 45-page report discusses the OECD's follow-up mechanisms, the Council of Europe's GRECO, the Inter-American Drug Abuse Control Commission, and the Caribbean Financial Action Task Force, with sections on the institutional setup and procedures of each mechanism as well as a schematic comparison.[78] The report does not offer clear recommendations on which elements to

104 *Organization of American States*

adopt, but the Working Group also sent the Permanent Council a proposal for its favored follow-up mechanism. In November, the Permanent Council forwarded this proposal (with some amendments) to the parties to the treaty. At this point, it included the idea that the newly created Commission of Experts would handle "the selection of topics under the convention to be reviewed, countries to be evaluated, and the issuance of a report that will be forwarded first to the states parties and then made public."[79]

In May 2001, the 17 parties to the IACAC met in Buenos Aires for the first Conference of the Parties. This meeting resulted in the "Report of Buenos Aires on the Mechanism for Follow-up on Implementation of the Inter-American Convention Against Corruption," which endorsed the creation of an intergovernmental mechanism consisting of a Conference of States Parties and a Committee of Experts. When this was formally confirmed by the General Assembly of the OAS in June 2001, it became the first—and thus far only—major addition to the agreement.[80]

Evidence of diffusion

Given the OAS's status as a pioneer among international organizations on the issue of addressing corruption, to what extent were the scope and design of the IACAC products of diffusion processes? In this section, I will discuss the reference models for the original convention, the second set of negotiations that resulted in the MESICIC review mechanism, and the role of non-state actors.

Reference models for the original IACAC

Publications authored by participants in the OAS negotiations served as unofficial *travaux préparatoires* for the agreement. Analysis of these sources sheds light on the reference models and source material that were used for much of the IACAC. Given that there were no binding agreements against corruption to emulate, the drafters were unable to draw on international models for the corruption-specific elements of the convention. Instead, the first 10 articles are innovations and/or inspired by member states' domestic legislation. The articles up to article VII, which contains the obligation to criminalize corruption through domestic laws, focus on the purpose of the convention, defining corruption, and outlining how jurisdiction will be established. These aspects of criminalization and jurisdiction were drafted over a period of time with significant inputs from legal experts and country delegations.

Organization of American States 105

Some sections of the treaty can be traced to specific initiatives by member states rather than the collaborative work of the Working Group and the Juridical Committee. For instance, the article on preventive measures (article III) was developed on the basis of US and Colombian proposals. Similarly, article XI, on "progressive development," which outlines additional ideas relating to criminalization, was drafted on the basis of suggestions from member states rather than international precedents. Unsurprisingly, as the United States was the main proponent of this doctrine, article VIII, with its permissive clause on banning transnational bribery, draws heavily on that country's FCPA. Finally, the controversial clause on illicit enrichment reflects a compromise brokered by Mexico and Colombia, but it was based on a decades-old piece of Argentinian legislation.[81]

While there was no corpus of treaties on the problem of corruption, the issue of international legal cooperation had been addressed in earlier agreements, and the availability of suitable reference models was reflected in the OAS's drafting process. According to the head of the Working Group on Probity and Public Ethics, the drafters drew particular inspiration from the 1988 UN Convention on Illegal Traffic in Narcotics and Psychotropic Substances, the 1981 Inter-American Convention on Extradition, and the 1992 Inter-American Convention on Mutual Assistance in Criminal Matters.[82] Indeed, article XIII (on extradition) largely mirrors the narcotics convention, while one of seven paragraphs is equivalent to rules in the OAS's own extradition convention.[83] Article XIV (on assistance and cooperation) contains a relatively broad commitment to provide the widest possible assistance, plus a reference to technical assistance. The final version goes beyond the original proposals of the Working Group and the Juridical Committee, which had merely advocated the provision of mutual legal assistance. The addition of technical cooperation among enforcement agencies seems to indicate a deliberate attempt to exceed the provisions in the closest reference model.

The US delegation introduced a clause based on the UN narcotics convention into article XV (confiscation of property),[84] while article XVI (on limiting bank secrecy) is inspired by but not a verbatim copy of the corresponding provision in the same document.[85] Article XVII (denial of corruption as a political offense) is a counter-measure to the OAS's own extradition convention, which allows states to deny an extradition request if the alleged crime is deemed to be a political offense. Article XVIII (declaration of a central authority) follows the model of the OAS's mutual legal assistance convention.[86]

106   *Organization of American States*

International reference models for MESICIC

By 1998/1999, when the OAS launched the process of developing a follow-up mechanism, the international situation had changed because other organizations had started to address the issue of corruption. Judging from the archival records, the OAS was influenced by both the OECD and the Council of Europe regarding the establishment of its follow-up mechanism. Two discrete diffusion mechanisms are evident: emulation and lesson-drawing.

At first, proponents of a mechanism within the OAS simply pointed out that the OECD and the COE—two well-known organizations that were undertaking comparable efforts to fight corruption—had created follow-up institutions. This is illustrated in the discussions of the November 1999 roundtable on potential benefits and problems with regional monitoring. In addition to US legal scholars and activists from Transparency International, the group included officials and academics from various Latin American countries and delegates from the OECD, the Council of Europe, and the World Bank. During the meeting, the OECD and COE follow-up mechanisms were discussed after representatives from the two organizations had given presentations. The experts noted that some member states were concerned that delegation to a follow-up mechanism might be too costly, could impede their sovereignty, and had the potential to give the United States undue influence in line with its anti-drug efforts. On the other hand, participants pointed out that follow-up mechanisms seemed to be crucial aspects of other regions' anti-corruption efforts: "Indeed, every other recent anti-corruption initiative has provided for a rigorous monitoring follow-up program."[87]

In another presentation, two lawyers outlined their analysis of the agreement's design, status of ratifications, and follow-up. They noted that the OAS convention was broader in scope than those adopted by the EU, COE, and OECD, but lacked follow-up and was hampered by a relatively poor ratification record. They then suggested that the latter problem was due in large part to member-state "concern over the lack of institutional support for implementation and enforcement." After summarizing the strengths of the OECD's follow-up mechanism, they closed with an appeal to OAS members to implement a similar procedure: "The adoption of a monitoring mechanism and other components of 'institutional support' will help ensure not only the ratification but also the implementation of the OAS Convention."[88]

Once this idea had been approved by the Permanent Council and the Working Group had been tasked with developing a workable proposal,

Organization of American States 107

emulation started to give way to lesson-drawing. The Working Group did not simply copy an existing model; rather, it reached out to delegates from other organizations. The OAS's Assistant Secretary for Legal Affairs at the time emphasized that "we learnt of the modalities under which these mechanisms have been structured and how effective they were, in order to take them into account when State Parties to the Convention consider it appropriate to take decisions in this regard."[89]

At the October 2000 meetings, high-level delegates from the COE, the OECD, and the Inter-American Drug Abuse Control Commission gave presentations to the Working Group, backed by written statements on their organizations' experiences.[90] The Working Group then conducted a relatively detailed analysis of the various follow-up models, noting similarities and differences, and published its findings in a report.[91] This suggests that discussions were conducted at a detailed, technical level, with strengths and weaknesses weighed carefully.

The lesson-drawing continued even after MESICIC was established. At its first meeting, the Committee of Experts discussed the experiences of other international organizations to guide the development of its procedural rules:

> The seminar studied four international evaluation and/or follow-up mechanisms, the experiences of which over the years was deemed of much use in the process on which the MESICIC was about to embark. Then, at its meetings held in the week of January 14 to 18, 2002, the Committee discussed a draft of its rules of procedure that had previously been drawn up by the Technical Secretariat.[92]

Non-state actors: experts and civil society

As mentioned earlier, two OAS committees were involved in developing a draft convention before the document was discussed at the intergovernmental Specialized Conference in Caracas. While the Working Group was open to all member states and thus resembled intergovernmental decision-making, in the Juridical Committee OAS staff acted with some delegated authority. Back in 1992, one member of the latter committee, Jorge Reinaldo Vanossi from Argentina, had published a study in which he had argued that corruption ought to be tackled through an international instrument. His proposal included several provisions that were ultimately incorporated within the OAS convention, such as "penalizing transnational bribery, lifting bank secrecy and preventing political asylum from being used by corrupt politicians to avoid accountability."[93]

108 *Organization of American States*

As the analysis in the previous section indicated, deliberations in expert-led groups helped to shape the final convention. On the other hand, the influence of international bureaucrats should not be exaggerated. After all, member-state delegations were constantly active in the Working Group, added their amendments in sessions of the Permanent Council, and were the main players at the Specialized Conference. Given the way that the drafts evolved over time, it is fair to say that these governmental delegations controlled the whole process.

As Monica Herz notes in her study of the OAS, civil society's influence within the organization generally grew and became more institutionalized in the course of the 1990s.[94] Non-state actors did not participate in an officially sanctioned way in the initial negotiations for the anti-corruption agreement. Indeed, Guerzovich and de Michele point out that governments and civil society representatives were mutually skeptical at first. This resulted in government leaders refraining from incorporating strong language on the role of civil society in the IACAC, whereas NGOs questioned the usefulness of a treaty that was endorsed by several leaders who were personally implicated in corruption scandals: "Some cynics asked, why trust a legal document promoted by Fujimori, Menem, or Dahik?"[95] However, attitudes started to change over subsequent years. The Assistant Secretary for Legal Affairs at the OAS at the time credited Transparency International with promoting a follow-up mechanism, and the same organization lobbied for more transparency within the review process after the establishment of MESICIC.[96] Today, civil society plays a larger official role in MESICIC than it does in the equivalent UN review mechanism.[97]

A similar pattern of gradually increasing participation is evident among multilateral financial institutions. These organizations were largely sidelined in the development and drafting of the IACAC, with observers insisting, "the legalization process in the Americas evolved almost completely detached from international financial institutions' efforts and agendas. They had no voice in the negotiation of the IACAC and MESICIC."[98] Only later did the OAS start to cooperate closely with the Inter-American Development Bank on the issue of anti-corruption.[99]

Conclusion

To explain the emergence of anti-corruption on the OAS agenda, and the subsequent pioneering role of that organization with respect to this issue, this chapter has traced the early diplomatic efforts of the United

Organization of American States 109

States and several Latin American allies. Internal signaling was the dominant motivation for the IACAC, with external signaling playing a much less important role. Several OAS member states had closely aligned interests, which led them to form a coalition under US leadership in favor of creating a binding agreement. Corruption was a worrying issue for the United States in the contexts of transnational drug crime and political instability. Latin American leaders were motivated by an urge to improve international cooperation—with extradition the main motivator for Venezuela—and to signal their reformist intentions to domestic constituencies. In addition, creating the IACAC offered collateral benefits. For the United States, the OAS was a vehicle through which it could set a precedent for banning transnational bribery. For the Latin American countries, the treaty could help to attract trade and foreign investment.

The IACAC was primarily developed through intergovernmental diplomacy and deliberation. While the legal experts in the OAS's Juridical Committee were tasked with producing a draft agreement, the final convention included many provisions that were based on inputs from member-state delegations and subsequent discussions. The United States contributed major sections of the text and lobbied successfully for the inclusion of several issues in the final document. Yet, the efforts of other delegations with respect to specific provisions were also rewarded. Civil society played a minor role in the negotiations, but was more active after the establishment of the MESICIC review process. As a factor shaping the scope and design of the agreement itself, however, NGOs were rather marginalized.

Because the OAS anti-corruption convention was the first of its kind, emulation and lesson-drawing from international sources played no role in the drafting of its provisions on prevention, criminalization, and jurisdiction. Instead, the articles in question are either entirely original or draw on domestic models. The sections on international cooperation, however, draw directly on existing international models. There is evidence of both normative emulation and lesson-drawing with respect to the provisions on extradition, mutual legal assistance, and assets. Regarding the development of the follow-up mechanism—MESICIC— the evidence points more clearly towards lesson-drawing, as the Working Group compared existing models and discussed their respective usefulness.

The OAS anti-corruption agreement laid the foundation for an effective follow-up mechanism, and the latter had a much greater impact than some of its early supporters probably envisaged. According to a 2009 newspaper article, a third of the individuals who signed

110 *Organization of American States*

the treaty were now in prison, and many of the prosecutions could be attributed to OAS cooperation.[100] Today, sub-regional organizations in the Americas generally defer to the OAS with respect to norms, but supplement it with smaller-scale, technical initiatives. This, along with the treaty's excellent ratification record, lends support to the argument that the IACAC was developed primarily in response to domestic and intra-group signaling motives, and that its member states now consider it to be relatively successful.

Notes

1 Summit of the Americas, *First Summit of the Americas: Declaration of Principles*, 1994, www.summit-americas.org/i_summit/i_summit_dec_en. pdf.

2 Summit of the Americas, *First Summit of the Americas: Plan of Action*, 1994, www.summit-americas.org/i_summit/i_summit_poa_en.pdf; OAS General Assembly, "Resolution 1294 (XXIV-O/94) on Probity and Public Ethics," in *Twenty-fourth Regular Session: Belém do Pará, Brazil, 6–10 June 1994: Proceedings*, vol. 1, 145–146.

3 OAS MESICIC, *Hemispheric Report of the Committee of Experts of the Mechanism for Follow-up on the Implementation of the Inter-American Convention Against Corruption, Fourth Round of Review*, SG/MESICIC/ doc.441/15 rev.1 (Washington, DC: Mechanism for Follow-up on the Implementation of the Inter-American Convention Against Corruption, 2015), www.oas.org/juridico/PDFs/mesicic_hem_rep_final_4_round.pdf.

4 OAS General Assembly, "Resolution 1477 on the Inter-American Program for Cooperation in the Fight Against Corruption," in *Twenty-seventh Regular Session: Lima, Peru, 1–5 June 1997: Proceedings*, vol. 1, 69–74.

5 Beatriz M. Ramacciotti, "Strengthening Probity and Public Ethics in the OAS Framework: Implementation of the Inter-American Program of Cooperation to Fight Corruption," *American University International Law Review* 15, no. 4 (2000): 780–786, at 784.

6 OAS General Assembly, "Resolution 1784 on the Mechanism for Follow-up on Implementation of the Inter-American Convention Against Corruption," in *Thirty-first Regular Session: San José, Costa Rica, 3–5 June 2001: Proceedings*, vol. 1, 56–64.

7 OAS, *Declaration of Managua: Meeting of the States Parties to the Inter-American Convention Against Corruption*, 2004, www.oas.org/juridico/ english/corr_managua_declen.pdf.

8 OAS MESICIC, *Conclusions and Recommendations on Concrete Measures to Strengthen MESICIC: First Meeting of the Conference of States Parties within the MESICIC Framework: 1–2 April 2004*, SG/MESICIC/ doc.103/04 rev.6 (Washington, DC: Mechanism for Follow-up on the Implementation of the Inter-American Convention Against Corruption, 2004), www.oas.org/juridico/english/followup_conf_concl.pdf.

9 OAS MESICIC, *Inter-American Program of Cooperation to Fight Corruption: Second Meeting of the Conference of States Parties, 20–21*

Organization of American States 111

November 2006, MESICIC/CEP-II/doc.5/06 rev. 2 (Washington, DC: Mechanism for Follow-up on the Implementation of the Inter-American Convention Against Corruption, 2006), www.oas.org/juridico/english/m esicic_conf_est_parte_II_prog_intam_en.pdf.

10 OAS MESICIC, *Recommendations of the Third Meeting of the Conference of State Parties of the MESICIC: 9–10 December 2010*, MESICIC/CEP-III/doc.4/10 rev. 1, 2010, www.oas.org/juridico/english/cepIII_recom_en.pdf; OAS General Assembly, "Resolution 2655 (XLI-O/11) on Follow-up on the Inter-American Convention Against Corruption and on the Inter-American Program of Cooperation to Fight Corruption," in *Forty-first Regular Session: San Salvador, El Salvador 5–7 June 2011: Proceedings*, vol. 1, 159–163; OAS MESICIC, *Recommendations of the Fourth Meeting of the Conference of States Parties of the MESICIC: 14–15 December 2015*, MESICIC/CEP-IV/doc.2/15 rev. 1 (Washington, DC: Mechanism for Follow-up on the Implementation of the Inter-American Convention Against Corruption, 2015), www.oas.org/juridico/PDFs/mesicic_cosp_iv_rec_eng.pdf.

11 Interview with OAS official, Washington, DC, May 2013.

12 OAS General Assembly, "Resolution 2655 (XLI-O/11)," 162.

13 OAS MESICIC, *Hemispheric Report of the Committee of Experts of the Mechanism for Follow-up on the Implementation of the Inter-American Convention Against Corruption: First Round of Review*, SG/MESICIC/doc.170/06 rev. 1 (Washington, DC: Mechanism for Follow-up on the Implementation of the Inter-American Convention Against Corruption, 2006), www.oas.org/juridico/english/mec_ron1_inf_hemis_en.pdf.

14 Carlos A. Manfroni and Richard S. Werksman, *The Inter-American Convention Against Corruption: Annotated with Commentary* (Lanham, MD: Lexington Books, 2003), 115.

15 OAS MESICIC, *Hemispheric Report of the Committee of Experts: First Round of Review*; OAS MESICIC, *Hemispheric Report of the Committee of Experts of the Mechanism for Follow-up on the Implementation of the Inter-American Convention Against Corruption: Second Round of Review*, SG/MESICIC/doc.227/08 rev. 1 (Washington, DC: Mechanism for Follow-up on the Implementation of the Inter-American Convention Against Corruption, 2008), www.oas.org/juridico/english/mec_ron2_inf_hemis.pdf; OAS MESICIC, *Hemispheric Report of the Committee of Experts of the Mechanism for Follow-up on the Implementation of the Inter-American Convention Against Corruption: Third Round of Review*, SG/MESICIC/doc.287/11 rev. 1 (Washington, DC: Mechanism for Follow-up on the Implementation of the Inter-American Convention Against Corruption, 2011), www.oas.org/juridico/PDFs/IIIinf_hemis_en.pdf; OAS MESICIC, *Hemispheric Report of the Committee of Experts: Fourth Round of Review*.

16 Florencia Guerzovich and Roberto de Michele, "The Anticorruption Agenda in Latin America: National and International Developments," in *Corruption and Politics in Latin America: National and Regional Dynamics*, ed. Stephen D. Morris and Charles H. Blake (Boulder, CO: Lynne Rienner Publishers, 2010), 193–218, at 195.

17 Gordon Mace and Dominic Migneault, "Hemispheric Regionalism in the Americas," in *The Ashgate Research Companion to Regionalisms*, ed.

112   *Organization of American States*

Timothy M. Shaw, J. Andrew Grant, and Scarlett Cornelissen (Farnham: Ashgate, 2012), 159–174, at 166–167.

18   Gordon Mace, Andrew F. Cooper, and Timothy M. Shaw, "Introduction," in *Inter-American Cooperation at a Crossroads*, ed. Gordon Mace, Andrew F. Cooper, and Timothy M. Shaw (Houndmills: Palgrave Macmillan, 2011), 1–19; Mace and Migneault, "Hemispheric Regionalism in the Americas."

19   Richard E. Feinberg, *Summitry in the Americas: A Progress Report* (Washington, DC: Institute for International Economics, 1997).

20   Jorge Garcia-Gonzalez, "The Organization of American States and the Fight against Corruption," in *Public Sector Transparency and Accountability: Making it Happen*, ed. OECD (Paris: OECD Publishing, 2002), 175–181, at 177.

21   Feinberg, *Summitry in the Americas*, 116–120.

22   Thomas W. Lippman, "After 20-year Campaign, US Balks at OAS Pact against Business Corruption," *Washington Post*, 7 April 1996.

23   Holger Moroff, "Internationalisierung von Anti-Korruptionsregimen," in *Dimensionen politischer Korruption: Beiträge zum Stand der internationalen Forschung*, ed. Ulrich von Alemann (Wiesbaden: VS Verlag für Sozialwissenschaften, 2005), 444–477, at 453; my translation.

24   Christopher F. Corr and Judd Lawler, "Damned if You Do, Damned if You Don't? The OECD Convention and the Globalization of Anti-bribery Measures," *Vanderbilt Journal of Transnational Law* 32 (1999): 1249–1344, at 1297.

25   Manfroni and Werksman, *The Inter-American Convention Against Corruption*, 110.

26   David A. Gantz, "Globalizing Sanctions against Foreign Bribery: The Emergence of a New International Legal Consensus," *Northwestern Journal of International Law and Business* 18, no. 2 (1997): 457–497, at 481.

27   "Cleaning up Latin America," *The Economist*, 6 April 1996.

28   Marco Arnone and Leonardo S. Borlini, *Corruption: Economic Analysis and International Law* (Cheltenham: Edward Elgar Publishing, 2014), 220.

29   Manfroni and Werksman, *The Inter-American Convention Against Corruption*, 78.

30   Feinberg, *Summitry in the Americas*, 199.

31   Jennifer L. McCoy and Heather Heckel, "The Emergence of a Global Anti-corruption Norm," *International Politics* 38, no. 1 (2001): 65–90, at 80.

32   Feinberg, *Summitry in the Americas*, 118–119, 140.

33   "Cleaning up Latin America."

34   Bruce Zagaris and Shaila Lakhani Ohri, "The Emergence of an International Enforcement Regime on Transnational Corruption in the Americas," *Law and Policy in International Business* 30, no. 1 (1999): 53–93, at 65; Guerzovich and de Michele, "The Anticorruption Agenda in Latin America," 193; McCoy and Heckel, "The Emergence of a Global Anti-corruption Norm," 80.

35   McCoy and Heckel, "The Emergence of a Global Anti-Corruption Norm"; Moroff, "Internationalisierung von Anti-Korruptionsregimen."

36   Edmundo Vargas Carreño, "The Inter-American Convention Against Corruption," paper prepared for the Conference on Transparency and

Organization of American States 113

Development in Latin America and the Caribbean, Washington, DC, 16–18 May 2000, 4.

37 Nancy Zucker Boswell, "Combating Corruption: Focus on Latin America," *Southwestern Journal of Law and Trade in the Americas* 3 (1996): 179–193, at 185–187.

38 Feinberg, *Summitry in the Americas*, 118; Darren G. Hawkins and Carolyn Shaw, "Legalising Norms of Democracy in the Americas," *Review of International Studies* 34, no. 3 (2008): 459–480.

39 Guerzovich and de Michele, "The Anticorruption Agenda in Latin America," 197.

40 Feinberg, *Summitry in the Americas*, 117.

41 Lukas Goltermann, Mathis Lohaus, Alexander Spielau, and Kai Striebinger, "Roads to Regionalism: Concepts, Issues, and Cases," in *Roads to Regionalism: Genesis, Design, and Effects of Regional Organizations*, ed. Tanja A. Börzel, Lukas Goltermann, Mathis Lohaus, and Kai Striebinger (Farnham: Ashgate, 2012), 3–21.

42 Tanja A. Börzel and Sören Stapel, "Mapping Governance Transfer by 12 Regional Organizations: A Global Script in Regional Colors," in *Governance Transfer by Regional Organizations: Patching Together a Global Script*, ed. Tanja A. Börzel and Vera van Hüllen (Houndmills: Palgrave Macmillan, 2015), 22–48.

43 Andean Community, *Declaración del Consejo Presidencial Andino sobre la Lucha contra la Corrupción* (Cartagena de Indias: Andean Community, 1999).

44 Andean Community, *DECISIÓN 668 Plan Andino de Lucha contra la Corrupción: El Consejo Andino de Ministros de Relaciones Exteriores*, 2007, https://perma.cc/9NT3-M8P6.

45 Olga Nazario, "A Strategy against Corruption," paper prepared for A 20/20 Vision: CARICOM Conference on the Caribbean, Washington, DC, 19–21 June 2007, www.cpahq.org/CPAHQ/CMDownload.aspx?Con tentKey=efd36893-8265-4a69-9370-350130278795&ContentItemKey=08b e8177-d8d4-454c-a4db-916395dc3078.

46 Nazario, "A Strategy against Corruption"; Mark T. Nance, "Naming and Shaming in Financial Regulation: Explaining Variation in the Financial Action Task Force on Money Laundering," in *The Politics of Leverage in International Relations: Name, Shame, and Sanction*, ed. H. Richard Friman (Houndmills: Palgrave Macmillan, 2015), 123–142.

47 CARICOM, *Report on Crime and Security: CARICOM Regional Task Force* (Trinidad and Tobago: CARICOM, 2002), 17.

48 CARICOM-SICA, *Plan of Action* (Belize City: CARICOM-SICA, 2007), 5.

49 MERCOSUR, *Acuerdo No. 18/02—Sobre el combate a la corrupción en las fronteras entre los Estados Parte del MERCOSUR, Bolivia e Chile: XII Reunión de Ministros del interior del MERCOSUR*, MERCOSUR/ RMI/ACTA No. 02/02—Anexo VI (2002).

50 MERCOSUR, *Comunicado Conjunto de los Estados Partes del Mercosur y Estados Asociados* (San Juan: Consejo del Mercado Común, 2010), 11.

51 US negotiators, in contrast, were certain that no domestic laws would have to be changed due to IACAC, which, for them, served to bring the other OAS member states to a level that was comparable to the existing

114 *Organization of American States*

US laws. See Peter J. Henning, "Public Corruption: A Comparative Analysis of International Corruption Conventions and United States Law," *Arizona Journal of International and Comparative Law* 18 (2001): 793–865, at 798.

52 OAS, *Permanent Council Resolution CP/Res. 154 (167/75): Behavior of Transnational Enterprises Operating in the Region and Need for a Code of Conduct to be Observed by Such Enterprises*, reprinted in: *American Society of International Law, International Legal Materials* 14, no. 5 (1975): 1326–1328.

53 Manfroni and Werksman, *The Inter-American Convention Against Corruption*, 10; OAS General Assembly, "Resolution 1294," 146.

54 Feinberg, *Summitry in the Americas*, 119.

55 The participants were Argentina, Bolivia, Chile, Colombia, Ecuador, Guatemala, Mexico, Panama, Paraguay, Peru, Trinidad and Tobago, Uruguay, Venezuela, and Brazil. See Rio Group, *Declarations of the Rio Group: Annexes I–IV to a Letter Dated 94/09/15 from the Permanent Representative of Brazil to the United Nations Addressed to the Secretary-General* (New York: United Nations, 1994), 2, http://hdl.handle.net/11176/44183.

56 Rio Group, *Declarations*, 9.

57 Feinberg, *Summitry in the Americas*, 119–120.

58 Feinberg, *Summitry in the Americas*, 144.

59 Feinberg, *Summitry in the Americas*, 120.

60 Summit of the Americas, *First Summit of the Americas: Plan of Action*, 4.

61 Manfroni and Werksman, *The Inter-American Convention Against Corruption*, x.

62 OAS Working Group on Probity and Public Ethics, *Draft Inter-American Convention Against Corruption*, OEA/Ser. G CP/GT/PEC-17/95 [document comparing the Venezuelan Draft to the Working Group draft] (1995).

63 OAS General Assembly, "Resolution 1346 (XXV-O/95) on Probity and Public Ethics," in *Declarations and Decisions Adopted by the General Assembly at its Twenty-Fifth Regular Session. Montrouis, Haiti, 5 June 1995*, 123–125, at 125.

64 Manfroni and Werksman, *The Inter-American Convention Against Corruption*, x; OAS Working Group on Probity and Public Ethics, *Draft Inter-American Convention Against Corruption*, OEA/Ser. G CP/GT/PEC-17/95.

65 OAS General Assembly, "Resolution 1346 (XXV-O/95) on Probity and Public Ethics," 124–125.

66 OAS Working Group on Probity and Public Ethics, *International Cooperation Against Corruption: Document Prepared by the Inter-American Juridical Committee in Compliance with the General Assembly Resolution 1346 (XXV-O/95)*, OEA/Ser.G CP/GT/PEC-22/95 (Washington, DC: OAS Working Group on Probity and Public Ethics, 1995), 15–19.

67 OAS Working Group on Probity and Public Ethics, *International Cooperation Against Corruption*, 20–22.

68 Carreño, "The Inter-American Convention Against Corruption," 7–9.

69 Carreño, "The Inter-American Convention Against Corruption," 10–11; Manfroni and Werksman, *The Inter-American Convention Against Corruption*, 20–21.

Organization of American States 115

70 Manfroni and Werksman, *The Inter-American Convention Against Corruption*, 86–89.

71 Manfroni and Werksman, *The Inter-American Convention Against Corruption*, 92.

72 Carreño, "The Inter-American Convention Against Corruption," 18; Manfroni and Werksman, *The Inter-American Convention Against Corruption*, 98–99.

73 Manfroni and Werksman, *The Inter-American Convention Against Corruption*, 111.

74 Garcia-Gonzalez, "The Organization of American States and the Fight against Corruption," 179–180.

75 Roundtable Participants, "Findings, Considerations, and Recommendations," *American University International Law Review* 15, no. 4 (2000): 808–811, at 811; Transparency International, "Program Design," *American University International Law Review* 15, no. 4 (2000): 766–768, at 767.

76 OAS General Assembly, "Resolution 1723 (XXX-O/00) on the Enhancement of Probity in the Hemisphere and Follow-up on the Inter-American Program for Cooperation in the Fight Against Corruption," in *Thirtieth Regular Session: Windsor, Canada, 4–6 June 2000: Proceedings*, vol. 1, 71–74.

77 Manfroni and Werksman, *The Inter-American Convention Against Corruption*, 112.

78 OAS Working Group on Probity and Public Ethics, *A Comparison of Follow-up Mechanisms for Enforcement of Commitments under International Agreements*, OEA/Ser.G CP/GT/PEC-87/00 (Washington, DC: OAS Working Group on Probity and Public Ethics, 2000), 36, www.oas. org/council/CAJP/docs/cp07574e04.doc; OAS Working Group on Probity and Public Ethics, *Report of the Chair of the Working Group on Probity and Public Ethics Regarding the Draft Recommendation on the Mechanism for Follow-up of Implementation of the Inter-American Convention Against Corruption*, OEA/Ser.G GT/PEC/doc.98/00 rev. 1 corr.1 (Washington, DC: OAS Working Group on Probity and Public Ethics, 2000), www.oas.org/council/CAJP/docs/cp07720e11.doc.

79 Manfroni and Werksman, *The Inter-American Convention Against Corruption*, 112.

80 OAS Working Group on Probity and Public Ethics, *Report of the Chair of the Working Group on Probity and Public Ethics on the First Conference of States Parties to the Inter-American Convention Against Corruption on the Mechanism for Follow-Up on Implementation of the Convention*, OEA/Ser.G CP/GT/PEC-120/01 rev. 1 (Washington, DC: OAS Working Group on Probity and Public Ethics, 2001), www.oas.org/council/CAJP/docs/cp08440e07.doc; OAS MESICIC, *Hemispheric Report of the Committee of Experts: First Round of Review*, 4–5; OAS General Assembly, "Resolution 1784."

81 Manfroni and Werksman, *The Inter-American Convention Against Corruption*, 18–68.

82 Carreño, "The Inter-American Convention Against Corruption," 15–17; United Nations, *Convention Against Illicit Traffic in Narcotic Drugs and Psychotropic Substances* (New York and Vienna: United Nations,

116   *Organization of American States*

1988), www.unodc.org/pdf/convention_1988_en.pdf; OAS, *Inter-American Convention on Extradition* (Caracas: Organization of American States, 1981), www.oas.org/juridico/english/treaties/b-47.html; OAS, *Inter-American Convention on Mutual Legal Assistance in Criminal Matters* (Nassau: Organization of American States, 1992), www.oas.org/juridico/english/treaties/a-55.html.

83   United Nations, *Convention Against Illicit Traffic in Narcotic Drugs and Psychotropic Substances*, article VI; OAS, *Inter-American Convention on Extradition*, articles II, VII.

84   Manfroni and Werksman, *The Inter-American Convention Against Corruption*, 92; United Nations, *Convention Against Illicit Traffic in Narcotic Drugs and Psychotropic Substances*, article V(5).

85   Carreño, *"The Inter-American Convention Against Corruption"*, 17; United Nations, *Convention Against Illicit Traffic in Narcotic Drugs and Psychotropic Substances*, articles V, VII.

86   OAS, *Inter-American Convention on Extradition*, article IV; OAS, *Inter-American Convention on Mutual Legal Assistance in Criminal Matters*, article III.

87   Transparency International, "Program Design," 767.

88   Lucinda A. Low and Jacqueline de Gramont, "The Inter-American Convention Against Corruption: Overview and Status at Three Years Since Its Inception," *American University International Law Review* 15, no. 4 (2000): 768–780, at 778–779.

89   Enrique Lagos, "The Future of the Inter-American Convention Against Corruption," paper prepared for the Conference on Transparency and Development in Latin America, Washington, DC, 16–18 May 2000, http s://web.archive.org/web/20050426235803/https://www.iadb.org/leg/Docum ents/Lagos%20Eng.pdf.

90   OAS Working Group on Probity and Public Ethics, *Order of Business for Thursday, October 19, 2000*, OEA/Ser.G CP/GT/PEC-94/00 (Washington, DC: OAS Working Group on Probity and Public Ethics, 2000); Mark Pieth, "Taking Stock: Making the OECD Initiative Against Corruption Work," OEA/Ser.G CP/GT/PEC-88/00 (Washington, DC: OAS Working Group on Probity and Public Ethics, 2000), www.oas.org/coun cil/CAJP/docs/cp07577e04.doc; Peter Csonka, "The Council of Europe: Activities for the Fight against Corruption," OEA/Ser.G CP/GT/PEC-89/ 00 (Washington, DC: OAS Working Group on Probity and Public Ethics, 2000), www.oas.org/council/CAJP/docs/cp07579e04.doc.

91   OAS Working Group on Probity and Public Ethics, *A Comparison of Follow-up Mechanisms for Enforcement of Commitments under International Agreements*.

92   OAS MESICIC, *Hemispheric Report of the Committee of Experts: First Round of Review*, 4–5.

93   Manfroni and Werksman, *The Inter-American Convention Against Corruption*, 2.

94   Monica Herz, *The Organization of American States (OAS): Global Governance away from the Media* (London and New York: Routledge, 2011).

95   Guerzovich and de Michele, "The Anticorruption Agenda in Latin America," 199.

Organization of American States 117

96 Lagos, "The Future of the Inter-American Convention Against Corruption," 7; Transparency International, *Anti-corruption Conventions in the Americas: What Civil Society Can Do to Make Them Work* (Berlin: Transparency International, 2006), 98, https://perma.cc/K456-W3HG.

97 Interview with OAS official, Washington, DC, May 2013.

98 Guerzovich and de Michele, "The Anticorruption Agenda in Latin America," 205.

99 OAS General Assembly, "Resolution 1477"; OAS MESICIC, *Inter-American Program of Cooperation to Fight Corruption.*

100 Gerardo Reyes and Frances Robles, "Summit of the Americas: Anticorruption Accord Was a First," *McClatchy DC*, 11 April 2009.

4 African Union

Development cooperation, non-state actors, and external reference models

- **History, design, and implementation**
- **Motives and drivers**
- **Tracing the drafts over time**
- **Evidence of diffusion**
- **Conclusion**

The African Union Convention on Preventing and Combating Corruption was adopted in 2003, making the AU the third continental organization to create a binding agreement, after the Organization of American States and the Council of Europe.[1] In this chapter, I summarize the key facts about the convention and then focus on two questions. First, which factors led the AU member states to draft and adopt this convention? Second, how did the negotiations and drafting proceed, and what explains the outcomes?

History, design, and implementation

In June 1998, the AU Assembly adopted a decision that commented on the activities of the African Commission on Human and Peoples' Rights and called for a meeting of experts. The goal was to "consider ways and means of removing obstacles to the enjoyment of economic, social and cultural rights, including fight against corruption and impunity and propose appropriate legislative and other measures."[2] The AU thus framed corruption as a human rights issue when it first mentioned the topic in a high-level document.

The African Union's Office of the Legal Counsel (OLC) was responsible for overseeing the project to develop an African legal instrument to combat corruption. Tiyanjana Maluwa led this office until 2001, but then left to take up a position within the United Nations.[3] He was succeeded by his deputy, Ben Kioko, who remained

African Union 119

at the head of the OLC until July 2012, when he became a judge of the African Court on Human and Peoples' Rights. The preparatory work and negotiations for the convention thus fell within Kioko's tenure, first as deputy and then as head of the OLC. Funding for consultancy work and the meetings that would be held on this issue over the coming years was mainly provided by the Swedish government, which signed a contract with the AU in November 1999.[4]

In September 2000, the OLC hired Adama Dieng as a consultant. He had recently ended his term as Secretary General of the International Commission of Jurists, a Geneva-based NGO working on human rights issues, and was about to become the Registrar of the International Criminal Tribunal for Rwanda. The AU handed him a twofold task. First, he was asked to submit a report on the implications of corruption for Africa and how the problem might be combated. Second, he was tasked with drawing up a draft convention that could serve as a starting point for the upcoming deliberations. Dieng submitted his report and the draft convention in December 2000. In line with the terms set out in his consultancy contract, the report addressed four issues: a list of the negative implications of corruption in Africa; suggestions on how to combat corruption effectively; suggestions on which actors should be involved; and a section on regional organizations' potential role in the fight against corruption. The draft convention itself was rather brief (see below).[5]

Consequently, two meetings of experts were scheduled for February and July 2001 to discuss Dieng's report and develop an anti-corruption document. However, the first of these was postponed, and the OLC hired another consultant to assist with the drafting process. The meeting eventually took place in Addis Ababa on 26–29 November 2001. It brought together delegates from 42 AU member states as well as 18 other delegations as observers and guests. The latter included delegates from AU bodies as well as representatives from international organizations, such as the UN Development Programme (UNDP), the UN Economic Commission for Africa (UNECA), and the World Bank, as well as civil society, such as Transparency International (TI) and the Southern African Human Rights Trust (SAHRIT).[6]

Delegates from the 42 member states reconvened for the second experts' meeting on 16–17 September 2002. Non-state delegations from SAHRIT, the Asian African Legal Consultative Organization, the African Development Bank (AfDB), the Organization of African Trade Union Unity, and TI also attended. This was followed by a ministerial-level meeting on 18–19 September, which was attended by delegates from all but two of the member states and the same civil society delegations.[7]

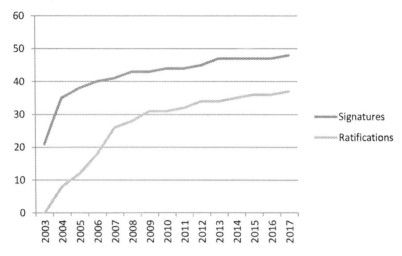

Figure 4.1 Signing and ratification of the AU convention
Source: Based on AU data.

Following these preparatory meetings, the AU Convention on Preventing and Combating Corruption was adopted at the second ordinary session of the AU Assembly in Maputo, Mozambique, on 11 July 2003. Since then, 48 AU member states have signed the document and 37 have ratified it (excluding the Western Sahara territory, which is recognized by the AU but not the UN). The convention officially entered into force in August 2006, when the threshold of 15 ratifications was reached. The fast pace of signatures and ratifications shows significant early momentum, with 35 states signing up within 18 months of adoption, and the bulk of ratifications taking place within five years. To put this into context, by 2012, a total of 27 AU treaties had entered into force, with an average of 33 ratifications, whereas 13 other treaties were yet to reach the required threshold. A more recent tally of treaty commitments by AU members suggests that the anti-corruption convention is typical in terms of both signatures and ratifications.[8]

As discussed in Chapter 2, the AU convention provides for a follow-up mechanism called the AU Advisory Board on Corruption (AU ABC). This would comprise 11 experts who would conduct research on corruption, advocate for the convention, and act as consultants to member states. Its annual budget was set at approximately 500,000 dollars. However, after adoption of the convention in 2006, it was another three years before the AU ABC was inaugurated as member states dragged their feet on nominating candidates.[9] It finally became operational when the

African Union   121

first group of 11 members was elected by the AU Assembly in January 2009. Since then, members have been elected biennially.

A 2011–2015 work plan for the AU ABC was developed in cooperation with UNECA and funded by the Swedish International Development Cooperation Agency (SIDA). This document was adopted in 2010, and the AU ABC then spent its first two years setting up procedural rules and reaching out to potential partners.[10] Consequently, one consultant lamented that it was a long time before the AU ABC was able to establish itself.[11] By June 2011, the second group of experts had been appointed, but the AU ABC still lacked a fully functioning secretariat. A questionnaire relating to national anti-corruption laws and strategies had been distributed to 31 AU member states, but only six had bothered to return it. Nevertheless, in 2011, UNECA expressed cautious optimism: "Given the relative [sic] poor commitment towards the implementation of [the convention] by member states, the establishment of the [AU ABC] is a starting point in committing all member states to implement the Convention."[12]

The following year, the AU ABC was relocated from the AU's headquarters to Arusha, Tanzania. Supported by additional funds from SIDA, its executive secretary was able to hire some permanent staff. Meanwhile, the elected members held meetings and collected information on the implementation of the convention in 27 member states. They then reported their findings to the AU's Executive Council. The AU's Assembly elected the fourth group of experts in January 2015 and the fifth two years later. As intended in the founding documents, all of these members serve on the board as part-time volunteers rather than full-time staff.[13]

Unfortunately, the AU ABC's track record and operational standards have not met expectations. At the end of 2014, the executive secretary had to step down in the midst of a scandal about his use of funds. Investigations by an AU task force and a private auditing firm found that guidelines for competitive tendering had not been followed, the executive secretary did not abide by rules for personal travel expenses, and the budget had not been spent in accordance with the board's stated priorities.[14] By April 2015, the AU leadership and SIDA were discussing their next steps and the AU ABC was virtually moribund, with only two staffers in Arusha and severe reputational problems, as testified by AU officials and development partners.[15] In 2018—a year in which the AU adopted the slogan "Winning the Fight against Corruption"—the heads of state declared their intention to reform a number of institutions, including the AU ABC. However, there has been no new work plan since the first one expired in 2015.[16]

122 *African Union*

In addition to the operational problems since the AU ABC's move to Arusha, the implementation of anti-corruption measures has been hindered by limited resources at the AU Commission, which serves as the organization's permanent secretariat in Addis Ababa. In April 2015, just one full-time staff member was working on corruption, and he had responsibility for another six portfolios, too. Therefore, especially in comparison with security issues, the good-governance portfolio seems to be underfunded and understaffed, which has led to skepticism about the likelihood of implementation.[17]

Motives and drivers

What motivated AU member states to negotiate and adopt the Convention on Preventing and Combating Corruption? First, we need to consider the context of other governance-related agreements reached by the African Union. In a report on the AU convention, Transparency International links it to a number of earlier documents, such as the African Charter on Human and Peoples' Rights. Yet, these agreements did not include corruption as a core issue: "The word corruption was first used at the Thirty-Fourth Ordinary Session of The Assembly of Heads of State and Governments in June 1998 in Ouagadougou, Burkina Faso."[18]

Diplomatic initiatives connected to donors

Outside the formal AU framework, African leaders had previously shown some interest in tackling corruption. For instance, in December 1994, the Africa Leadership Forum held a workshop on "Corruption, Democracy and Human Rights in East and Central Africa." This meeting was funded by the European Commission and attended by a diverse group of government, development cooperation, business, and civil society representatives. Among the attendees were two leading figures from the newly established Transparency International (Lawrence Cockcroft and Jeremy Pope) and an Ethiopian activist who would later become one of the elected members the AU ABC (Costantinos Berhe-Tesfu). The workshop's summary report insists that Western governments must accept part of the blame for corruption in Africa, and the recovery of assets is mentioned as one of the priorities for international cooperation. It also announces the participants' intention to put corruption on the agenda at the next AU Assembly, and there is a clear reference to anti-corruption efforts in the Americas:

African Union 123

[The workshop] called on African leaders to follow the excellent example set by the leaders of the Americas at the initiative of Ecuador at their Hemispheric Summit in Miami last week, by being prepared honestly and openly to face up to the problems of corruption, and without trying to hide it under the carpet or pretending that it is under control. Only in an environment of honesty and frankness can effective international instruments be developed and enforced.[19]

It is unclear how the Summit of the Americas found its way into the workshop's purview. The closest personal or geographic links to Miami were the World Bank official and the two delegates from Transparency International. Irrespective of who made the connection, however, this appears to be the first mention of another international initiative as a potential reference model for the AU's anti-corruption agreement.

Another initiative that addressed corruption outside of the official channels of the AU, but still on a continental scale, was the Global Coalition for Africa (GCA). Convened under the auspices of the World Bank (WB), this forum brought together government officials from a number of African and OECD countries. Corruption was first discussed at two GCA meetings in 1995 and 1997. Unsurprisingly, given its close connection to the World Bank, the forum initially addressed bribery and corruption from a development perspective, with a focus on the WB's own and other donor-funded projects. This was a pressing governmental issue for several African states: for instance, the WB suspended its aid to Tanzania and Kenya in the latter half of the 1990s amid concerns about corruption. However, contributions were also invited from civil society and parliamentarians; and, in a bid to make the GCA more appealing to a wide range of actors, its scope was eventually broadened to include international business transactions as well as development projects.[20] In 1999, the GCA held a third meeting in Washington, DC. This concluded with high-level representatives from 11 African countries signing an agreement titled "Principles to Combat Corruption in African Countries."[21]

The preamble to this agreement refers to the "devastating effects of corruption on the social, economic and political foundations of nations, and on their economic and social development and efforts to eradicate poverty." It also notes recent "regional efforts" by the OAS, the OECD, and the UN General Assembly to tackle corruption. As a result, the 25 "principles" display a very broad approach to criminalization and prevention. Anti-corruption measures are not framed specifically in terms of development cooperation or procurement;

124 *African Union*

instead, they follow the general logic of safeguarding the rule of law. The final principle asks signatories to "[c]onsider the elaboration and adoption of an African convention for combating corruption based on the foregoing principles, and encourage the establishment of a global anti-corruption convention."[22]

These early initiatives were not immediately successful in putting corruption on the AU agenda. At the 1995 AU Assembly of member-state leaders, there was no mention of corruption in any of the declarations or decisions, which suggests that the African Leadership Forum had little impact. Indeed, it would be another three years before the Assembly finally tasked the Secretary General with convening a meeting of experts to consider ways of tackling the problem. Of course, this decision fell in the middle of the GCA's series of meetings, so it may be fair to say that the World Bank played a significant role in setting the AU wheels in motion.

However, the OLC needed an institutional partner to finance the anti-corruption project, so it turned to the Swedish embassy for support. Legal Counsel Kioko prepared a funding proposal in consultation with a contact at the embassy and Adama Dieng, who would later be hired as a consultant. The embassy agreed to his request and donated 1.2 million krona (approximately 140,000 dollars) to the AU in November 1999.[23] This money allowed the organization to hire external experts and convene meetings. There is no evidence that the Swedish government subsequently attempted to set the agenda or initiate the drafting process.[24]

Another donor-related initiative on anti-corruption was the African Governance Forum II, held in Ghana in July 1998 and sponsored by the regional office of the UNDP. One meeting on "accountability and transparency" led to a research project to gather data on national anti-corruption measures. However, there is no mention of this forum in later official AU documents, and little evidence of any link between the initiatives, aside from a single suggestion from the UNDP that joint meetings should be held.[25]

Bribery and illicit financial flows

Besides the forums attended by African leaders and development partners, there were other motivations and initiatives that did not involve external actors directly.

Dieng's December 2000 report takes a more antagonistic stance towards OECD countries than is typically found in documents that address the issue of development cooperation. Indeed, it concludes by

African Union 125

drawing attention to the flow of capital from Africa to wealthy countries:

> African Organizations such as OAU, ADB, ECOWAS and SADC have a critical role to play in combatting corruption, illicit enrichment, plundering of foreign exchange resources and the shameful transfer of capital to the bank strong rooms of the West. Good governance, the promotion and strengthening of measures to combat corruption should be a priority objective ...
> Corruption will only disappear if it is brought out to light. It is necessary for Africa to speak with one voice. Banks increase their profits with funds stashed away by corrupt leaders and billions of dollars that could have been used to build schools, hospitals and create employment opportunities are misappropriated and transferred to major multinational banks in western countries at a time when children are dying from hunger in Africa.[26]

This argument has since been reformulated under the label "illicit financial flows" and has recently gained considerable traction among civil society organizations, UN institutions, the OECD itself (as part of its "Strategy on Development"), and the World Bank. In the Nyanga and Nairobi Declarations, representatives from national TI chapters across Africa urged Western countries to repatriate assets. Several books and reports have also highlighted the magnitude of financial outflows from the continent, and the World Bank has launched an initiative to help with the recovery of assets.[27] The UN, OECD, and WB were still showing little interest in this issue in the late 1990s, yet combating the outflow of capital had been high on the agenda for some African policymakers as early as 1994, when they emphasized "the need to repatriate the monies stolen from different African countries ... [and transferred to rich] countries as investment funds."[28]

International cooperation against corruption was championed by African activists and experts because it offered a chance to stop the outflow of capital and could improve access to assets that were deposited outside of African countries' jurisdictions. These were very attractive causes for African leaders as they not only sent a positive signal to domestic audiences but also had the potential to secure financial benefits if implemented. They also provided a counterbalance to foreign aid conditionality and donors' reform demands. The argument about the secretion of African riches in foreign bank accounts raised the issues of hypocrisy and domestic policy shortcomings among countries that had traditionally pushed for reform abroad. Therefore, all African

126 *African Union*

heads of state, including corrupt and cynical leaders who sensed an opportunity to shift the blame for their own misdeeds, could be expected to support it, at least rhetorically.

Another issue was transnational bribery. Transparency International's Jeremy Pope addressed this problem at the 1994 African Leadership Forum. He argued that developing countries' appeals to OECD trade and investment partners had to be taken more seriously, but suggested that the organization was at least on the right track:

> At long last, too, in the OECD there is recognition that there are, for example, too many countries where corporations can pay bribes abroad and claim these as tax deductible expenses in their home countries. Laws that permit companies to behave in this way encourage bribery.[29]

By pointing the finger at OECD member states, Pope sought to underline the changing international environment. African leaders were invited to signal their own support for the anti-bribery movement by adopting a regional anti-corruption agreement. As with the financial flows argument, African governments—in cooperation with NGOs such as TI—took the opportunity to criticize their European and US counterparts over transnational bribery and thereby reversed the two sides' traditional roles.

For both transnational bribery and asset recovery, however, an agreement among African countries would be of limited use in a functionalist sense. The former had already been addressed by the OECD when the AU negotiations started. Therefore, it could have been only a partial motivation for the African leaders, as a statement of support for the OECD initiative or as a reminder to foreign trade and investment partners to honor their previous commitment. Illicit financial flows and asset recovery, on the other hand, had not yet been addressed, as the UN convention would not be opened for signatures until late 2003. Reaching an agreement among African nations and no other parties would be of little functional utility, as the assets in question were held elsewhere. That said, though, addressing the issue in an African convention would at least create a precedent for a strongly worded UN convention.[30]

Sub-regional initiatives

As discussed in Chapter 2, the AU differs from the OAS in that there is no division of labor with sub-regional organizations. While article XXI of the AU convention states that it supersedes all other agreements on the issue of corruption, the SADC and ECOWAS protocols are still active. This could be dismissed as a simple accident of history given that SADC and ECOWAS happened to adopt their agreements before the continent-wide AU convention was drafted. However, two facts suggest that there was rather more to the duplication of anti-corruption efforts. First, members of SADC and ECOWAS continued to ratify their protocols even after the AU's convention was opened for signatures. Second, the East African Community has continued to negotiate its regional protocol long after the AU convention entered into force. The relationship between the AU and these sub-regional groups sheds considerable light on the motivations behind all anti-corruption agreements.

Figure 4.2 shows that the SADC protocol and the AU convention reached their respective ratification thresholds to enter into force in 2005 and 2006, respectively. Shortly thereafter, the former reached almost universal ratification among its 15 members. By contrast, ECOWAS struggled to reach its ratification threshold, but the protocol finally entered into force in 2015 thanks to a ninth ratification by Niger; Senegal then became the tenth state party the following year.[31] Interestingly, though, the non-parties to the regional protocols in both ECOWAS and SADC have ratified the AU convention. This suggests that these organizations are split over whether to prioritize their local protocols. Overall, however, the steady flow of ratifications in both

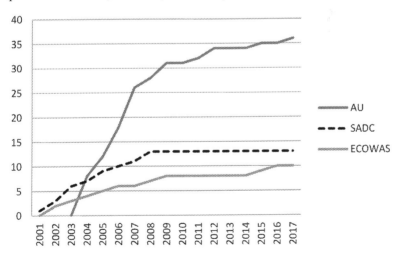

Figure 4.2 Ratification of African anti-corruption agreements
Source: Based on organizations' official data.

128 *African Union*

SADC and ECOWAS, at least until the late 2000s, suggests that these protocols were not discarded in favor of the AU agreement. In the meantime, the EAC is still in a prolonged process of negotiating its own regional protocol. All five members of this organization ratified both the AU and the UN anti-corruption conventions between 2004 and 2009. Yet, since 2007, with support from EU and UNDP funds, the EAC has worked on developing regional agreements on good governance, with a protocol on corruption one element of this. One of the contentious issues is whether anti-corruption agencies should have prosecutorial powers, which would go beyond the standard set in either the AU convention or the UNCAC. Another suggestion is that a protocol among the five East African states would allow for closer cooperation in asset recovery. However, the small size of the group increases the risk that government officials will be named and shamed. These issues have all slowed the drafting process to a crawl. One draft protocol was transferred to a sub-committee of the EAC in the hope of resolving the outstanding issues in 2013. At the time of writing it was still unclear how member states intended to proceed, although a meeting to discuss the revisions had been scheduled for June 2018, suggesting that the project was still being pursued.[32] Moreover, the region's national anti-corruption bodies have held regular meetings under the auspices of the East African Association of Anti-corruption Authorities since 2007.[33]

What drives these sub-regional initiatives, and how do they relate to the AU's anti-corruption efforts? The ongoing process at the EAC seems to be driven partially by the need to address shortcomings in existing documents. Yet, overall, the evidence suggests that these protocols primarily serve as signals to donors, and they have certainly been driven by strong support from external actors. The SADC case illustrates this close relationship with external partners. In 1998, the Summit (the SADC's highest decision-making body) rejected a proposed "Declaration Against Corruption" in remarkably explicit terms:

> [T]he Summit observed that large scale corruption was a foreign phenomenon dating back to the colonial era ... The Summit also raised other concerns regarding the potential implications of signing a SADC Declaration Against Corruption: (a) The Declaration would be used as a yardstick and criteria against which qualification for development assistance from SADC's international cooperating partners would be measured and granted. (b) It would give credence to the notion that corruption, particularly of a large scale

African Union 129

nature, was an African phenomenon. This would be an indictment on SADC and its Member States.[34]

Clearly, safeguarding the organization's relationship with external donors was the main consideration during the Summit's debate of this proposal. One important issue was the conceptualization of corruption as a consequence of colonial—Western—influence rather than a local—African—problem.[35] The leaders' intention was to reject the narrative of African societies as inherently corrupt by blocking the initiative. More pragmatically, they were cautious about adopting a declaration that might be interpreted as an admission of responsibility. But an even more specific and logical argument was that the anti-corruption proposal would provide a yardstick for external valuation and aid conditionality. In short, in 1998, the SADC leaders were extremely wary of external criticism, viewing even a non-binding, general statement against corruption as a reputational risk rather than a possibly beneficial signal to donors.

However, over the next three years, they changed their strategy completely. In November 2000, a meeting of SADC ministers of justice adopted a draft anti-corruption protocol. The following August, the SADC Summit adopted it.[36] The organization's official records do not specify what led to this unprecedented shift, but civil society in the region had been lobbying tirelessly since the 1998 Summit. In 1999, South Africa hosted the 9th International Anti-corruption Conference. By then, the leaders' concern about donors using an anti-corruption agreement as a benchmark had probably already started to give way to anxiety about the impact of TI's indices and the World Bank's assessments. In addition, all of the Southern African leaders were contributors to the GCA initiative. Hence, in response to pressure from donors and civil society actors, it is highly plausible that they concluded that the adoption of a regional anti-corruption agreement was more of an advantageous signal than a risk to their international and domestic reputations.[37]

After the protocol's entry into force in 2005, it was 10 years before the member states established the SADC Anti-corruption Committee, which is supposed to oversee follow-up, according to article XI of the protocol. A press release from April 2015 noted that SADC officials were meeting with several anti-corruption officials from the region and pledged to speed up the process. Three months later, the committee held its first meeting and announced it would develop a plan of action to make the protocol operational.[38] This is further strong circumstantial evidence in support of the notion that anti-corruption

130 *African Union*

agreements under the condition of aid inflows are best explained as one-off signals rather than genuine attempts to facilitate effective regional cooperation. The sluggish ratification process for the ECOWAS protocol suggests a similar logic is at play within that organization.

There are two possible mechanisms by which donors may motivate the adoption of binding agreements. First, member states may face direct pressure from development partners to address corruption. Signaling their commitment through a sub-regional agreement thus makes sense, both in reaction to such pressure and as a general means to try to enhance their legitimacy. Research has shown that Africa is particularly prone to overlapping regionalism, with topics covered by several organizations at the same time.[39] For instance, in the field of human rights, African governments have created documents at the continental level as well as numerous sub-regional protocols. However, the governments then tend to ratify fewer of these documents than their UN counterparts. It seems that they view *drafting* new instruments as reputationally beneficial, but the UN documents are given much higher priority when it comes to ratification and implementation.[40]

Second, a rather prosaic driver of activism at the regional level may be the desire to attract funding. By creating a regional initiative and potential follow-up activities, a regional organization and its member states may gain access to extra resources. For staffers at the international level, who face severe resource constraints and are under constant pressure to secure external funding, this can be a powerful motive. Yet, ultimately, projects that are perceived to be driven by external agency—such as the AU's anti-corruption initiative—are prone to suffer from efficiency and legitimacy deficits.[41] Two long-time observers of the AU judged that its "top-down approach to corruption appears to have been aimed at hoodwinking donors and is unlikely to succeed."[42] Therefore, the impact of donor funding may explain the prevalence of redundant and superfluous agreements in Africa, which stands in stark contrast to the neat division of labor in the Americas.

Summary: donor agendas and African leaders' incentives

Early anti-corruption efforts in Africa were connected to the initiatives of multilateral institutions and donor governments, resulting in a strong link to aid and development goals. The GCA exemplifies this approach as it ultimately produced a document that emphasized prevention in the context of development. Yet, African leaders were not merely following their development partners' agenda. As the early SADC deliberations illustrate, governments were mindful of aid

African Union 131

conditionality and the impact that a negative image based on alleged corruption might have. Yet, just a few years later, there was a change of heart and it was decided that addressing the issue at the highest political level was a better plan of action than trying to resist external suggestions and pressure from international civil society organizations. The inflow of aid and donors' corresponding expectations were the major driving forces behind the anti-corruption efforts at the AU. Therefore, these regional efforts seem to mirror the logic of national reforms due to external pressure.[43] The external dimension also explains why African states continue to develop functionally redundant agreements. Overlapping protocols add value not necessarily because they offer practical solutions but because they seem to address donors' concerns and attract financial support. In this way, the benefits of sub-regional initiatives have undermined support for the AU convention.

Another line of argument also encouraged the AU to reach an agreement on corruption. Financial flows out of Africa were problematized in public statements, expert analyses, and official documents, and the prospect of recovering assets from abroad was a strong incentive for African leaders to join the international anti-corruption movement. However, this second motivation presented these leaders with a dilemma: in functional terms, the AU was not the most appropriate forum in which to address illicit financial flows. After all, the proceeds of corruption generally flow to havens in countries that lie far beyond the reach of any African organization. Therefore, even early observers of the drafting process noted that African governments might be better served by lobbying for strong language in the forthcoming UN anti-corruption convention.[44] Thus, the prospects for the AU convention were constrained from the very start by the organization's limited ability to address the underlying issues.

Tracing the drafts over time

Over the course of roughly three years, the African Union's draft anti-corruption agreement developed in several stages. Two early drafts were submitted by Adama Dieng (in late 2000 as part of his consultancy contract) and the Ethiopian delegation to the AU (in October 2001, shortly before the first experts' meeting). Yet, neither of these became the official working document for subsequent negotiations. Instead, the Office of the Legal Counsel presented a consolidated draft that incorporated proposals from a variety of sources. This document was then revised following discussions in two sessions of intergovernmental meetings.

132   *African Union*

Adama Dieng's draft

Adama Dieng's draft convention contains 15 substantial articles, followed by 5 very brief articles on the modalities of ratification and other formalities.[45] It starts with a list of offenses to be criminalized (articles I–II), including quid pro quo exchanges as well as corrupt practices other than bribery. However, no clear definitions are offered. Articles III–IV ask states to establish adequate sanctions and public-sector preventive measures. The brief article V extends prevention to the private sector. (The draft does not contain an article VI or VII, probably due to an administrative error.) Article VIII introduces the notion of a follow-up mechanism, consisting of "up to 15" individual experts appointed by states parties. Article IX deals with jurisdiction (territory, citizenship of offender, effect on citizens). Articles X–XV, which are longer and more detailed than the earlier ones, then address international cooperation by covering general principles, extradition, confiscation, punitive measures, and collaboration among national authorities.

In total, the draft amounts to 2200 words, which makes it by far the shortest of those discussed in this chapter. However, brevity should not be confused with limited scope; in fact, a wide range of issues are mentioned, albeit briefly. While the language on international cooperation is comparable in both length and design to the other drafts, the sections prior to article X lack detail. Overall, the document appears to be a list of items for future discussion, rather than a fully fledged international agreement.

Ethiopia's draft

In contrast to Dieng's draft, the document submitted by the Ethiopian government follows a structure similar to conventions produced by other regional organizations.[46] It contains 18 substantial articles, followed by 6 on technical issues relating to accession and other issues. The first three articles provide definitions of public officials and property, name international cooperation and domestic anti-corruption mechanisms as the treaty's principal goals, and obligate states parties to cooperate in general terms. Articles IV and V then define corrupt practices and urge states to criminalize them. Article VI is a nonbinding clause on illicit enrichment, while article XI asks signatories to criminalize money laundering.

The bulk of the draft—articles VII to X and XII to XVIII—is concerned with cooperation among the signatories. States are asked to

African Union 133

provide mutual legal and technical assistance (article VII), specifically in the areas of asset seizure (article VIII), bank secrecy (article IX), and extradition (article X). Article XII then states that parties should consider returning confiscated assets to countries that request assistance. Articles XIII and XIV clarify that cooperation among states should continue even if crimes were committed before the treaty entered into force ("temporal application") and that members may enter into additional agreements with one another. Article XV states that parties to the treaty may transmit information they have gathered from their investigations to other states in the absence of a request for assistance. According to articles XVI–XVIII, states should establish central authorities to handle these requests, communicate directly with one another, and report on progress. Finally, articles XIX–XXIV are technical in nature. They cover signature, ratification, accession, and entry into force of the treaty (with blank spaces left for the insertion of threshold rules). Also, it is declared that the AU will be the place of deposit, and that the document will be registered with the UN.

In sum, the Ethiopian draft focuses on criminalizing acts of corruption (with money laundering and illicit enrichment covered in separate articles) and encouraging international cooperation. There is no mention of domestic enforcement or prevention.

Office of the Legal Counsel draft

The OLC prepared its draft in time for the first experts' meeting, and it was subsequently updated to reflect their discussions. The draft that was distributed to member states ahead of the first meeting contains 19 substantial articles, plus 6 of a technical nature.[47] Article I provides definitions of several terms. Article II then outlines five objectives, adding policy harmonization and development to the goals mentioned in other drafts. Article III adds five principles for parties to consider, including human rights and democracy. Article IV defines acts of corruption, then article V(1) specifies that these are to be criminalized. In article VII, illicit enrichment is added as another aspect of corruption to be outlawed, but this is qualified with a reference to national laws. Article X requires states to establish jurisdiction based on territory, nationality, or lack of extradition options.

Contrary to the earlier drafts, the OLC document addresses prevention in some detail in articles V (legislative and other measures), VI (public service), VIII (private sector), and IX (civil society). Another addition is article XI, which references the African Charter on Human and Peoples' Rights to ensure that those accused of corruption receive a fair trial.

134 *African Union*

Articles XII–XVIII are concerned with international cooperation. All of the familiar aspects are covered: extradition, confiscation and return of assets, bank secrecy, mutual legal assistance, national central authorities, and relationships with other treaties. In addition, article XVI is specifically labeled "international cooperation." It addresses cooperation with "developed countries," "countries of origin of multi-nationals," and "financial organizations," all with the stated goal of reducing corruption.

Article XIX introduces a follow-up mechanism. Much like the proposal in article VIII of Dieng's draft, this will consist of "independent experts of the highest integrity and recognized competence in matters relating to combating and preventing corruption" based on proposals by member states and elected by the AU Executive Council. However, this article modifies Dieng's suggestion by reducing the size of the committee to 11 members and specifying a list of tasks.

The final clauses are contained in articles XX–XXV. Besides regulating accession and entry into force (article XX), they allow for reservations and denunciation by member states (articles XXI and XXIII). According to article XII, a two-thirds majority of AU member states will be required to amend the treaty.

Results of the first experts' and diplomats' meeting, November 2001

The African Union held an experts' meeting and then a diplomats' meeting to discuss the anti-corruption convention between 26 and 29 November 2001. The OLC draft was used as the starting point, and most of its clauses were adopted with no or only minor amendments.[48] However, one section of article IV, which lists the acts that should be categorized as corruption, was bracketed as the participants could not agree on whether to include embezzlement (diversion of funds). The participants also agreed to add a new article VI, which obligates state parties to outlaw the laundering of proceeds of corruption.

The clauses on preventive measures for the public sector in article VII (article VI in the OLC draft) were discussed at length. Consequently, one provision became more demanding: rather than a one-off declaration at the time of appointment, public officials were required to make continuous declarations about their assets throughout their tenure. On the other hand, two subsequent sections were made slightly less impactful: article VIII (formerly VII) on illicit enrichment was bracketed after some delegates argued that it was not a core aspect of anti-corruption; and article XI (formerly X) on jurisdiction was widened to allow for the establishment of jurisdiction on the basis of effect. The

African Union   135

latter addition allows states to claim jurisdiction when an action "affects the vital interests of the State Party, or the deleterious harmful consequences or effects of such offences impact on the State Party." The last substantial amendment was made to article XX (formerly XIX), which concerns the establishment of a follow-up mechanism—the Advisory Board. The new version stresses that this body will indeed have a strictly advisory role:

> Subsequently, a new clause 3 was added to stipulate that members of the Board should serve in their personal capacity ... The rest of the clauses were adopted with amendments to ensure that the Board was focused on its advisory role in the fight against corruption.[49]

Results of the second experts' meeting, September 2002

Further meetings were held from 16 to 19 September 2002, first among experts, then among ministers. As mentioned earlier, a much smaller number of observers attended these sessions. Just five non-state organizations—the South African Human Rights Trust, Transparency International, the African Development Bank, the inter-regional consultative Asian African Legal Consultative Organization, and a group of African trade unions known as the Organization of African Union Unity—sent delegations.

In light of the broad consensus that was reached at the 2001 meetings, the second experts' meeting was able to focus on resolving just two contentious clauses. With respect to article IV, regarding the scope of issues to be defined as corruption, the debate revolved around whether to include embezzlement of public funds. Relatedly, the experts discussed whether to include private-sector employees as potential subjects. After considerable deliberation, they decided to opt for the broadest possible scope. According to the amended clause IV.1(d), states must criminalize the diversion of public funds by a public official "or any other person."

Regarding article VIII, the discussion focused on whether illicit enrichment should be considered corruption. This was more of a technical issue, because establishing illicit enrichment as an offense was made a permissive clause (i.e., subject to national law), and clause 2 merely provides more leeway to accommodate national legislative precedent. By retaining clause VIII.2, the delegates gave members the final say on whether to criminalize illicit enrichment outside the framework of corruption, but asked them to ensure that it would still be subject to corruption-related international cooperation.

136 *African Union*

In addition to these two issues, discussions addressed three more articles. Regarding article V, on legislative and other measures, one of the civil society delegations proposed various amendments, all of which were rejected. However, two new articles were added: namely, article IX (access to information) and article X (funding of political parties). Both are designed to be obligatory, although the wording, which encourages states to introduce measures in line with anti-corruption goals, is rather vague.[50]

Finally, input from the observer delegations was reflected in a change to article XII (formerly X), concerning the role of civil society:

> [T]he Meeting expanded former Article 10 to strengthen the participation of civil society in the monitoring process and to ensure consultation with civil society in the implementation of the Convention ... Furthermore, the Meeting accepted to include a provision stipulating free access of the Media to information on corruption and related offences having due regard to national legislation.[51]

Results of the ministerial meeting, September 2002

A two-day ministerial conference was convened following the conclusion of the second experts' meeting. It was intended to finalize the draft and allow for adoption by heads of state at a later date. The official report indicates that the ministerial representatives approved the vast majority of the experts' amendments and additions. Articles IV, V, VIII, IX, and X—all of which had been discussed during the preceding meeting—were adopted in full.[52] Similarly, the new article XII, on civil society and the media, was accepted with only minor adjustments in the form of more hortatory language regarding desired outcomes. With respect to clause XIII.1(d), on effects-based jurisdiction—which had been added in the 2001 experts' meeting—it was decided that states could claim jurisdiction on the basis of their perception of negative effects. Regarding article XV, on extradition rules, although delegates discussed rules for domestic enforcement in lieu of extradition, the article remained unchanged aside from some minor adjustments to the wording.

The only substantial addition was made to article XVI, which deals with confiscation of the proceeds of corruption, including outside of the offender's home country. In all of the previous drafts, section 1 of this article had declared that parties should introduce measures to ensure that their authorities will be able to (a) trace and (b) confiscate such proceeds. Now, though, the new clause XVI.1(c) demanded legislation on the "repatriation of proceeds of corruption." Therefore, the principle of returning assets to a damaged party was included in the convention for the first time.

Adoption in 2003 and subsequent changes

A few minor linguistic and cosmetic changes were made to the text between the final ministerial conference and the official adoption of the convention by heads of states at the second ordinary session of the Assembly of the African Union, held in Maputo, Mozambique, on 11 July 2003. The substance of the document remained unchanged, however.[53]

Unfortunately, some significant inconsistencies were introduced during the translation process. One legal scholar from the United States, Peter Schroth, was so concerned that he contacted the OLC to point out the problems and later published his critique:

> A starting place for discussion of the AU Convention is its four versions, in French, English, Portuguese and Arabic, all of which, according to article 28, are equally authentic. The four texts often say different things. At some points, one or more of the texts obviously does not make sense, so officials and courts may look to the versions in one or more other languages—if they can find them and read them, neither of which is a trivial matter—in the hope of learning what was intended. Worse, at several points, the texts do make sense in each language, so that the differences, sometimes major, may never be suspected.[54]

In reaction, the Algerian delegation to the AU supplied updated, corrected versions of the French and Arabic texts.[55] However, none of the substantial issues raised by Schroth or other critics was addressed. The convention has not been amended since it was opened for signature.

Evidence of diffusion

Having traced the evolution of the drafts, what role did mechanisms of diffusion play in this process? In this section, I discuss international and transnational agreements that may have been reference models for the AU convention on the basis of information provided by the drafters themselves, either in the official archives or in interviews.

138   *African Union*

International reference models

The report that Adama Dieng submitted as part of his consultancy contract in late 2000 clearly mentions several sources of inspiration for the AU convention. Indeed, it contains a total of eight pages on "the role of sub-regional, regional, continental and international organizations" in the fight against corruption and points out that some African countries are already working with the World Bank, International Monetary Fund, Transparency International, and donor agencies in the field of public procurement. Dieng then highlights a number of international initiatives:

> In 1996, the UN General Assembly adopted a declaration against corruption in business related transaction. Similar initiatives were adopted within the EU which has finally defined a complete strategy to combat corruption. The same is true of the Council of Europe ... For several years now, the World Bank, UNDP, ADB have taken effective measures to support the efforts of African countries in the area of the transparent management of public affairs.[56]

The report explicitly refers to regional organizations in Europe, the United Nations, and the two main international financial institutions—the IMF and the WB. Emphasis is placed on interactions between African governments and donors. While the COE and the EU are not discussed in great depth, the report dedicates almost four pages to the World Trade Organization and the World Bank. However, this discussion provides few details on scope or legal design; rather, it presents summaries of the two organizations' approaches.

Additionally, Dieng refers to the International Labor Organization, the UN Conference on Trade and Development, the UN General Assembly, and specific UN Economic and Social Council documents, then lists nine important aspects of anti-corruption best practice:

- Prevention:
  - ethics legislation;
  - public-sector training;
  - civil servants' asset declarations;
  - whistleblower mechanisms;
  - ethics monitoring by a dedicated body; and
  - public-sector hiring practices.

African Union 139

- Domestic enforcement:

  - "draconian measures [against] corruption and impunity"; and
  - disciplinary measures in the public sector.

- Follow-up:

  - pan-African and regional initiatives to facilitate implementation.

The Ethiopian draft, in comparison, mentions no reference models. That said, it is an obvious example of direct copying. The acts of corruption that it specifies are based on the list of public-sector corrupt practices in the OAS convention, plus the private-sector clause in the Council of Europe's Criminal Law Convention. Moreover, most of the articles on international cooperation (XIII–XVIII) are verbatim copies of the respective provisions in one or other of these two reference models. The section on illicit enrichment is also lifted directly from the OAS agreement. Finally, the wording of articles VIII, XI, and XII—on how to deal with the proceeds of crime—is taken straight from the UN Convention on Transnational Organized Crime.[57]

At the first AU experts' meeting in November 2001, Legal Counsel Kioko made an introductory statement that provides valuable information on the documents that served as reference models for the OLC.[58] Three binding international documents are mentioned: the SADC protocol, the OAS convention, and the OECD convention. All of these were available to the Legal Counsel prior to the start of negotiations. Indeed, the US ambassador to Ethiopia, David Shinn, had sent copies of the OAS and OECD conventions to an assistant secretary general at the AU as early as March 1998:

> At Mauritius National Day, I mentioned our interest in talking with appropriate persons in the [AU] concerning the possibility of an anti-corruption convention for Africa. You, in turn, asked that I send you a copy of the Inter-American Convention Against Corruption. I am enclosing a copy of the Convention with this letter, together with several other items on the subject of corruption that I thought you might find interesting.[59]

The Legal Counsel at the time, Tiyanjana Maluwa, received copies of the letter and the attached documents. The two conventions, as well as a couple of explanatory texts taken from the respective websites, were then archived by the Office of the Legal Counsel. Indeed, they are among the first items in the folders that contain all of the material

140   *African Union*

relating to negotiations about the AU convention. This indicates that both Maluwa and his deputy (and successor) Kioko must have been aware of the OAS and OECD models well in advance of those negotiations. The paper trail is less obvious with respect to the SADC protocol. In fact, I was unable to find a single copy of this document in the AU archives in Addis Ababa (although this may be because documents from sub-regional African organizations have been filed at a separate location). However, in June 2001, a Zimbabwean NGO, the Southern African Human Rights Trust (SAHRIT), sent a letter to the Legal Counsel, requesting an invitation to the upcoming experts' meeting, given that SAHRIT had "facilitated the drafting" of the SADC protocol (which had not yet been adopted). Therefore, even if there were no direct communication between SADC and AU officials, the Legal Counsel was certainly reminded of the ongoing anti-corruption efforts in Southern Africa.[60]

Clear evidence of the OAS and SADC agreements as reference models can also be found in a letter from Tiyanjana Maluwa to Adama Dieng in which the former invited the latter to attend the first experts' meeting. The invitation, which was sent on 31 October 2001, includes an explanation of why the draft that was distributed to the delegates differed from Dieng's earlier version:

> As far as the Convention is concerned, we have introduced some major amendments by incorporating some of the concepts and elements contained in the Inter-American Convention Against Corruption, the Draft SADC Protocol Against Corruption as well as a Draft Convention Against Corruption prepared by the Federal Democratic Republic of Ethiopia.[61]

As the SADC protocol is mentioned in the same sentence as the OAS convention and the Ethiopian draft, it must have been a reference model, even though it is absent from the official records. Indeed, this private letter is even stronger evidence than Kioko's statement to the experts' meeting: while the latter might have felt the need to honor all of the delegates at the table by drawing attention to their respective anti-corruption efforts, there was no reason for Maluwa to mention the SADC protocol unless it had been a genuine point of reference.

In his statement to the experts' meeting, Kioko mentioned two other important documents. The first of these, the GCA's "Principles to Combat Corruption," had already been signed by 15 AU member states, which opened a channel for their introduction in the AU document. More directly, in messages sent to the Legal Counsel, GCA staff actually urged AU officials to incorporate the principles in the convention.[62] Second, the Ethiopian draft may be interpreted as either an attempt to set the agenda at the upcoming discussions or simply a gesture of goodwill as the host country. Either way, Kioko's reference to this draft somewhat obscures the fact that inspiration for the AU agreement may be traced to the Council of Europe. Dieng made multiple references to COE documents in his report, and the Ethiopian draft copied articles verbatim from its Criminal Law Convention, yet there was no explicit mention of the Council of Europe in the course of the first experts' meeting.

Research and outreach by the Legal Counsel

The evidence from the archival record was supported by interviewees' testimonies. For instance, I learned that the Office of the Legal Counsel tried to incorporate existing initiatives into its decision-making. However, it lacked the necessary resources to survey all of the potential reference models systematically and evaluate their respective strengths and weaknesses:

> At that time, we were two lawyers in the AU Legal Department, dealing with *all* the legal issues affecting the AU. So, we did not have the time for any research. What we did was engage a consultant, who came up with a report and a draft. And there were clear terms of reference of what he had to take into account. Among other things, he had to check what is out there, and what we could learn from elsewhere. But we ourselves did not sit down and say, "Let's look at other models and do this and this." No—we didn't have the time.[63]

This statement confirms that staffers at the AU were forced to rely on a single external consultant—Adama Dieng—to provide the initial survey. However, his report failed to provide either an in-depth comparison of alternative approaches or a guide to best practice. Therefore, the Office of the Legal Counsel, perhaps realizing the limits of Dieng's document, augmented his draft by drawing on some readily available sources—that is, those that had been provided by external actors. Given its resource and time constraints, the OLC was unable to set up meetings to exchange information with officials from other international organizations; nor did it conduct additional research to corroborate what Dieng had proposed.

142 *African Union*

This helps to explain why the AU devised a unique follow-up mechanism that relies on 11 experts to provide research and assistance with implementation of the convention in member states. This body has no precedent in earlier anti-corruption initiatives. In contrast to the OAS, which held meetings with numerous representatives from other organizations to learn about their follow-up experiences, the AU drafters did not have the resources to conduct any such research. It seems that Dieng and Kioko assumed that member states would reject a strong follow-up mechanism and designed the Advisory Board accordingly. Moreover, my interviewees confirmed that lesson-drawing or mimicry based on international reference models played no part in this process. However, the Advisory Board's structure is very similar to the African Commission on Human and Peoples' Rights, which apparently served as the principal model. Rather than lesson-drawing from international or even national anti-corruption sources, the drafters chose a model that was already well established in the AU context and had proved to be relatively uncontroversial among the organization's members.[64]

Archived correspondence shows that the OLC attempted to establish ties with various international actors and invited experts to the official meetings that were organized to discuss the anti-corruption project. This was a highly successful strategy with respect to the 2001 meetings, as delegates from the World Bank, the UNDP and UNECA, civil society, and other organizations all attended. The second round of meetings was smaller in scale, and only five non-state delegations participated. Indeed, several institutions declined their invitations. Meanwhile, AU officials were invited to various anti-corruption events but attended only a few, if any. For instance, Kioko seems to have declined invitations to attend the Global Forum on Fighting Corruption and Safeguarding Integrity, which held its first meeting in Washington, DC, in 1999 and its second in The Hague two years later; the GCA's 2001 meeting in Washington, DC; and an "Africa Workshop" at the International Anti-corruption Conference. Nevertheless, the host of invitations signaled to the Legal Counsel and his colleagues that these international actors were all following the AU's anti-corruption efforts closely.

Inputs from civil society

It is impossible to determine whether the Legal Counsel invited observers into the drafting process in the hope of gaining access to their expertise or primarily to increase the legitimacy and prestige of the negotiations. Either way, though, non-state actors certainly enjoyed significant access. As one observer points out, the first experts' meeting was characterized by an atypical balance between relatively ill-prepared government representatives and many well-informed non-state delegations:

> [A]part from a few countries, such as South Africa, Ghana, Uganda, over three quarters of the states were represented by individuals mostly drawn from their embassies and missions, without the expertise required and whose ability to deal with the issues in sufficient depth proved quite limited. It might be added, in this connection, that the participation of the African Commission on Human and Peoples' Rights, as well as of several observers and guests ... had considerable influence in shaping the contents of the Convention. Contrary to well established practice, this participation was actively sought [by the Legal Counsel].[65]

Whatever the underlying motivation for inviting them, the non-state delegations were not mere observers; they were also free to make comments during the sessions. This was a novelty at the time: while the African Union increasingly paid attention to civil society,[66] it did not have a long-standing tradition of involving non-state actors. As a result, the civil society delegates pushed for the inclusion of several issues in the final convention. Transparency International, according to its own records, focused on the financing of political parties, access to information rights, the protection of whistleblowers, and asset recovery—that is, aspects of prevention, domestic enforcement, and international cooperation.[67] It also insisted on the establishment of the Advisory Board as a follow-up mechanism in the face of opposition from several country delegations.[68]

All of the NGO participants were introduced as experts, rather than activists, in the hope of reducing resistance from member states. This cooperation among AU officials and civil society was facilitated by personal connections among the legal experts, and TI was able to make several recommendations through the Legal Counsel, rather than in direct statements. Indeed, the OLC and TI—which had also been in contact with Dieng—agreed on a non-confrontational, cooperative strategy before the first meeting began in order to circumvent opposition from member states. Participants felt that this strategy was successful. For instance, because the TI delegation included an expert on civil law, it was able to assist during the discussions whenever delegates were uncertain about how specific clauses might be implemented in different legal systems.

144 *African Union*

The OLC acted as a strategic gatekeeper, admitting only those NGOs that it felt were supportive of the non-confrontational approach: "We were also careful in who we invited ... We invited those we knew would give constructive proposals to help discussions. More like experts."[69] This correlates with Tallberg and colleagues' findings in their analysis of NGO influence on IO decision-making: civil society actors are more likely to be effective when their input is framed as expert knowledge rather than confrontational, partisan advocacy.[70] AU officials wanted to avoid confrontation and instead formed a coalition with outside experts to overcome intransigence among the member-state delegations:

> I knew [civil society] would be able to assist us. Quite often it is the secretariat that has a good idea, and [member states] don't have an interest in the matter. Therefore, it is member states who are trying to protect [against] what they feel is an assault on their sovereignty ... But I knew that civil society would be, if you like, on our side in dealing with this issue.[71]

Overall, the delegates from Transparency International and the other NGOs succeeded in presenting themselves as experts rather than confrontational activists. Consequently, they managed to influence the outcome of the discussions.[72] Civil society and the Legal Counsel shared the goal of developing a relatively strong document and cooperated to overcome government skepticism. As the final text shows, their efforts were worthwhile because, in addition to retaining all of the original provisions from the OLC draft, the convention contained several others that were added during the negotiations. This is further evidence of global diffusion shaping local decisions. Nevertheless, skeptical member states did enjoy some success as they managed to limit the degree of obligation and subsequently implementation of the convention.

Conclusion

As this chapter has shown, external influence played a crucial role in persuading the African Union to draft an anti-corruption agreement and then shaping the scope and legal design of that agreement. During the 1990s, African governments were under severe pressure from donors and civil society to address the problem of corruption. On the one hand, the World Bank and national development agencies demanded reforms to curb fraud and inefficiency in the aid sector. On

African Union 145

the other, scholars and activists drew attention to foreign bribes and damaging capital outflows. Therefore, adopting a binding anti-corruption agreement not only allowed African leaders to signal their commitment to donors who were worried about the pernicious impact of corruption on development projects but also enabled them to speak out against transnational bribery and illicit financial flows. Judging from the archival record of meetings and communications, the first of these two motivations played the greater role.

The drafting and negotiation processes permitted significant input from non-state actors. The AU's Legal Counsel played a key role in drafting the agreement and gave legal experts and advocates access to the negotiations. The archival record reveals that member states' involvement was largely limited to just two sets of meetings, during which a coalition of progressive non-state actors and governments argued the case for a strong agreement amid opposition from a group of skeptical member states. While the delegates made some changes to the draft text in the course of these meetings, the overall structure remained intact. The OLC, which acted as organizer, drafter, and agenda-setter, thus had a decisive impact on the final outcome, enjoying a level of influence that went far beyond what might be expected of a mere facilitator of an intergovernmental process. In other words, the development of the AU convention deviated significantly from the traditional pattern of strictly intergovernmental decision-making.

From the early preparatory stages onwards, the Legal Counsel consulted with external legal experts, and funding for the project was provided by the Swedish embassy. Clearly, several earlier agreements served as reference models for the AU, with the OAS convention and the SADC protocol particularly important inspirations. The AU's adoption of numerous aspects of these agreements may be interpreted as either lesson-drawing or emulation. Claims of lesson-drawing must be qualified, however, because of the limited resources that were available. With only two lawyers—for whom the anti-corruption convention was just one of many ongoing tasks—the OLC did not have the capacity to conduct a thorough comparative legal analysis of previous agreements or talk to experts from other organizations. Given these internal constraints, any external actors who supplied their reference models to the AU enjoyed a privileged position, at least initially. The archival record indicates that the OAS and OECD agreements were provided early in the drafting process, whereas the Council of Europe did not contact the AU decision-makers. Nevertheless, the latter did become a reference model via the Ethiopian draft.

146 *African Union*

To conclude, external reference models had a significant influence on the AU's anti-corruption agreement. International actors were highly successful in lobbying for the start of negotiations, in marked contrast to their efforts with the SADC a few years earlier. External actors also contributed to the drafting process—both actively, by submitting suggestions, and indirectly, as reference models. AU officials commissioned an initial study in an effort to draw lessons from previous agreements, but resource constraints in the OLC meant that "availability bias" associated with bounded rationality was inevitable.[73]

The subsequent history of the agreement suggests that this prevalence of external drivers in the drafting process translated into a lack of support among member states and a consequent decoupling of rhetoric and implementation. Sub-regional agreements by SADC and ECOWAS were developed in parallel, apparently to serve as additional signals of conformity with international expectations and to attract further funding. This explains why overlapping agreements were and continue to be drafted. Africa is thus on a very different trajectory from the Americas (in terms of division of labor) and Europe (in terms of functional differentiation). In addition, the UNCAC is now the main instrument through which to address the recovery of assets from jurisdictions outside of Africa and transnational bribery. Consequently, implementing and supporting the AU's own anti-corruption convention seem to be very low on the list of priorities for the organization's member states. The recent scandal surrounding the Advisory Board might be a symptom of that negligence, and follow-up at the regional level remains dependent on support from development partners. Stakeholders who supported far-reaching commitments at the regional level have been left frustrated and disillusioned by these developments, so it seems likely that support for the AU convention will continue to ebb away in the future.

Notes

1 Until 2001/2002, the African Union was known as the Organization of African Unity (OAU). During the transition period, both names were used in parallel. For simplicity and consistency, I use the current name throughout this chapter.

2 Organization of African Unity, *Annual Activities of the African Commission on Human and Peoples' Rights*, AHG/Dec. 126 (XXXIV) (Ouagadougou, Burkina Faso: OAU, 1998), https://au.int/sites/default/files/decisions/9543-1 998_ahg_dec_124-131_xxxiv_e.pdf.

3 Personal communication with Tiyanjana Maluwa, 2014.

4 African Union, "Study on Corruption in Africa and Draft African Convention for Combating Corruption," inter-office memorandum from Legal

African Union 147

Counsel to Director of Political Department, 22 December 2000, a.i. CAD. CAB/LEG/24.12/99/Vol.VI (36).

5 African Union, "Letter of Appointment/Consultancy Contract," from Director of Administration/Finance Department to Adama Dieng, plus reply from Adama Dieng, 13 September 2000, CAB/LEG/24.12/36/Vol.I; Adama Dieng, *Corruption in Africa: Legal, Political, Economic and Other Implications* (Addis Ababa: African Union, 2000).

6 African Union, "Study on Corruption in Africa and Draft African Convention for Combating Corruption"; African Union, "Project for the Elaboration of an OAU Convention for Combating Corruption," inter-office memorandum from Legal Counsel to Secretary General, 21 August 2001, CAB/LEG/24.12/7/Vol.II (9); African Union, "Report of the Experts/Diplomats Meeting to Consider the Draft OAU/AU Convention on Combating Corruption and the Draft OAU/AU Convention on Combating Corruption," inter-office memorandum from Legal Counsel to all Directors of Departments, Executive Secretaries, Secretary General to the ACHPR, 7 December 2001, CAB/LEG/24.12/123/Vol.II.

7 African Union, "Report of the Second Experts' Meeting on the Draft AU Convention on Combating Corruption and Related Offenses," Expt/AU/Conv/Comb/Corruption/Rpt.l(II) (2002); African Union, "Report of the Ministerial Conference on the Draft African Union Convention on Preventing and Combating Corruption," Min/AU/Conv/Comb/Corruption/Rpt.1(II) Rev.1 (2002).

8 African Union, *Executive Council, Twenty-first Ordinary Session: Report on the Status of OAU/AU Treaties (as at 11 July 2012)*, EX.CL/728(XXI) Rev.1 (2012); State of the Union Coalition, *Continental Compliance Report 2014* (Nairobi, Kenya: AU, 2015), 1–10, www.fahamu.org/resources/SOTU-Continental-Compliance-Report-2014-English1.pdf.

9 African Union, *Executive Council, Thirteenth Ordinary Session: Report on the Election of the Members of the Advisory Board on Corruption within the African Union*, EX.CL/448(XIII) (2008); African Union, *Executive Council, Fourteenth Ordinary Session: Report on the Election of the Members of the Advisory Board on Corruption within the African Union*, EX.CL/492 (XIV) (2009).

10 African Union, *Executive Council, Seventeenth Ordinary Session: Report on the Activities of the African Union Advisory Board on Corruption*, EX.CL/603(XVII) (2010); African Union, *Executive Council, Eighteenth Ordinary Session: Report on the Activities of the African Union Advisory Board on Corruption*, EX.CL/651(XVIII) (2011).

11 Phone interview with former UNDP official, April 2015.

12 African Union, *Executive Council, Nineteenth Ordinary Session: Report of the African Union Advisory Board on Corruption*, EX.CL/680(XIX) (2011); United Nations Economic Commission for Africa, *Combating Corruption, Improving Governance in Africa: Regional Anti-corruption Programme for Africa (2011–2016)* (Addis Ababa: UNECA, 2011), 13, http://repository.uneca.org/handle/10855/23273.

13 African Union, *Executive Council, Twenty-fifth Ordinary Session: Report of the Activities of the African Union Advisory Board against Corruption*, EX.CL/860(XXV) (2014); African Union, *Assembly of the Union, Twenty-*

148 *African Union*

fourth Regular Session: Decision on the Election of Eleven Members of the African Union Advisory Board on Corruption, Dec.549(XXIV) (2015).

14 African Union, *Executive Council, Twenty-sixth Ordinary Session: Report of the African Union Advisory Board on Corruption on the Implementation of Decision EX.CL/DEC.847(XXV) Adopted by the Executive Council in Malabo in June 2014*, EX.CL/879(XXVI) (2015).

15 Interview with AU official, Addis Ababa, April 2015; interview with AU OLC official, Addis Ababa, April 2015; interview with Swedish embassy official, Addis Ababa, April 2015.

16 African Union, *Summary of the Key Decisions and Declarations of the 31st African Union Summit* (2018), https://perma.cc/L5NV-87XM.

17 George Mukundi Wachira, *Consolidating the African Governance Architecture*, SAIIA Policy Briefing No. 96 (Johannesburg: SAIIA, 2014), 4, http s://perma.cc/YSL2-LPAB; Samuel M. Makinda, David Mickler, and F. Wafula Okumu, *The African Union: Addressing the Challenges of Peace, Security, and Governance* (London: Routledge, 2016), 71–96.

18 Transparency International, *Understanding the African Union Convention on Preventing and Combating Corruption and Related Offenses* (Berlin: Transparency International, 2005), 13.

19 Ayodele Aderinwale, "Summary Report," in *Corruption, Democracy and Human Rights in East and Central Africa: Workshop in Entebbe, Republic of Uganda, 12–14 December 1994*, ed. Ayodele Aderinwale (Lagos: Africa Leadership Forum, 1994), 5–16, at 13.

20 Alhaji B. M. Marong, "Toward a Normative Consensus against Corruption: Legal Effects of the Principles to Combat Corruption in Africa," *Denver Journal of International Law and Policy* 30, no. 2 (2002): 99–129, at 110.

21 Benin, Botswana, Ethiopia, Ghana, Mali, Malawi, Mozambique, Senegal, South Africa, Tanzania, and Uganda signed. Thus, the initiative was not tied to a specific sub-region but combined states from West, East, and Southern Africa. See Global Coalition for Africa, "Principles to Combat Corruption in African Countries," CAB/LEG/24.12/88/Vol.II.

22 Global Coalition for Africa, "Principles to Combat Corruption in African Countries," 2–4.

23 Adama Dieng, Fax message to Ben Kioko, Office of the Legal Counsel, 14 March 1999, CAB/LEG/24.12/7/Vol.I; African Union, "Project on the Elaboration of an OAU Convention against Corruption," 30 March 1999, CAB/LEG/24.12/19/Vol.I; African Union, "Grant Agreement between Sweden and OAU," press release 93/99, attached to "Agreement between the Swedish Embassy and the Organization of African Unity Regarding a Convention against Corruption," CAB/LEG/24.12/20–21/Vol.I.

24 Interview with Swedish embassy official, Addis Ababa, April 2015; phone interview with former AU OLC official, August 2015.

25 African Union, "Public Service Ethics in Africa Project: Mid-term Report," inter-office memorandum from Assistant Secretary General for Administration and Conferences to Secretary General, 4 January 2000, CAB/LEG/24.12/17/Vol.I.

26 Dieng, *Corruption in Africa*, 33–34.

27 Transparency International, *The Nyanga Declaration on the Recovery and Repatriation of Africa's Wealth* (Nyanga, Zimbabwe: Transparency International, 2001); Transparency International, *Nairobi Declaration on*

African Union 149

International Obligations and the Recovery and Repatriation of Africa's Stolen Wealth (Nairobi, Kenya: Transparency International, 2006); Léonce Ndikumana and James K. Boyce, *Africa's Odious Debts: How Foreign Loans and Capital Flight Bled a Continent* (London: Zed Books, 2011); AfDB/GFI, *Illicit Financial Flows and the Problem of Net Resource Transfers from Africa: 1980–2009* (Tunis and Washington, DC: AfDB/GFI, 2013); OECD, *Illicit Financial Flows from Developing Countries: Measuring OECD Responses* (Paris: OECD, 2014); UNECA, *Report of the High Level Panel on Illicit Financial Flows from Africa* (Addis Ababa: UNECA, 2015), http://repository.uneca.org/handle/10855/22695; Emile van der Does de Willebois, Emily Halter, Robert Harrison, Ji Won Park, and J. C. Sharman, *The Puppet Masters: How the Corrupt Use Legal Structures to Hide Stolen Assets and What to Do about It* (Washington, DC: World Bank, 2011).

28 Aderinwale, "Summary Report," 13.
29 Jeremy Pope, "Corruption in Africa: The Role for Transparency International (TI)," in *Corruption, Democracy and Human Rights in East and Central Africa*, ed. Aderinwale, 142–154.
30 Transparency International, *Anti-corruption Conventions in Africa: What Civil Society Can Do to Make Them Work* (Berlin: Transparency International, 2006), 16, https://perma.cc/JC3Z-2UUG.
31 ECOWAS, *National Anti-corruption Institutions in West Africa (NACIWA) General Assembly Resolutions: 13–15 July 2016* (Cotonou: ECOWAS, 2016), https://perma.cc/LE4R-8WX8.
32 Fred Oluoch, "Regional Agencies Seek More Powers to Fight Corruption," *East African*, 28 June 2014; East African Community, "Meeting to Redraft Protocol on Preventing and Combatting Corruption" (2018), https://perma.cc/M6AB-TJBW.
33 Achieng Akena, *Challenges and Opportunities in Combatting Corruption within the AU Legal Framework*, working paper (2011), 12, www.academia.edu/4848030/CHALLENGES_AND_OPPORTUNITIES_IN_COMBATTING_CORRUPTION_WITHIN_THE_AU_LEGAL_FRAMEWORK.
34 SADC, *Record of the Summit: Grand Baye, Republic of Mauritius, 13–14 September 1998*, 14–15.
35 Munyae M. Mulinge and Gwen N. Lesetedi, "Interrogating Our Past: Colonialism and Corruption in Sub-Saharan Africa," *African Journal of Political Science* 3, no. 2 (1998): 15–28; Munyae M. Mulinge and Gwen N. Lesetedi, "Corruption in Sub-Saharan Africa: Towards a More Holistic Approach," *African Journal of Political Science* 7, no. 1 (2002): 51–77.
36 SADC, *Record of the Council of Ministers: Blantyre, Republic of Malawai, 9–11 August 2001*; SADC, *Record of the Summit: Blantyre, Republic of Malawai, 12–14 August 2001*.
37 Transparency International, *Anti-corruption Conventions in Africa*, 15–16; IACC, *Programme for the the 9th International Anti-corruption Conference: Global Integrity: 2000 and Beyond—Developing Anticorruption Strategies in a Changing World* (Durban, South Africa: International Anticorruption Conference, 1999), https://perma.cc/93WY-4U3A; Indira Carr, "Corruption, the Southern African Development Community Anti-corruption Protocol and the Principal–Agent–Client Model," *International Journal of Law in Context* 5, no. 2 (2007): 147–177.

150 *African Union*

38 SADC, "News: SADC and SACC to Fight Corruption," 23 April 2015, www. sadc.int/news-events/news/sadc-and-sacc-fight-corruption/; SADC, "News: SADC Anti-corruption Committee (SACC) Meeting, 2–3 July 2015," 6 July 2015, www.sadc.int/news-events/news/sadc-anti-corruption-committee-sacc-m eeting-2-3-july-2015/.

39 Malte Brosig, "Overlap and Interplay between International Organisations: Theories and Approaches," *South African Journal of International Affairs* 18, no. 2 (2011): 147–167.

40 Frans Viljoen, "Human Rights in Africa: Normative, Institutional and Functional Complementarity and Distinctiveness," *South African Journal of International Affairs* 18, no. 2 (2011): 191–216; Tiyanjana Maluwa, "Ratification of African Union Treaties by Member States: Law, Policy and Practice," *Melbourne Journal of International Law* 13 (2012): 1–49.

41 Interview with UNDP official, Addis Ababa, May 2015; Julia Gray, "Donor Funding and Institutional Expansions in International Organizations: Failures of Legitimacy and Efficiency," unpublished manuscript (2014).

42 Samuel M. Makinda and F. Wafula Okumu, *The African Union: Challenges of Globalization, Security, and Governance* (London: Routledge, 2008), 65.

43 Stephen P. Riley, "The Political Economy of Anti-corruption Strategies in Africa," *European Journal of Development Research* 10, no. 1 (1998): 129–159; Stephen P. Riley, "Western Policies and African Realities: The New Anti-corruption Agenda," in *Corruption and Development in Africa: Lessons from Country Case-studies*, ed. Kempe Ronald Hope and Bornwell C. Chikulo (Basingstoke and New York: Macmillan and St. Martin's Press, 1999), 137–158; UNECA, *African Governance Report II* (Oxford: Oxford University Press, 2009), 226; John Gbodi Ikubaje, "Democracy and Anti-corruption Policies in Africa," *Ugandan Journal of Management and Public Policy Studies* 6 (2014): 38–56, at 47.

44 Transparency International, *Anti-Corruption Conventions in Africa*, 15–16.

45 Dieng, *Corruption in Africa*, 35–44.

46 African Union, "Letter from the OAU General Secretariat to Ministry of Foreign Affairs of the Federal Republic of Ethiopia," 11 October 2001, attached to "Note Verbale OAU-1/9/01 from the Ethiopian FM, Including Draft Convention," 9 October 2001, CAB/LEG/24.12/22/Vol.II.

47 African Union, "Experts' Meeting to Consider Draft OAU Convention on Combating Corruption, 26 to 29 November 2001, Addis Ababa, Ethiopia," inter-office memorandum from Legal Counsel to all Assistant Secretaries General, all Directors of Departments, etc., 25 October 2001, CAB/LEG/24.12/35/Vol.II.

48 African Union, "Report of the Experts/Diplomats Meeting to Consider the Draft OAU/AU Convention on Combating Corruption and the Draft OAU/AU Convention on Combating Corruption."

49 African Union, "Report of the Experts/Diplomats Meeting to Consider the Draft OAU/AU Convention on Combating Corruption and the Draft OAU/AU Convention on Combating Corruption," 10.

50 African Union, "Report of the Ministerial Conference on the Draft African Union Convention on Preventing and Combating Corruption," 10–11.

51 African Union, "Report of the Second Experts' Meeting on the Draft AU Convention on Combating Corruption and Related Offenses," 5.

African Union 151

52 African Union, "Report of the Ministerial Conference on the Draft African Union Convention on Preventing and Combating Corruption"; African Union, "Draft AU Convention on Combating Corruption and Related Offenses," Expt/Draft/AU/Conv/Comb/Corruption (II) Rev.4 (2002).

53 African Union, "Report of the Ministerial Conference on the Draft African Union Convention on Preventing and Combating Corruption," Annex; African Union, *Convention on Preventing and Combating Corruption* (Maputo: AU, 2003), https://perma.cc/2G42-SXW7.

54 Peter W. Schroth, "The African Union Convention on Preventing and Combating Corruption," *Journal of African Law* 49, no. 1 (2005): 24–38, at 25.

55 African Union, "Harmonization of the French and Arabic Texts of the African Convention on Preventing and Combating Corruption," inter-office memorandum from Legal Counsel to Conference Directorate, 26 March 2004, BC/OLC/24.12/31/Vol.V.

56 Dieng, *Corruption in Africa*, 27–28.

57 United Nations, *Resolution 55/25 Adopted by the General Assembly: United Nations Convention Against Transnational Organized Crime (November 15, 2000)*, A/RES/55/25, www.unodc.org/pdf/crime/a_res_55/res5525e.pdf.

58 African Union, "Report of the Experts/Diplomats Meeting to Consider the Draft OAU/AU Convention on Combating Corruption and the Draft OAU/AU Convention on Combating Corruption," 4–5.

59 US Embassy, Addis Ababa, "Letter from Ambassador David Shinn to Ambassador Ahmed Haggag," 16 March 1998, CAB/LEG/24.12/2/Vol.I.

60 According to a report by the regional UN office, SAHRIT indeed "played a crucial role in facilitating the preparation of the SADC Protocol against Corruption and providing technical assistance to the SADC Legal Office." See Ugljesa Zvekic, "Editor's Introduction," in *Corruption and Anti-corruption in Southern Africa: Analysis Based on the Results of the Regional Seminar on Anti-corruption Investigating Strategies with Particular Regard to Drug Control for the SADC Member States* (Pretoria: UNODC Regional Office for Southern Africa, 2002), 4–9, at 4; SAHRIT, "Letter to the OAU Office of the Legal Counsel," 13 March 2001, CAB/LEG/24.12/1/Vol.II.

61 African Union, "Letter from Legal Counsel Tiyanjana Maluwa to Adama Dieng," 31 October 2001, CAB/LEG/24.12/36/Vol.II.

62 Global Coalition for Africa, "Principles to Combat Corruption in African Countries."

63 Phone interview with former AU OLC official, August 2015.

64 Akere Muna, *The African Union Convention Against Corruption* (Berlin: Transparency International, 2004), https://web.archive.org/web/2012030404 2118/http://www.transparency.org/content/download/8549/55114/file/Muna2 004_introduction_AUconvention.pdf.

65 Kolawole Olaniyan, "Introductory Note to African Union (AU): Convention on Preventing and Combating Corruption," *International Legal Materials* 43, no. 1 (2004): 1–4, at 2.

66 Thomas Kwai Tieku, "Explaining the Clash and Accommodation of Interests of Major Actors in the Creation of the African Union," *African Affairs* 103, no. 411 (2004): 249–267.

67 Transparency International, *Understanding the African Union Convention on Preventing and Combating Corruption and Related Offenses*, 14.

152 *African Union*

68 Phone interview with TI Africa expert, August 2015; phone interview with former AU OLC official, August 2015.

69 Phone interview with former AU OLC official, August 2015.

70 Jonas Tallberg, Thomas Sommerer, Theresa Squatrito, and Christer Jönsson, *The Opening up of International Organizations: Transnational Access in Global Governance* (Cambridge: Cambridge University Press, 2013).

71 Phone interview with former AU OLC official, August 2015.

72 From a critical perspective, these outside actors command very little input legitimacy and are driven by a narrow ideological mission. I thank the anonymous reviewer for highlighting this point. See, for example, Janine R. Wedel, "High Priests and the Gospel of Anti-corruption," *Challenge* 58, no. 1 (2015): 4–22.

73 Kurt Weyland, *Bounded Rationality and Policy Diffusion: Social Sector Reform in Latin America* (Princeton, NJ: Princeton University Press, 2007).

5 Conclusion
Lessons to draw from the global patchwork

- **Enforcement, compromises, and illusionary giants**
- **Signaling motives as scope conditions**
- **Anti-corruption as an instance of diffusion**
- **Implications and contribution to the literature**
- **Outlook: can these agreements be effective?**

I address three important questions in this chapter. First, how can the landscape of international anti-corruption agreements be systematized? Second, under which conditions do states adopt such agreements? Third, to what extent have these developments followed the logic of diffusion? I also discuss the implications of my findings and this book's contribution to the literature before concluding with some thoughts on the effectiveness of global anti-corruption agreements.

International organizations around the world are addressing the issue of corruption. The most prominent case is the United Nations Convention Against Corruption, which entered into force in 2005 and had 186 states parties at the time of writing. However, several regional organizations had already adopted agreements before the UN's convention was even drafted. These documents obligated the organizations' member states to fight corruption, both domestically and transnationally. Since 1996, binding agreements have been adopted by continental as well as sub-regional organizations in Europe, the Americas, and Africa. It cannot be said that every regional organization has chosen to address corruption, yet, compared with the international legal environment in 1995, when there was not a single binding agreement on the issue, it is now firmly established on the global agenda.

After addressing the initial impetus for this "eruption,"[1] this book has focused on the contrasting outcomes of anti-corruption efforts by asking: which factors explain the similarities and differences among international anti-corruption agreements? I have attempted to answer

154   *Conclusion*

this question by investigating the scope and legal design of these agreements. In simple terms, the former encompasses *what* is covered in a given agreement. Anti-corruption agreements may address prevention (how should member states prevent corruption at the domestic level), criminalization (which acts are defined as illegal), jurisdiction (where should governments apply these rules), domestic enforcement (which standards will regulate the severity of sanctions and so on), and international cooperation (how will states cooperate in the fight against corruption). Detailed analysis of the various anti-corruption agreements revealed a total of 57 elements that fit within one or other of these categories (see Chapter 2).

Legal design relates to *how* the drafters of the agreements addressed these issues. In this regard, I was guided by the legalization framework.[2] Across the various scope elements, cases vary with respect to degree of obligation. Clauses are binding if they insist on implementation by all states parties. Alternatively, clauses may be permissive or optional. In the former case, an obligation is qualified by an escape clause or a contingency, such as compatibility with domestic law. In the latter, a clause is marked as optional, hortatory, or aspirational. The basic distinction is thus between mandatory and non-mandatory provisions. In addition to obligation, delegation is another crucial aspect of legal design. In this regard, I have analyzed the follow-up mechanisms that have been established at the international level to monitor the implementation of the agreements. Here, peer review is the gold standard: when agreements stipulate this as a follow-up mechanism, thorough scrutiny of member states' implementation and compliance practices as well as naming and shaming are facilitated.

Enforcement, compromises, and illusionary giants

On the basis of analysis of scope and legal design, international organizations may be differentiated into four groups (see Table 5.1). Members of the first group have not adopted any binding agreements. The legal design of their anti-corruption agreements, if they have even drafted any, therefore falls well short in terms of obligation. No agreement has been reached on binding minimum standards for domestic anti-corruption measures or rules of international cooperation to combat corruption. ASEAN, the East African Community, MERCOSUR, CARICOM, and the Andean Community all fall within this category.

The members of the second group may be labeled "illusionary giants." Their agreements predominantly contain legally binding

Conclusion 155

Table 5.1 Four groups of cases

Scope	Obligation	Delegation	Type of agreement
–	–	–	No binding agreement
Broad	High	Low	Illusionary giants
Narrow	Mixed	High	Enforcement cooperation
Mixed	Mixed	Medium	Compromise plus peer review

provisions and cover multiple aspects of prevention, criminalization, jurisdiction, domestic enforcement, and international cooperation. In other words, they combine broad scope with high levels of obligation. However, they are also characterized by a lack of delegation. The absence or weakness of follow-up mechanisms—and especially peer review—is what turns these agreements into illusionary giants. From afar, they appear to be far-reaching, yet a closer look reveals significant limitations. SADC, ECOWAS, and the African Union fall within this category. All three of these African organizations created supposedly binding agreements between 2001 and 2003, but they have not subsequently amended them or created strong follow-up mechanisms.

Third, some agreements can be labeled "enforcement cooperation." These contain mandatory provisions on a relatively narrow range of issues, mainly focusing on criminalization, jurisdiction, enforcement, and cooperation. This set of rules is then backed up by a follow-up mechanism. The core agreements adopted by the OECD and the Council of Europe fit into this category. The EU's anti-corruption agreement is another example of enforcement cooperation because, while it does not entail a peer-review mechanism that is explicitly focused on anti-corruption, the overall structure of the EU means that compliance with its anti-corruption treaties is still monitored.

Finally, the Organization of American States and the United Nations have both adopted agreements that combine preventive and other measures. In these cases the mixture of binding and non-binding provisions reflects compromises and trade-offs in the drafting and negotiation processes. A few years after the treaties entered into force, member states in both organizations agreed to establish follow-up mechanisms. As a result, they have broader scope and lower average obligation than the ideal type of enforcement cooperation, but stronger follow-up than the illusionary giants. The Council of Europe also falls within this category due to its additional documents and the decision to assess them in peer review. Thus, the COE, OAS, and UN agreements may be labeled "compromises plus peer review." While scope

156 *Conclusion*

and legal design vary significantly among them, all three occupy positions between enforcement cooperation and illusionary giants. This categorization leaves the League of Arab States as an outlier. Its 2010 convention has a broader scope than the illusionary giants, displays the varying degrees of obligation typically associated with the compromise type, but it includes no peer review. Unfortunately, a lack of information on the development of this convention and its implementation make further analysis impossible.

Signaling motives as scope conditions

Why do some organizations adopt binding anti-corruption agreements, while others do not? Which factors lead to agreements developing into illusionary giants, enforcement cooperation, or compromises plus peer review? My analysis has been guided by three assumptions. First, decision-making in international organizations is interdependent, so choices in one case affect those in the others. Second, drafting and negotiation processes are typically dominated by member states, but non-state actors, such as IO bureaucrats or NGOs, may also have an influence. Third, member states design international agreements to serve as signals to domestic, intra-group, and/or external audiences. These signaling motives are scope conditions for the effects of diffusion.

The comparative part of this book focused on the logic of signaling motives to explain the variation in outcomes (see Table 5.2). The OECD, EU, COE, and OAS agreements all correspond to the notions that there is a trade-off between scope and obligation, and that member states seeking to signal to domestic audiences or other members of the group will adopt a follow-up mechanism. However, it is more difficult to differentiate between domestic and intra-group signaling, and to determine the extent to which they lead to different results. Empirically, all of the organizations that have opted for enforcement cooperation or compromises fit both descriptions: they are both highly democratic (domestic signaling) and contain entrepreneurial member states that set the agenda (intra-group signaling). In the EU and the COE, Western European governments sought to create agreements to commit their Eastern neighbors to good governance. In the OECD and the OAS, the US government was the main norm entrepreneur. The configuration of cases thus limits further exploration of these arguments.

The SADC, ECOWAS, and AU cases all support my hypothesis about external signaling: the creation of anti-corruption agreements in

Conclusion 157

Table 5.2 Signaling motives and outcomes

Signaling motive	Operationalization		Outcome	Cases
Domestic	High democracy levels	→	Enforcement cooperation	EU, OECD
Intra-group	Agenda-setting process	→	Compromise plus peer review	COE, OAS, UN
External	High aid inflows	→	Illusionary giants	SADC, ECOWAS, AU
None/low levels of the above		→	Deference/ division of labor	MS, CAN, CARICOM
		→	Significant delay	LAS, EAC
		→	No binding agreement	ASEAN

these organizations was driven by the need to address outsiders' concerns about corruption, because international donors and multilateral institutions have intensified the fight against bribery and fraud in development cooperation. The resulting "illusionary giant" pattern of broad commitments paired with a lack of meaningful follow-up is the most likely response of member states that are primarily interested in the collateral consequences of treaties.

The clearest case of opting out also conforms to my hypothesis: ASEAN, with its relatively undemocratic and not particularly aid-dependent membership, has chosen not to address corruption in a binding agreement. ASEAN members have little interest in creating a mandatory agreement as a signal because they face minimal pressure from either within the organization or from donors due to their low levels of both democracy and development aid. However, the picture becomes more complicated when one considers the IO laggards. The League of Arab States' adoption of an anti-corruption convention came as a surprise even to anti-corruption activists.[3] According to the signaling motives hypothesis, the relatively undemocratic LAS, with its low to medium levels of incoming development aid, should not have been particularly interested in formulating such an agreement. Further research may explain why it chose to do so.

A less significant challenge to the explanatory model is posed by the East African Community. Depending on political developments in that region, it could well be that this organization soon adopts its own anti-corruption agreement. This would be in line with my argument about pursuing the collateral consequences of agreements. The fact that

158 *Conclusion*

negotiations have been ongoing for many years suggests that, while external signaling is a strong motive, as yet this has been insufficient to overcome general concerns about sovereignty and specific disagreements among member states.

Finally, the Central and Latin American organizations MERCOSUR, the Andean Community, and CARICOM illustrate that signaling motives are context-dependent. In these cases, the prerequisite of democratic governance is met, but the member states have chosen to defer to the OAS on the issue of anti-corruption, resulting in a division of labor throughout the Americas. Once a regional compromise-plus agreement has been established, sub-regional organizations have no incentive to create additional documents unless their motive is external signaling (see below).

Anti-corruption as an instance of diffusion

In Chapter 2, I analyzed the extent to which the drafters of conventions have directly copied the provisions of earlier agreements. This served as a plausibility probe for the hypothesis that negotiation and drafting processes in each organization are influenced by those in others. The results are clear: approximately one-quarter of the clauses contained within the documents under investigation were copied verbatim from other agreements, with the OAS by far the most widely cited reference model, followed by the COE and the EU. Given that my measure systematically *underestimates* the true effects of diffusion for methodological and conceptual reasons, this comparative evidence lends strong support to the assumption of interdependent decision-making.

To assess the role played by diffusion processes in more detail, I then presented case studies of the Organization of American States and the African Union. These covered member states' motivations, the drafting and negotiation processes, the interplay with sub-regional organizations, and evidence of diffusion. Both the OAS and the AU are continental-level organizations with political mandates and diverse memberships. Yet, I expected the primary motivation in the former to be signaling among member states and to domestic constituents, while the latter would be driven by a desire to send a signal to an external audience of donors.

For the OAS, I did indeed find evidence of a mostly intergovernmental process. A coalition of activist member states, headed by the United States, pushed for the adoption of the convention. The decision to become active was primarily driven by a wish to harmonize policies

Conclusion 159

among members, fulfill election promises, and signal credible reforms to domestic constituencies. There was also some evidence of an external component, as the United States used the OAS to set a precedent for the OECD, while the Latin American governments hoped to attract foreign investors.

Given the pioneering nature of the OAS convention, its drafting was not heavily influenced by other anti-corruption treaties. Instead, several member states submitted their own domestic legislation as reference points and lobbied for its incorporation. That said, the drafters did rely on reference models—other OAS treaties and UN documents—for the sections on international cooperation. It is unclear whether this was an example of lesson-drawing in the sense of a comprehensive search for best practice. On the other hand, when it comes to the design of the OAS's follow-up mechanism—MESICIC—which was a later addition to the convention, the evidence certainly points to lesson-drawing. The OAS commissioned a study to identify and compare other organizations' review processes, and the drafters met with representatives from all of these organizations. This is in line with the expectation that member states will try to identify best practice if they are motivated to design an agreement that is suitable for domestic and intra-group signaling. The deliberations over MESICIC also marked a change in the role of non-state actors. Whereas civil society had been marginalized in the early negotiations for the convention itself, the move to create a follow-up mechanism was partly driven by pressure from civil society activists and legal experts.

The case study of the African Union provides a stark contrast to the OAS. The process of drafting the AU convention was driven by a small group of legal experts from the AU Commission, external consultants, and civil society. The Office of the Legal Council, which acted as both drafter and agenda-setter, used the existing SADC and OAS conventions as reference models. This may be characterized as lesson-drawing with bounded rationality, which in practice was heavily conditioned by the availability of documents and the OLC's limited capacity to conduct research. An external consultant was hired but failed to deliver a comprehensive assessment of the possible options. AU staffers could not conduct extensive research due to resource constraints, and they were repeatedly contacted by activist governments and non-state actors who lobbied for their preferred models. As a result, the most readily available OAS, SADC, and (indirectly through an Ethiopian proposal) COE documents became the main inspirations. One might have expected the AU drafters to emulate European reference models for added legitimacy, given that European development partners

160 *Conclusion*

comprised the primary external audience, but there was no evidence for this.

During the drafting and negotiation phases, the OLC opened the door for input from non-state actors, who were invited and contributed to the relevant meetings. Transparency International and the AU staff worked together, whereas member-state delegations merely reacted to their proposals, usually with the intention of diluting them. The expectation that attenuated delegation within the drafting process leads to more influence for outside actors was thus confirmed. Given their privileged access to negotiations, civil society actors were able to exert more pressure on the government delegations than is generally expected in IO decision-making. This path to the anti-corruption convention mirrors the AU's efforts to protect democracy through the development of an anti-coup norm, which was advanced by staffers at the AU Commission in conjunction with external experts in the face of reluctance among several member states.[4]

Besides confirming the divergent signaling motives among member states, the two case studies thus reveal major differences in how drafting and negotiations unfold in practice. In both cases, there was evidence of feedback effects in diffusion processes: the OAS convention introduced foreign bribery to international law, creating a precedent for the OECD; and the AU convention addressed asset recovery while negotiations over the UNCAC were ongoing. Additional research may explore the extent to which the design of agreements in one forum might be driven by motives to influence outcomes in another. In sum, different mechanisms of diffusion are of crucial significance when agreements are negotiated and designed in international organizations.

Implications and contribution to the literature

By developing a framework to compare international agreements, mapping the variations among those agreements, constructing a typology of outcomes, and explaining the scope and legal design of the conventions, I feel this book makes a valuable contribution to the anti-corruption literature. Moreover, it is relevant to broader debates in international relations.

First, the book contributes to the debate about scope conditions in diffusion research. Recent survey articles have pointed to the need to identify conditions that affect the workings of diffusion mechanisms.[5] I urge researchers working on diffusion to apply the notion of signaling to conceptualize these conditions. The signaling perspective on international law provides a framework that can accommodate expectations

Conclusion 161

corresponding to factors such as regime type and the composition of international organizations. Integrating diverse factors into a single analytical perspective helps to clarify the arguments. The logic of signaling captures the causal mechanisms linking, for instance, regime type and willingness to adopt an agreement: democratic governments do not embrace anti-corruption measures because they are somehow normatively superior; rather, they do so because such agreements send useful signals to their most important audiences. Future studies of diffusion in other policy areas or other cases could probe the generalizability of this approach, which I feel should be amenable to different contexts. In practical terms, signaling offers a bridge between diffusion research and rationalist–functionalist accounts of international legal design.

In the context of domestic and intra-group signaling, I expected to find incentives and persuasion from sources within the organization paired with lesson-drawing. In the context of external signaling, I assumed that incentives and persuasion from outside actors, competition for external resources, and normative emulation of external reference models would be the most prevalent mechanisms. The evidence lent support to these hypotheses. Yet, the association between signaling motives and specific mechanisms is not clear cut. My findings do not indicate that the AU's draft authors deliberately chose to mimic rather than draw lessons; bounded rationality and the availability bias played much larger roles. Meanwhile, the OAS's decision to introduce a peer-review mechanism may be interpreted as legitimacy-driven as much as lesson-drawing. Future research might incorporate additional cases to explore the extent to which signaling motives systematically correlate with diffusion mechanisms.

Additionally, the case studies in this book illustrate the methodological issues that are invariably associated with the empirical study of diffusion mechanisms. Chapters 3 and 4 demonstrate both the merits and the challenges of qualitative case-study research on diffusion. One such challenge is to consider observable implications.[6] The diffusion mechanisms defined in the literature serve as a heuristic to search for relevant influences. At the same time, however, archival sources and interviews do not always allow for reliable distinction between mechanisms that may be observationally equivalent. My case studies showcase the usefulness as well as the limitations of different types of data.

The study of diffusion mechanisms is linked to broader debates about decision-making in international organizations. Clearly, non-state actors sometimes play important roles. This applies to civil society

162   *Conclusion*

organizations as well as IO bureaucrats. The negotiation and drafting processes in the African Union demonstrate the power of IO staff and experts, who are often overlooked in international relations theory. Beyond enjoying some autonomy as part of a principal–agent relationship, these actors can cooperate in informal networks that influence the decision-making within organizations. The collaboration between the Legal Counsel, development partners, and experts in the AU illustrates that individual initiatives can be significant. This book's findings are relevant for research into NGO access, bureaucratic politics, and non-traditional forms of delegation within IOs.[7] Linking this back to the research program on diffusion, the task ahead is clear: similar to what Solingen has suggested by naming potential "agents of diffusion," researchers who are interested in interdependent decision-making in international organizations are advised to consider much more than government actors alone.[8] However, one unfortunate consequence of this may be that theoretical expectations become more convoluted and difficult to assess empirically.

This book also contributes to research on comparative regionalism, and particularly the literature that focuses on how international organizations promote standards in the areas of democracy, human rights, the rule of law, and good governance.[9] The preceding chapters have shown that anti-corruption agreements were a regional phenomenon before they became a global one. While the UNCAC has now been widely ratified and draws attention and resources to the global level, regional peer-review mechanisms have proved their worth and remain active. In this sense, this book's findings support the notion that, while "a global script is emerging, it is patched together by different inter- and transnational actors, among which regional organizations play an increasingly prominent role."[10] The explanatory model developed in this book should be generalizable to other aspects of governance transfer.

A nascent research program in international relations is exploring so-called "overlapping regionalism," in which regional organizations share some member states and overlap in terms of their mandates and activities.[11] For the field of anti-corruption, the analysis is relatively clear: in the Americas, MERCOSUR, the Andean Community, and CARICOM have created a division of labor by deferring to the OAS on this issue. In Europe, the COE and EU agreements exist in parallel, and most of the member states of those organizations have also signed the OECD convention. Yet, this overlap is mitigated by the fact that the agreements are functionally differentiated: the EU and OECD conventions are quite narrow and address different issues, whereas the

COE agreement provides a broader framework. These findings are consistent with the prevalence of domestic and intra-group signaling in these cases. Creating a separate agreement among a subset of actors would signal a decrease in their commitment to the initial agreement. Hence, unless some specific audience emerges and demands just that, the situation should remain stable. The European Union is an interesting case in this regard, as the European Commission might create its own monitoring mechanism in the future.

In Africa, by contrast, sub-regional organizations have adopted discrete anti-corruption protocols that are broad in scope and contain mandatory commitments. Their existence could be dismissed as an accident of history: after all, ECOWAS and SADC were only marginally ahead of the AU in adopting their protocols. Yet, African states continue to ratify sub-regional documents, and negotiations about another protocol are ongoing in the East African Community. This is congruent with the logic of external signaling and points to competition as a mechanism of diffusion. Overlap and redundancy result from states seeking to benefit from the collateral consequences of creating agreements. As organizations in Africa continue to compete for external funding, the adoption of new anti-corruption initiatives modeled on other African and global reference models is likely to persist. This is not specific to anti-corruption, but rather typical for the region.[12] Signaling to external audiences seems conducive to ever more overlap and redundancy, but future research should investigate whether this varies by issue area. If a policy field is dominated by a small number of key players, as in the case of anti-corruption, external signaling might be prevalent. In other policy fields, however, different causes of overlap might be more important.

Finally, how does this study relate to the World Society Approach (WSA)? I agree with the general premise of diffusion. More precisely, the evidence seems to be consistent with the notions of normalization and world time, given that the international agreements under discussion emerged more or less simultaneously over a short period of time. Jakobi argues that anti-corruption continues to spread in line with World Society now that the initial set of agreements has been established.[13] Indeed, considering the recent adoption of a UN follow-up mechanism, one might diagnose a (reluctant) race to the top. In this sense, the WSA provides a persuasive argument about the overall long-term trend.

Yet, this book's findings also contradict some WSA claims. In a 2014 article, Kim and Sharman claim that individualistic anti-corruption norms are being "theorized" because they fit the dominant modernist

164 *Conclusion*

world culture. They argue that international anti-corruption initiatives have emphasized individual accountability rather than country-level reform: "Establishing the individual guilt of corrupt leaders has been regarded as superior to collective punishment of whole countries, which affects both perpetrators and innocent victims alike."[14] I find this assessment somewhat inconsistent with the evidence as the agreements under discussion cover prevention and many other issues that relate to national governments. Peer review is designed to identify non-compliant *states*, not individual leaders. Similarly, naming and shaming with reference to indices such as the CPI affects whole economies. Kim and Sharman rightly point out that some governments and advocates lobby for increased prosecution of individual offenders. However, that approach is not the only game in town. Anti-corruption agreements address myriad issues, and elsewhere I have shown that some sections are highly contested.[15] Short of declaring all of them to be elements of the same core of modernist norms, the WSA provides little analytical leverage.

Outlook: can these agreements be effective?

My investigation of the politics behind the international anti-corruption consensus informs expectations about its impact. Motives to create agreements differ among organizations, and their design is affected by diffusion mechanisms. Because "the path to institutional reform tells us much about the probable performance of the reform," it makes no sense to expect similar results and effects across the board.[16] Thus, observers as well as practitioners must consider the peculiarities of different international agreements. Transnational and local activists should tailor their efforts to those agreements that are most compatible with their agendas. More broadly, international agreements offer points of reference and leverage when corruption impacts transnational business, investment, or development cooperation. When it comes to the extradition of offenders or the recovery of assets, the parties involved can base their requests on one of several agreements, and thus should weigh their options carefully.

Despite the emergence of anti-corruption agreements and the associated activism around the world, it must be noted that blind spots remain. Critics point out that the US government, as the single most important champion of anti-corruption measures, has blocked any attempt to tackle the input side of politics. As a result, international agreements fail to address the necessary "balance between the criminal law and acceptable campaign finance practices that permit donors to

Conclusion 165

purchase access to and influence with a candidate."[17] Regulating political deal-making is difficult to reconcile with a technocratic, rule-based approach to anti-corruption. Even before Donald Trump announced his candidacy, critical observers noted that some arrangements in recent presidential campaigns would have triggered federal investigations if they had involved foreign officials. Since then, debates about corruption in the United States have gained extra impetus, to put it mildly.[18] Future research will show whether this translates into changes in foreign policy, as happened after the Watergate scandal.

Notwithstanding the debate about the strengths and weaknesses of individual international agreements, the trend towards more formal commitments to combat corruption paired with peer review, which has now reached the global level, might result in little change on the ground. After all, there is minimal evidence that these efforts have translated into strong legal regimes in all of the participatory states, let alone less corruption. In addition, the more intrusive or innovative measures are often phrased as non-binding suggestions. This is especially true in the UNCAC, imposing severe limits on the potential of the most widely ratified instrument.[19] Even if international agreements are perfectly transposed into domestic systems, corrupt practices do not necessarily cede to the rule of law. In systematically corrupt states, transparency rules and codes of conduct are unlikely to make much of a difference on their own.[20] Unless national judicial bodies are given the power and resources to investigate irregularities in procurement, legal changes will have no effect on illicit practices. National anti-corruption agencies, heralded as among the most effective innovations on the basis of the experiences of Hong Kong and Singapore, have now been introduced across the globe. Yet, their impact remains uncertain, with observers pointing out that they are often manipulated by corrupt incumbents to discredit the opposition. Even when laws have been enacted, the elusive "political will" is still necessary to tackle corruption. Binding international commitments and specialized national institutions do not necessarily lead to the consistent application of laws.[21]

The empirical record in terms of international cooperation is equally mixed. States make use of mutual legal assistance based on anti-corruption treaties. For the United States, the UN and OAS instruments are most relevant in this regard.[22] But it seems hyperbolic to speak of widespread, systematic usage. In the area of transnational bribery, the OECD's provisions for sanctions against bribe-paying corporations are enforced only selectively, and half of the member states have never imposed a sanction for foreign bribery. Various reasons are

166   *Conclusion*

given for this inactivity, "ranging from judicial cooperation difficulties to plain conflict between policy goals of states."[23]

So, what can be done to improve the situation? In development cooperation, regional integration, and transnational business, fighting corruption has become a mantra over the last two decades. Yet, it is by no means certain that international treaty commitments will succeed in overcoming the fundamental tensions between economic and ethical goals. Perhaps self-commitment and self-regulation should be accompanied by interventions led by third parties. Kaczmarek and Newman have shown that extraterritorial enforcement of the US Foreign Corrupt Practices Act has encouraged governments to start enforcing their own anti-bribery laws.[24] This finding suggests that implementation practices may be subject to diffusion, too, now that the underlying norms and policy ideas have spread around the world. If this is indeed the case, the clutter of international agreements and national laws with extraterritorial jurisdiction might turn out to be surprisingly effective in comparison with a universally accepted but much weaker and vaguer agreement.

A second proposal relates to the connection between the transnational and domestic layers. Mungiu-Pippidi argues that the UNCAC will have the greatest chance of success if it encourages domestic demands for change, echoing the progress made in human rights: "What the international community should do to increase its impact is to think of UNCAC implementation and review as mechanisms for stirring collective action."[25] A number of scholars have argued for an approach linked to human rights, proposing that domestic and/or international courts should enforce anti-corruption commitments.[26]

A third strategy is to prosecute former and current officials and make every effort to seize their assets, particularly those that have been secreted outside of their home jurisdictions. Thus far, the World Bank and the UN Office on Drugs and Crime, as well as a number of civil society actors, have led the way on the issue of asset recovery, with their work resulting in the Stolen Asset Recovery Initiative (StAR) in 2007.[27] However, this has proved challenging due to the inherent difficulty of tracing illegally acquired assets and the investigators' limited resources. There have been a number of high-profile cases, but it seems too early to speak of a trend towards more frequent or more widespread prosecutions.[28] Nevertheless, such efforts can help to secure justice, compensate victims, and improve public-goods provision in impoverished countries. High-profile cases might also raise awareness and expectations among the public, which could help to constrain corrupt activities. Finally, leaders might be deterred from engaging in

Conclusion 167

grand corruption if they can no longer expect to control the proceeds and enjoy the associated lifestyle in the world's most desirable destinations.

Quite a few building blocks have been put into place to reduce the opportunities for and payoffs from corruption across the world. Now that the concept of anti-corruption has spread among international organizations and individual states, implementation and enforcement are the key challenges. While there is no abundance of success stories, optimists can at least point to a few promising trends: a mechanism of peer review has been established at the United Nations; practitioners and legal experts are developing and sharing ideas and best practice models; and prosecutors have an unprecedented array of cross-border tools at their disposal. In conclusion, anti-corruption remains an enormous challenge, but there are countless opportunities for incremental progress.

Notes

1 Patrick Glynn, Stephen J. Kobrin, and Moisés Naím, "The Globalization of Corruption," in *Corruption and the Global Economy*, ed. Kimberly Ann Elliott (Washington, DC: Institute for International Economics, 1997), 7–27.
2 Kenneth W. Abbott, Robert O. Keohane, Andrew Moravcsik, Anne-Marie Slaughter, and Duncan Snidal, "The Concept of Legalization," *International Organization* 54, no. 3 (2000): 17–35.
3 Interview with TI treaty expert, Berlin, February 2014.
4 Thomas F. Legler and Thomas Kwai Tieku, "What Difference Can a Path Make? Regional Democracy Promotion Regimes in the Americas and Africa," *Democratization* 17, no. 3 (2010): 465–491; Julia Leininger, "Against All Odds: Strong Democratic Norms in the African Union," in *Governance Transfer by Regional Organizations: Patching Together a Global Script*, ed. Tanja A. Börzel and Vera van Hüllen (Houndmills: Palgrave Macmillan, 2015), 51–67.
5 Tanja A. Börzel and Thomas Risse, "When Europeanisation Meets Diffusion: Exploring New Territory," *West European Politics* 35, no. 1 (2012): 192–207, at 198–204; Etel Solingen, "Of Dominoes and Firewalls: The Domestic, Regional, and Global Politics of International Diffusion," *International Studies Quarterly* 56, no. 4 (2012): 631–644, at 640–641.
6 Judith Kelley, "Assessing the Complex Evolution of Norms: The Rise of International Election Monitoring," *International Organization* 62, no. 2 (2008): 221–255, at 232–236.
7 Jonas Tallberg, Lisa M. Dellmuth, Hans Agné, and Andreas Duit, "NGO Influence in International Organizations: Information, Access, and Exchange," *British Journal of Political Science* 48, no. 1 (2018): 213–238; Jonas Tallberg, Thomas Sommerer, Theresa Squatrito, and Christer Jönsson, *The Opening up of International Organizations: Transnational Access in Global Governance* (Cambridge: Cambridge University Press, 2013); Ian

168 *Conclusion*

Johnstone, "Law-making by International Organizations: Perspectives from IL/IR Theory," in *Interdisciplinary Perspectives on International Law and International Relations: The State of the Art*, ed. Jeffrey L. Dunoff and Mark A. Pollack (Cambridge: Cambridge University Press, 2013), 266–292.

8 Solingen, "Of Dominoes and Firewalls," 634.

9 Börzel and van Hüllen, eds., *Governance Transfer by Regional Organizations.*

10 Tanja A. Börzel and Vera van Hüllen, "Patching Together a Global Script: The Demand for and Supply of Governance Transfer by Regional Organizations," in *Governance Transfer by Regional Organizations*, ed. Börzel and van Hüllen, 245–259, at 257.

11 Diana Panke and Sören Stapel, "Exploring Overlapping Regionalism," *Journal of International Relations and Development* 21, no. 3 (2018): 635–662.

12 Malte Brosig, "Overlap and Interplay between International Organisations: Theories and Approaches," *South African Journal of International Affairs* 18, no. 2 (2011): 147–167.

13 Anja P. Jakobi, *Common Goods and Evils? The Formation of Global Crime Governance* (Oxford: Oxford University Press, 2013).

14 Hun Joon Kim and J. C. Sharman, "Accounts and Accountability: Corruption, Human Rights, and Individual Accountability Norms," *International Organization* 68, no. 2 (2014): 417–448, at 439.

15 Ellen Gutterman and Mathis Lohaus, "What is the 'Anti-corruption' Norm in Global Politics?," in *Corruption and Norms: Why Informal Rules Matter*, ed. Ina Kubbe and Annika Engelbert (London: Palgrave Macmillan, 2018), 241–268.

16 Zachary Elkins and Beth A. Simmons, "On Waves, Clusters, and Diffusion: A Conceptual Framework," *Annals of the American Academy of Political and Social Science* 598, no. 1 (2005): 33–51, at 48.

17 Peter J. Henning, "Public Corruption: A Comparative Analysis of International Corruption Conventions and United States Law," *Arizona Journal of International and Comparative Law* 18, no. 3 (2001): 793–865, at 854.

18 Mike Koehler, "The Uncomfortable Truths and Double Standards of Bribery Enforcement," *Fordham Law Review* 84, no. 2 (2015): 525–561, at 545–550; Matthew Stephenson, "Tracking Corruption and Conflicts in the Trump Administration," GAB: The Global Anticorruption Blog, 2018, https://perma.cc/6RYF-5L2Q.

19 Paul M. Heywood, "Introduction: Scale and Focus in the Study of Corruption," in *Routledge Handbook of Political Corruption*, ed. Paul M. Heywood (London and New York: Routledge, 2015), 1–13, at 1–2; Cecily Rose, *International Anti-corruption Norms: Their Creation and Influence on Domestic Legal Systems* (Oxford: Oxford University Press, 2015), 125–131; Peter W. Schroth, "The United Nations Convention against Doing Anything Serious about Corruption," *Journal of Legal Studies in Business* 12, no. 2 (2005): 1–22.

20 Anna Persson, Bo Rothstein, and Jan Teorell, "Why Anticorruption Reforms Fail: Systemic Corruption as a Collective Action Problem," *Governance* 26, no. 3 (2012): 449–471; Alina Mungiu-Pippidi, *The Quest for Good Governance: How Societies Develop Control of Corruption* (Cambridge: Cambridge University Press, 2015), 221–226; Alina Mungiu-Pippidi

Conclusion 169

and Ramin Dadašov, "When do Anticorruption Laws Matter? The Evidence on Public Integrity Enabling Contexts," *Crime, Law and Social Change* 68, no. 4 (2017): 387–402.

21 Kevin E. Davis, "The Prospects for Anti-corruption Law: Optimists versus Skeptics," *Hague Journal on the Rule of Law* 4, no. 2 (2012): 319–336, at 330–331; Samuel De Jaegere, "Principles for Anti-corruption Agencies: A Game Changer," *Jindal Journal of Public Policy* 1, no. 1 (2012): 79–120; Njoya Tikum, "Guest Post: Time to Go beyond Anti-corruption Agencies in Sub-Saharan Africa," GAB: The Global Anticorruption Blog, 2016, http://globalanticorruptionblog.com/2016/01/21/guest-post-time-to-go-beyo nd-anti-corruption-agencies-in-sub-saharan-africa/; John Hatchard, *Combating Corruption: Legal Approaches to Supporting Good Governance and Integrity in Africa* (Cheltenham: Edward Elgar Publishing, 2014), 28–33.

22 Phone interview with US official, June 2013.

23 Sarah C. Kaczmarek and Abraham L. Newman, "The Long Arm of the Law: Extraterritoriality and the National Implementation of Foreign Bribery Legislation," *International Organization* 65, no. 4 (2011): 745–770; Fritz Heimann, Ádám Földes, and Sophia Coles, *Exporting Corruption: Progress Report 2015: Assessing Enforcement of the OECD Convention on Combating Foreign Bribery* (Berlin: Transparency International, 2015), http://files.transparency.org/content/download/1923/12702/file/2015_ExportingCorruption_OECDProgressReport_EN.pdf; OECD, *2016 Data on Enforcement of the Anti-bribery Convention: Special Focus on International Co-operation* (Paris: OECD Working Group on Bribery, 2017), www.oecd.org/daf/anti-b ribery/Anti-Bribery-Convention-Enforcement-Data-2016.pdf; Mungiu-Pippidi, *The Quest for Good Governance*, 188.

24 Kaczmarek and Newman, "The Long Arm of the Law."

25 Mungiu-Pippidi, *The Quest for Good Governance*, 225.

26 Ndiva Kofele-Kale, *The International Law of Responsibility for Economic Crimes: Holding State Officials Individually Liable for Acts of Fraudulent Enrichment* (Aldershot: Ashgate, 2006); Martine Boersma and Hans Nelen, eds., *Corruption and Human Rights: Interdisciplinary Perspectives* (Antwerp: Intersentia, 2010); Mark L. Wolf, "The World Needs an International Anti-corruption Court," *Daedalus* 147, no. 3 (2018): 144–156.

27 Gretta Fenner Zinkernagel, Charles Monteith, and Pedro Gomes Pereira, eds., *Emerging Trends in Asset Recovery* (Bern: Peter Lang, 2013); J. C. Sharman, *The Despot's Guide to Wealth Management: On the International Campaign against Grand Corruption* (Ithaca, NY: Cornell University Press, 2017).

28 Ivan Pavletic, *The Political Economy of Asset Recovery Processes* (Basel: Basel Institute on Governance, 2009), https://forum.assetrecovery.org/publi cations/403; Larissa Gray, Kjetil Hansen, Pranvera Recica-Kirkbride, and Linnea Mills, *Few and Far: The Hard Facts on Stolen Asset Recovery* (Washington, DC: World Bank, 2014).

Appendix 1
List of anti-corruption documents

Table A1.1 Overview of relevant anti-corruption documents

UN	1975 Resolution 35/14 (Corrupt Practices of Transnational and Other Corporations) 1996 Resolution 51/59 (Code of Conduct for Public Officials) 1997 Declaration against Corruption and Bribery in International Commercial Transactions *2001 Convention Against Transnational Organized Crime ***2003 Convention Against Corruption** *2009 CoP Decision to create a review mechanism
OECD	1994 Recommendations on Bribery 1996 Recommendations on Tax Deductibility of Bribes ***1997 Convention on Combating Bribery of Foreign Public Officials** 1998 Recommendations on Ethical Conduct 2006 Recommendations on Bribery and Export Credits 2008 Recommendations on Enhancing Integrity 2009 Recommendations on Tax Measures 2009 Recommendations on Further Combating Bribery 2010 Recommendations on Lobbying
EU	*1995 Convention on Protection of the EC Financial Interests 1996 EP Resolution on Combating Corruption *1996 Protocol to the EC Financial Interests Convention ***1997 Convention on Corruption Involving Officials** *1997 Second Protocol to the EC FI Convention 2003 Framework Decision on Combating Corruption in the Private Sector 2006 EP Resolution on Aid Effectiveness and Corruption in Developing Countries 2011 Commission Communication on Fighting Corruption

List of anti-corruption documents 171

COE	*1990 Convention on … Seizure and Confiscation of the Proceeds from Crime 1996 Programme of Action Against Corruption 1997 Twenty Guiding Principles ***1999 Civil Law Convention on Corruption** ***1999 Criminal Law Convention on Corruption** 2000 Model Code of Conduct 2003 Common Rules Against Corruption in Party and Campaign Funding ***2003 Additional Protocol to Criminal Law Convention** *2005 Convention on … the Proceeds of Crime and Terrorism
OAS	1975 Resolution 154 (Behavior of Transnational Enterprises) ***1996 Inter-American Convention Against Corruption** *2001 Creation of follow-up mechanism MESISIC 2006 Inter-American Program on the Fight Against Corruption 2008 Model Code of Conduct
MERCOSUR	2002 Decision on Combating Corruption at the Borders
CAN	2006 Andean Plan on the Fight Against Corruption
AU	***2003 Convention on Preventing and Combating Corruption** 2011 Charter on Values and Principles of Public Services
ECOWAS	***2001 Protocol on the Fight Against Corruption**
SADC	***2001 Protocol Against Corruption**
EAC	2010 Draft corruption convention
LAS	***2010 Arab Anti-corruption Convention**

Notes: Asterisks indicate hard law; bold print indicates major anti-corruption instruments that address multiple issues.

Appendix 2
Additional data on scope conditions

What correlation is there between foreign aid inflows and control of corruption? Irrespective of the direction of causality between those two variables, one may assume that countries with high aid inflows might also have problems with curtailing corruption. Both variables, after all, could be driven by similar underlying factors. In addition, aid inflows could themselves increase the likelihood of graft. Indeed, there appears to be a strong correlation (see Figure A2.1).

Similarly, the ability to control corruption is correlated with GDP per capita. This is logical, given that foreign aid inflows and GDP per

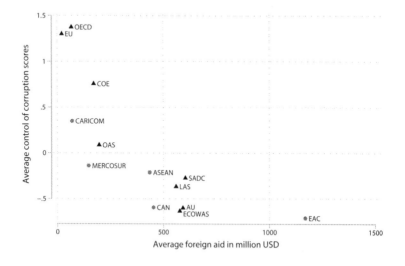

Figure A2.1 Control of corruption and foreign aid inflows
Note: Triangles indicate organizations that have adopted binding agreements; circles indicate those that have not.

Additional data on scope conditions   173

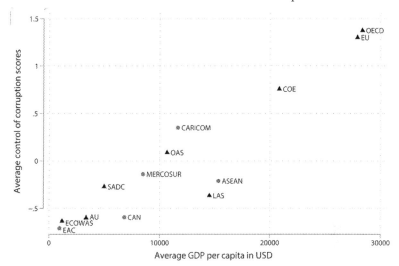

Figure A2.2 Control of corruption and GDP per capita
Note: Triangles indicate organizations that have adopted binding agreements; circles indicate those that have not.

capita are negatively correlated. In fact, the relationship appears linear if plotted at the level of regional organizations (see Figure A2.2). The relationship between regime type and control of corruption is less straightforward (see Figure A2.3). Those organizations with a highly democratic membership display higher levels of control of corruption among member states, but this correlation seems to disappear at lower levels of democratic governance. Intuitively, this is plausible, since hierarchical autocratic regimes might be both more willing and more able to crack down on corrupt practices than either "democracies with deficits" or hybrid regimes.

Bearing these correlations in mind, the most important question concerns their impact on organizations' adoption of binding agreements. In all three figures, this is indicated by how the data points are displayed: black triangles mark those organizations that have adopted at least one binding agreement since 1995; gray circles indicate those that have not. Looking at the distribution along the y-axis—which maps the "control of corruption" variable in all three graphs—it becomes clear that those organizations with the lowest functional pressure to improve their anti-corruption governance have all adopted agreements (COE, OECD, and EU). Those with member states that struggle to curtail corruption show mixed results. If corruption levels

174 *Additional data on scope conditions*

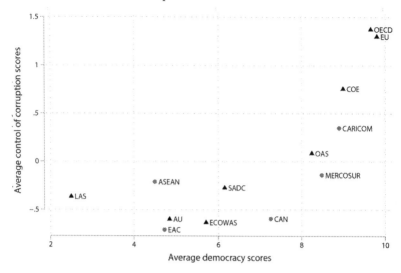

Figure A2.3 Control of corruption and democracy
Note: Triangles indicate organizations that have adopted binding agreements; circles indicate those that have not.

were driving treaty adoption in a straightforward manner, or if they were deterring states from drafting agreements in general, a clearer pattern would be evident.

The different factors plotted along the x-axis in the three graphs also yield inconclusive results. Looking at GDP per capita, we see the same group of organizations as in the case of control of corruption (COE, EU, and OECD), which suggests a positive correlation with treaty adoption. Again, however, the results are mixed below the highest levels. Aid inflow is equally unconvincing as a stand-alone predictor of binding agreements. There are both positive and negative values of the dependent variable at low and medium/high levels of foreign aid, and the same can be said for regime type, as the cases without binding agreements span almost the whole range of the distribution. Therefore, we need to consider the interactions among these factors as well as the broader regional signaling context to make sense of the variation in the results.

Appendix 3
List of interviews

Table A3.1 List of interviews

No.	Interviewee(s)	Date	Location
1	Official, OAS MESICIC Secretariat	May 2013	Washington, DC
2	Official, US Department of State	June 2013	By phone
3	Treaty expert, Transparency International	February 2014	Berlin
4	Official, World Bank (Stolen Asset Recovery)	April 2014	Washington, DC
5	Official, World Bank (Stolen Asset Recovery)	May 2014	By phone
6	Retired official, US Bureau of Government Ethics	June 2014	Vienna
7	Official, GRECO	June 2014	Vienna
8	Official, UN Office on Drugs and Crime	June 2014	Vienna
9	Legal scholar (US)	January 2015	Berlin
10	Former official, UNDP Africa and local Transparency International chapter	April 2015	By phone
11	Official, EU delegation to the AU	April 2015	Addis Ababa
12	Official, ECOWAS liaison with the AU	April 2015	Addis Ababa
13	Official, Department for Political Affairs, AU Commission	April 2015	Addis Ababa
14	Officials, UN Economic Commission for Africa	April 2015	Addis Ababa
15	Official, GIZ Office for Cooperation with the AU	April 2015	Addis Ababa

176 *List of interviews*

No.	Interviewee(s)	Date	Location
16	Official, Office of the Legal Counsel	April 2015	Addis Ababa
17	Official, Swedish embassy, Ethiopia	April 2015	Addis Ababa
18	Officials, UN Economic Commission for Africa	April 2015	Addis Ababa
19	Official, SADC liaison with the AU	April 2015	Addis Ababa
20	Official, Office of the Legal Counsel	April 2015	Addis Ababa
21	Official, EAC liaison with the AU	April 2015	Addis Ababa
22	Official, AU Commission (same as no. 12)	April 2015	Addis Ababa
23	Official, UNDP Africa	May 2015	Addis Ababa
24	US/Ethiopian legal scholar	May 2015	Addis Ababa
25	Official, Political Affairs Department, EAC	June 2015	By phone
26	Africa expert and delegate, Transparency International	August 2015	By phone
27	Former official, Office of the Legal Counsel	August 2015	By phone
28	Asset recovery expert, NGO	February 2016	By phone

Notes: All interviews were conducted under the condition of anonymity and lasted between 20 minutes and two hours. Several experts and officials provided background information by email or during informal communication.

Bibliography

Abbott, Kenneth W. and Duncan Snidal, "Values and Interests: International Legalization in the Fight Against Corruption," *Journal of Legal Studies* 31, no. S1 (2002): 141–177.

Arnone, Marco and Leonardo S. Borlini, *Corruption: Economic Analysis and International Law* (Cheltenham: Edward Elgar Publishing, 2014).

Börzel, Tanja A. and Vera van Hüllen, eds., *Governance Transfer by Regional Organizations: Patching Together a Global Script* (Houndmills: Palgrave Macmillan, 2015).

Dunoff, Jeffrey L. and Mark A. Pollack, eds., *Interdisciplinary Perspectives on International Law and International Relations: The State of the Art* (Cambridge: Cambridge University Press, 2013).

Hathaway, Oona A., "Between Power and Principle: An Integrated Theory of International Law," *University of Chicago Law Review* 72, no. 2 (2005): 469–536.

Jakobi, Anja P., *Common Goods and Evils? The Formation of Global Crime Governance* (Oxford: Oxford University Press, 2013).

Kaczmarek, Sarah C. and Abraham L. Newman, "The Long Arm of the Law: Extraterritoriality and the National Implementation of Foreign Bribery Legislation," *International Organization* 65, no. 4 (2011): 745–770.

Manfroni, Carlos A. and Richard S. Werksman, *The Inter-American Convention Against Corruption: Annotated with Commentary* (Lanham, MD: Lexington Books, 2003).

McCoy, Jennifer L. and Heather Heckel, "The Emergence of a Global Anti-corruption Norm," *International Politics* 38, no. 1 (2001): 65–90.

Sandholtz, Wayne and Mark M. Gray, "International Integration and National Corruption," *International Organization* 57, no. 4 (2003): 761–800.

Sharman, Jason C., *The Despot's Guide to Wealth Management. On the International Campaign against Grand Corruption* (Ithaca, NY: Cornell University Press, 2017).

178   *Bibliography*

Simmons, Beth A., Frank Dobbin, and Geoffrey Garrett, "Introduction: The International Diffusion of Liberalism," *International Organization* 60, no. 4 (2006): 781–810.

Snider, Thomas R. and Won Kidane, "Combating Corruption through International Law in Africa: A Comparative Analysis," *Cornell International Law Journal* 40, no. 3 (2007): 691–748.

Tallberg, Jonas, Thomas Sommerer, Theresa Squatrito, and Christer Jönsson, *The Opening up of International Organizations: Transnational Access in Global Governance* (Cambridge: Cambridge University Press, 2013).

Wouters, Jan, Cedrid Ryngaert, and Ann Sofie Cloots, "The International Legal Framework against Corruption: Achievements and Challenges," *Melbourne Journal of International Law* 14, no. 1 (2013): 1–76.

Index

activists *see* non-state actors
African Development Bank (AfDB)
119, 135
African Leadership Forum
122–124, 126
African Union (AU) 47, 49–51,
54–55; Advisory Board on
Corruption (ABC) 120–122, 142,
146; motives to adopt an agreement 122–131; Office of the Legal
Counsel (OLC) 118–119, 124,
133–134, 139–146, 162; relationship with other organizations in
the region 126–130, 163; *see also*
African Union Convention on
Preventing and Combating
Corruption; *see also*
anti-corruption agreements
African Union Convention on
Preventing and Combating
Corruption: drafting and negotiation process 118–122, 131–137;
language problems 137; ratification
record 120, 127–128; reference
models for 122–124, 138–146;
scope and legal design 66–71,
131–137; *see also* African Union
agency *see* diffusion; *see also* member
states; *see also* non-state actors
agenda-setting, global 2–7, 12–13, 28;
see also non-state actors; *see also*
Transparency International
aid *see* development aid
Andean Community (CAN) 9, 47,
54, 93–94, 154, 158, 162

anti-corruption agencies 47–49, 57,
64, 94, 128, 165
anti-corruption agreements: dates of
their adoption 9–10, 43–44, 49–51;
explanations for adoption or
absence 51–56, 172–174; in Africa
47, 54; in the Americas 46–47, 54;
in Asia 48–49; in Europe 44–46;
with global reach 47–48; *see also*
benchmarks; *see also* legal design;
see also ratification; *see also* scope;
see also typology of agreements
Arab Anti-Corruption Convention
see League of Arab States
asset recovery 61, 166–167; in the
OAS 92, 99; relationship between
AU, OECD, and UNCAC
124–126, 128, 131, 143;
Asia-Pacific Economic Cooperation
(APEC) 49, 54
Asian Development Bank (ADB)
49, 54
Association of South-East Asian
Nations (ASEAN) 9–10, 48–50,
54, 56, 154, 157
AU Advisory Board on Corruption
see African Union
audiences *see* signaling

benchmarks, anti-corruption
agreements as 15–16, 128–129,
164; *see also* Transparency
International
Berhe-Tesfu, Costantinos 122
binding commitment *see* legal design

180 *Index*

bounded rationality *see* diffusion
Bribe Payers Index (BPI) *see*
Transparency International
bureaucrats in international
organizations *see* non-state actors

Caldera, Rafael 91–93
CAN *see* Andean Community
Caribbean Community
(CARICOM) 47, 54, 93–95,
154, 158, 162
Chile 49, 88, 91–92, 97–98
civil society *see* non-state actors
collateral consequences *see* signaling
Cockcroft, Lawrence 122–123
Cold War 4–5, 71, 92
commitment problems 33–34;
see also signaling
competition *see* diffusion
compliance 15, 32–35, 60–63, 71–72,
87–88, 154–155; *see also* follow-up
mechanisms; *see also* signaling
compromise plus peer review *see*
typology of agreements
conference of states parties: for the
OAS convention 46, 86–87, 104;
for UNCAC 48
consultants *see* non-state actors
Control of Corruption (World Bank)
52, 55, 172–174
copy and paste (between documents)
72–74, 139; *see also* diffusion
corruption: definition of 13–14;
effects of 4–6, 93, 123–126;
domestic laws against 14;
measurement 52, 172–174;
scandals/cases 1, 4, 33, 45, 93,
109–110
Corruption Perceptions Index (CPI)
see Transparency International
Council of Europe 4, 9–10, 44,
49–51, 53, 56, 162–163; as
reference model 74, 103, 106–107,
138–141, 145, 158; scope and
legal design 66–72, 154–158;
see also anti-corruption
agreements
criminalization, provisions for 59–60;
provisions in comparison 64–67;
see also scope

deference: to the OAS 54, 93–95;
patterns in comparison 157–158,
162–163
delegation *see* legal design; *see*
follow-up mechanisms
democratization 3–4, 11, 33, 53–55,
88, 92–93, 96, 156–158; *see also*
signaling
development aid 52–56; as motive to
create anti-corruption agreements
15, 34–35, 71, 122–124, 128–131,
144–145, 156–157; *see also*
signaling; *see also* World Bank
Dieng, Adama 119, 124–125,
131–132, 138–143, 159
diffusion 2, 11, 25–26, 37–39;
evidence 72–76, 103–109, 122–124,
138–146, 158–161; mechanisms
26–27, 35–36, *38*, 74–76;
observable implications 74–76,
161; scope conditions 11–12,
31–32, *38*, 156–158, 160–161;
see also signaling
domestic enforcement, provisions for
60–61; lack of provisions in the
OAS convention 102–106;
provisions in comparison 64–67;
see also scope
donors *see* development aid
drug trafficking: driving force in the
OAS 91, 97, 109; UN convention
as reference model 105–106

East African Community (EAC) 9,
47, 54–55, 128; challenging the
explanatory model 157–158
Economic Community of West
African States (ECOWAS) 9, 47,
54, 127–130, 163; scope and legal
design 66–71, 154–158; *see also*
African Union; *see also*
anti-corruption agreements
Eigen, Peter 6
emulation *see* diffusion
enforcement *see* domestic
enforcement
enforcement cooperation *see*
typology of agreements
Ethiopian draft AU convention
132–133, 139–141

Index 181

European Union (EU) 4, 9–10, 44–46, 74, 162–163; influence on African organizations 122, 128, 138; scope and legal design 66–71, 154–158; *see also* anti-corruption agreements; *see also* development aid
experts: opinion on corruption 5–6; *see also* non-state actors; *see also* Transparency International
extradition 61, 164, 132–134; motive in OAS negotiations 91–92, 95–98, 109; OAS convention as reference model 105

follow-up mechanisms 62–63, 69–72, 162; in the AU 47, 120–122; in the COE 44; in the EU 45–46; in the OECD 46; in the OAS 46, 87–88; in the UN 48, 72, 165; logic of peer review/naming and shaming 15, 128, 154, 164–165; *see also* benchmarks
foreign aid *see* development aid
Foreign Corrupt Practices Act (FCPA) *see* United States of America
Free Trade Area of the Americas *see* Summit of the Americas
functionalism *see* rational design of agreements

Global Coalition for Africa 123–124, 129–130, 140–142; *see also* World Bank
globalization 4, 92
good governance and (anti-)corruption 12, 14–15, 122, 128, 156, 162
Group of States against Corruption (GRECO) *see* Council of Europe

human rights and (anti-)corruption 33, 118, 133, 162, 166

illicit enrichment 59, 101, 132–133, 135, 139
illicit financial flows *see* asset recovery

illusionary giants *see* typology of agreements
Implementation Review Group (IRG) *see* United Nations Convention Against Corruption
incentives *see* diffusion
Inter-American Convention Against Corruption (IACAC): as a reference model 74, 139–140; drafting and negotiation process 84–88, 96–102, 106–110; ratification record 85–86, 106; reference models for 103–109; scope and legal design 66–71, 96–104, 154–158; *see also* Organization of American States
Inter-American Convention on Extradition *see* extradition
Inter-American Convention on Mutual Assistance in Criminal Matters *see* mutual legal assistance
interdependent decision-making *see* diffusion
International Anti-Corruption Conference 129, 142
international cooperation (related to anti-corruption), empirical record of 109–110, 165–166; provisions for 61; provisions in comparison 64–67; *see also* asset recovery; *see also* extradition; *see also* follow-up mechanisms; *see also* scope
International Monetary Fund (IMF) 5–6, 138
institutional design *see* legal design
isomorphism *see* World Society Approach

jurisdiction, effects-based 132–136; extraterritoriality of 166; provisions in comparison 60, 65–67; *see also* scope

Kioko, Ben 118–119, 124, 139–142

laggards and leaders *see* anti-corruption agreements
League of Arab States (LAS) 48, 54–56, 74; challenging the

182 *Index*

explanatory model 157; scope and legal design 66–72, 156–158; *see also* anti-corruption agreements
learning *see* diffusion
legal design: analytical framework 7–9, 61–64; comparison between international agreements 9–10, 64–70, 153–156; *see also* follow-up mechanisms; *see also* scope; *see also* typology of agreements
legalization *see* legal design
lesson-drawing *see* diffusion
locking in domestic reforms 33, 92–93

Maluwa, Tiyanjana 118, 139–140
Mauro, Paolo 6
member states: as key decision-makers 31–32, 38–39; role in AU negotiations 143–146; role in OAS negotiations 108–110; *see also* signaling
MERCOSUR 46, 54, 93–95, 158, 162
Mérida Convention *see* United Nations Convention Against Corruption
MESICIC *see* Organization of American States
mimicry *see* emulation
military rule and anti-corruption 93
monitoring *see* follow-up mechanisms
mutual legal assistance: OAS convention as reference model 105; *see also* international cooperation

naming and shaming *see* benchmarks; *see* follow-up mechanisms
non-state actors: agency in IO decision-making 28–30; evidence of their influence 107–108, 141–146, 161–162; *see also* agenda-setting; *see also* Transparency International
norm entrepreneurs *see* agenda-setting; *see* non-state actors
normative pressure *see* diffusion

obligation *see* legal design
observable implications *see* diffusion
Office of the Legal Counsel *see* African Union
OLAF *see* European Union
Organisation for Co-Coperation and Development (OECD): anti-bribery convention 9–10, 12, 14–15, 46, 49–51, 53–56, 70–72, 94, 155–157; as a reference model 48, 102–103, 106–107, 139–140; criticism 124–126, 165; joint initiative with the ADB 49; influenced by OAS negotiations 90–91; scope and legal design 66–71, 154–158; *see also* United States; *see also* anti-corruption agreements
Organization of African Unity (OAU) *see* African Union
Organization of American States (OAS) 46; Juridical Committee 99–100, 107; MESICIC (follow-up mechanism) 69–70, 86–88, 102–104; motives to adopt an agreement 88–93, 95–96, 108–109; relationship with other organizations in the region 93–96, 162; Working Group on Probity and Public Ethics 85, 97–99, 100–102; *see also* anti-corruption agreements; *see also* Inter-American Convention Against Corruption
organized crime *see* drug trafficking
outliers *see* anti-corruption agreements
overlapping regionalism *see* regionalism

peer review *see* follow-up mechanisms
persuasion *see* diffusion
Pope, Jeremy 122–123, 126
prevention, provisions for 57–59; provisions in comparison 64–71; *see also* anti-corruption agencies; *see also* scope
principal-agent perspective 28–30, 162; *see also* non-state actors
prohibition regimes 3, 36

Index 183

ratification: of international treaties 3, 43–44, 50–51; of African agreements 120, 127–130; of the OAS agreement 85–86, 106
rational design of agreements (theory) 33, 36, 161
reference models *see* copy and paste; *see also* diffusion
regime type *see* democratization
regionalism 12, 162; overlap between organizations 10, 56, 130–131, 146, 162–163; *see also* deference
Rio Group 97–98

Schroth, Peter 137
scope conditions *see* diffusion
scope (of documents): analytical framework 7–9, 57–61; comparison between cases 9–10, 64–70, 153–156; *see also* legal design; *see also* typology of agreements
signaling, international law as 11–13, 31–32, 156–158, 160–161; to domestic audiences 33, 92–93; to intra-group audiences 33–34, 71, 95–96; to external audiences 34–35, 71, 128–131; *see also* development aid; *see also* diffusion
Southern African Development Community (SADC) 47, 54; as a reference model 140; initial reluctance to adopt an anti-corruption agreement 128–129; scope and legal design 66–71, 154–158; *see also* African Union; *see also* anti-corruption agreements
Southern African Human Rights Trust (SAHRIT) 119, 140
Southern Common Market *see* MERCOSUR
Summit of the Americas 7, 84–85, 88–92, 97–99, 123; *see also* Organization of American States
Swedish involvement in AU negotiations 119, 121, 124; *see also* development aid

transnational bribery 5, 46, 90–91, 96, 100–101, 109, 126, 145–146; *see also* OECD; *see also* United States of America
Transparency International: delegates in meetings and negotiations 103, 106–108, 122–123, 126, 143–144, 160; as global agenda-setters 6–7, 28, 92; using indices to rank and pressure governments 6–7, 15, 164; *see also* non-state actors
trade *see* globalization
treaty ratification *see* ratification
typology of agreements 70–72, 154–158; *see also* anti-corruption agreements; *see also* legal design; *see also* scope

United Nations Convention on Illegal Traffic in Narcotics and Psychotropic Substances *see* drug trafficking
United Nations Convention on Transnational Organized Crime: as reference model 139
United Nations Development Program (UNDP) 119, 124, 128, 138, 142
United Nations Economic Commission for Africa (UNECA) 119, 121, 142
United Nations Convention against Corruption (UNCAC) 3, 15, 47–48, 74, 146, 165–167; Implementation Review Group 48, 72; scope and legal design 66–72, 154–158; *see also* anti-corruption agreements
United Nations Office on Drugs and Crime (UNODC) 166
United States of America: FCPA and foreign bribery in the OECD 5, 90–91, 166; role in OAS negotiations 89–92, 95–96, 97–99; shortcomings of the anti-corruption approach 164–165

Vanossi, Jorge Reinaldo 107
Vargas Carreño, Edmundo 97–99

184 *Index*

Venezuela: advocating for an anti-corruption agreement 92, 97, 109; draft OAS convention 85, 99–100; *see also* Caldera, Rafael
verbatim copies *see* copy and paste; *see also* diffusion

Wolfensohn, James 6; *see also* World Bank

World Bank (WB) 5–6, 15, 166; demanding anti-corruption reforms in Africa 122–124, 129; delegates in meetings and negotiations 106, 119, 123–124, 142; governance indicators 52; *see also* benchmarks; *see also* Global Coalition for Africa
World Society Approach (WSA) 12, 36–37, 163–164

Printed in the United States
by Baker & Taylor Publisher Services